PELICAN BOOKS

A HISTORY OF NEW ZEALAND

Keith Sinclair, born in Auckland in 1922, is a Professor of History at the University of Auckland. During the Second World War he served in the army at home and the navy overseas. He has held visiting fellowships at the Institute of Commonwealth Studies, London, Cambridge University and the Australian National University, Canberra. He has written a number of books on New Zealand history and many articles on New Zealand, Malaysian, and Commonwealth history, as well as four small volumes of verse. Several of his books have won awards for historical and prose writings. Professor Sinclair is married, with four sons.

A HISTORY OF
NEW ZEALAND

BY

KEITH SINCLAIR

PENGUIN BOOKS

Penguin Books Ltd, Harmondsworth, Middlesex, England
Viking Penguin Inc., 40 West 23rd Street, New York, New York 10010, U.S.A.
Penguin Books Australia Ltd, Ringwood, Victoria, Australia
Penguin Books Canada Ltd, 2801 John Street, Markham, Ontario, Canada L3R 1B4
Penguin Books (N.Z.) Ltd, 182–190 Wairau Road, Auckland 10, New Zealand

—

First published 1959
Reprinted 1960
Revised edition 1969
Reprinted 1973, 1976
This revised and enlarged edition published
simultaneously in Pelican Books and Allen Lane 1980
Reprinted 1984, 1985

—

—

Reproduced, Printed and bound in Great Britain by
Cox & Wyman Ltd, Reading
Set in Monotype Imprint

To the authors of New Zealand's histories
(the pioneers in whose tracks I have laboriously followed),
and especially to J. B. Condliffe
and to the memory of W. T. G. Airey,
J. C. Beaglehole and W. P. Reeves,
this book is respectfully dedicated.

CONTENTS

CONTENTS

LIST OF MAPS

AUTHOR'S NOTE TO THE REVISED
AND ENLARGED EDITION

THIS book was first published in 1959. It was extensively revised for a new edition in 1969. The present edition includes further revisions in detail. Part Three is enlarged to include two new chapters discussing events from 1939 to 1978.

PROLOGUE

THE FISH OF MAUI

Ka tito au,	I sing,
Ka tito au,	I sing,
Ka tito au ki a Kupe,	I sing of Kupe,
Te tangata	The man
Nana i topetope	Who cut up
Te whenua.	The land.
Tu ke a Kapiti,	Kapiti stands apart,
Tu ke Mana,	Mana stands apart,
Tu ke Arapawa.	Arapawa stands apart.
Ko nga tohu tena	These are the signs
A taku tupuna,	Of my ancestor,
A Kupe,	Of Kupe,
Nana i whakatomene	Who explored
Titapua.	Titapua.
Ka tomene au	It was I explored
Te whenua-e!	The land!

A song sung by Te Rauparaha

IN the beginning Papa and Rangi, the earth and the sky, mother and father of the gods, lay close together with their children huddled between them in the darkness. To hide her nakedness, Rangi covered Papa with plants and trees; shell-fish were placed in the sea, reptiles, animals, and birds in the vegetation. All things led a miserable existence in this cramped world, so the gods plotted to drive their father away. After many stratagems had failed, Tane, the god of trees and birds, succeeded in breaking his parents' embrace and pushing the sky away from the earth. The rain, the dew, and the rising mist are the tears of these first parents, who lament their separation even to the present day.

All the gods stayed with their mother except Tawhiri, the god of winds, who went with his father and sent down great storms to attack his rebellious brothers. The forest trees of Tane crashed to the ground; Tangaroa, the fish-god, fled to the sea; the deities of the plants crept back to their mother's arms. Only Tu, the god of uncreated man, remained erect in that primeval storm. In his anger with his cowardly brothers he turned against their flocks; ever since he has netted the fish, speared the birds, eaten the fern-root and the sweet potato, chopped down trees for houses or canoes.

Beneath the earth there lay the underworld of *po*, darkness; above were the ten skies in which the gods set the sun, the moon and the stars to give light. When the universe was arranged according to their wishes, they decided to create mankind. Out of red soil they shaped the first woman, the Earth-formed-maid. Tane gave her life by breathing in her nostrils. He mated with her and the Dawn-maid was born. Tane then took his daughter for wife and she bore him another daughter. The Dawn-maid asked Tane 'Who is my father?' When, from his evasive reply, she guessed that their relations had been incestuous, she fled to the Underworld, where she took the name of the Great-lady-of-darkness, and remained to gather in the souls of her descendants.

Eventually the Maori Adam was born. In those far days men were like gods and the gods like men. One of the first men, the hero Maui, thought that Ra, the sun, moved too fast, so Maui and his brothers snared him when he emerged from his nightly lair. Then, while Ra was held fast, Maui beat him with the jaw-bone of his grandmother, Murirangawhenua, until, bruised and aching, he had to crawl across the sky ever more.

One day Maui went out fishing with his brothers. Though they had little food or water, he induced them to sail far to the south, into unknown waters, until he decided to try his luck. He then hit himself on the nose and smeared blood on the jaw-bone of his grandmother. With this charmed bait, with that prodigious hook, after a long struggle he fished the North Island of New Zealand, *Te Ika a Maui* – the Fish of Maui – up from the deep seas.

At last Maui met his match when he tried to secure immortality for mankind by killing the goddess of death.

> Death came to the mighty
> When Maui was strangled
> By the Great-lady-of-the-night,
> And so it remained in the world.

His fish lay forgotten in the mists and storms of the Great Ocean of Kiwa, hidden from all men.

According to a Maori tradition widely spread among the tribes, New Zealand was discovered by Kupe, who cut up Maui's fish into our present islands. 'His feat was to divide the land. He saw only two beings, Crow and Fantail. Kupe did not settle. He returned across the sea. He left his mark here, but he himself returned. . . .' So relates one version of the legend recorded over a century ago.

When he reached Hawaiki, the ancestral home of the Maoris, he allegedly gave directions for reaching *Tiritiri o te Moana*, the Gift of the Sea, an ancient name for New Zealand. Because of quarrels or hunger, or by accident, others went to the new land. The names of many of these early settlers, like Turi and Toi, are still remembered.

Most of the Maori tribes trace their descent from ancestors who came in great ocean-going canoes, *Tainui, Te Arawa, Aotea, Takitimu, Tokomaru* and many others. One or two traditions suggest that some of these canoes sailed at about the same time – in the so-called 'Fleet'. They arrived about two dozen generations ago, judging from some genealogies, which led some early European students of Maori lore, as interested in the precise facts as in the marvels of their feat, to date their arrival in A.D. 1350.

Some evidence has suggested that the Hawaiki of legend was in the Society Islands (Tahiti); some points to the Marquesas Islands. It was certainly in Eastern Polynesia, but exactly where, if there was indeed only one point of origin, is unknown.

In the even more distant past the Polynesians had come in their sailing canoes across the Pacific, island by island, from the East Indies. Some common vocabulary in the Maori and Malay languages remains to remind us of this prehistoric relationship. The Maori word for death, *mate*, is *mati* in Malay; *ika* (fish) is *ikan*; *rua* (two) is *dua*; *rima* (five) is *lima*.

Earlier still, they probably came from south China. It may be, too, that some ancestors of the Polynesians had sailed from South America on rafts, like the *Kon Tiki*, bringing the sweet potato and other plants.

Most of New Zealand's human history is shrouded in pre-literate time. When does legend become fact, tradition change into history? When do the gods and culture heroes become men? The archaeologist's trowel reaches further into the past than genealogical memory, if less far than myth.

Excavation and radio-carbon dating have in recent years revealed that by the eleventh or twelfth century A.D. people of East Polynesian origin were living on sites scattered along the thousand-mile length of the country. It is evident from this fact that the original settlement must have occurred long before, certainly by the eighth century. Thus New Zealand has a pre-history of at least a thousand years before the arrival of Europeans and written records, and possibly longer.

It was once thought, because of a Maori tradition, that the aboriginal inhabitants, the *tangata whenua* or 'men of the land', as the Maoris called their precursors, were darker than the Maori and probably Melanesian. This was not impossible, for Melanesians reached Fiji; but no Melanesian remains have been found in New Zealand. From the design of their stone adzes, fish-hooks and personal ornaments, we know that the first inhabitants to leave any traces (or any as yet discovered) came from East Polynesia.

These early New Zealand Polynesians are generally called moa-hunters because of the association in their graves, and on their village or camp sites, of their characteristic implements and the bones and eggs of the moa. *Moa* was the Polynesian word for the domestic fowl, but these early inhabitants of New Zealand, having, it seems, brought no moa with them, applied the word to the wingless birds which ranged in flocks on the grasslands of both islands. The moa was in New Zealand the equivalent of such grazing animals as the American buffalo, the Australian kangaroo, or the European and Asian sheep, goats and cattle.

The moa-hunters killed enormous numbers of one *genus* of moa, the *Euryapteryx gravis*, a squat and massive bird about the height of a man. In some places they also ate the *Dinornis*, a moa ten feet high. The moa must have been an easy prey and a wonderful food supply for the fortunate men who found them. They had many other uses. Dead chieftains were buried with large reel necklaces made from sections of moa thigh-bones, and water bottles made of perforated eggs, as well as stone implements to take on their journey to the spirit land.

'Moa-hunter' is a useful name to distinguish the inhabitants in the archaic phase of New Zealand Polynesian culture from the 'Maori' whom the Europeans met. But in a sense it is misleading, for the moa-hunters outlived their prey. Indeed they helped exterminate it. By the time the Europeans came the Maoris had forgotten or almost forgotten the existence of the moa – almost no references to it can be found in Maori legend.

The moa-hunters were a stone-age, fishing and hunting people. An astonishing number of pits of all shapes and sizes have been discovered on a few sites which they occupied. Though some of these may have been sunken dwellings, it seems that most were storage pits for *kumara* (sweet potato) or possibly for *taro*. There is also evidence of 'made' soils, fertilized with wood ash and other substances and loosened by adding gravel, on very ancient sites. In other words, agriculture was practised at an early date.

Their villages were unfortified and placed in the open and, although they were hunters, they seem to have possessed no weapons of war, unless they were made of perishable wood. So they do not appear to have been a fighting folk.

They manufactured many types of stone adzes, including the beautiful tanged quadrangular, all of East Polynesian origin. Their chevroned amulets and bone necklaces have a strange, remote beauty. In many caves one can still see paintings or etchings which may be their work.

Of their culture not much more may be said. Their religion, their genealogies, like most of their customs, are lost in the silences of prehistoric time. But no doubt more evidence of their life will be dug up, while more may be imagined. Anyone who has stood in an archaeologist's trench on a hot summer day and recovered from the shells and stone flakes of a midden a broken fish lure of fossilized wood, or from the fatty burnt soil of an oven a bone fish-hook, still embedded in a fish skull where the fisherman carelessly threw it away, knows that life on a New Zealand beach has not altogether changed.

'Classical' Maori culture, as it was seen by Europeans in the eighteenth century, though still Polynesian, was strikingly different from that of the early inhabitants. The varied and useful moa-hunter 'adze kit', for instance, had been discarded in favour of a standardized quadrangular adze with no grip and polished on all surfaces; necklaces had given way to ear-rings and pendants, notably the greenstone *hei-tiki*. There had been marked changes in the design of fish-hooks and many other artifacts. Some of these new forms have Polynesian parallels, while others seem to be New Zealand innovations. Warfare had become endemic. There was now a formidable array of weapons, including the short, spatulate clubs, *mere* and *patu*. The landscape was dominated, especially in the north, by the palisaded, terraced hilltop fortress, the *pa*.

The reasons for these changes, which could have been the result either of local cultural evolution or of alien intrusion, presumably by further Polynesian immigrants, or of both circumstances, are unknown. Archaeologists generally incline to the former view, that moa-hunter culture merged into Maori. But no intermediary phase has been found. Nor is it yet clear in which locality Maori culture evolved. In some places the two cultures co-existed for a time. A radio-carbon dating suggests that in the seventeenth century people using 'moa-hunter' or 'archaic' artifacts lived on an island a few miles away from a great Maori *pa* on the site of modern Auckland. All that is certain is that moa-hunter culture existed earlier than Maori.

Some scholars still seek to reconcile archaeological evidence with Maori tradition. In their view Maori culture came with the supposed 'Fleet' in the fourteenth century and superseded that of the earlier people. This is an opinion which faces great problems, notably that no one can say where so recent an immigration could have come from, for many elements in Maori culture have no known Polynesian parallels. Certainly its principal material items do not seem to have been assembled elsewhere in a single place.

Recently the traditionalists have come under heavy fire. The assumption that New Zealand was settled intentionally presupposes that a Polynesian explorer could have discovered the country, returned home, and instructed his people on the geography of the South Pacific. But this is extremely difficult to believe. The Polynesian seaman could not fix his position if he were blown off course, nor accurately determine his drift in a current or wind. Well-authenticated Polynesian voyages, out of sight of land, of two or three hundred miles are impressive enough, but it seems impossible that the Polynesians could accurately have navigated distances of one or two thousand miles. If they ever knew how to do so, it is hard to explain why they had forgotten the art by the time the European navigators arrived, and knew so little of the geography of the Pacific.

Andrew Sharp who, in *Ancient Voyagers in Polynesia* (1963), advanced the arguments outlined here, believed that the Pacific Islands, including New Zealand, were peopled as a result of the unintentional travels of Polynesians who, setting off on short voyages, were blown off course, or lost their way, so that they could not return to their native island. There was a variant form of this one-way voyaging. It is believed that Polynesians sometimes, voluntarily or otherwise, went into exile; sailed off with their families and foodplants and animals in search of the new islands which, their past experience assured them, must still lie ahead. If so, though their destinations were accidental, their settlements were intentional.

The traditional view of New Zealand's origins is not entirely altered by this theory. Instead of successive waves of voluntary immigrants we must imagine the occasional arrival of castaways, flotsam and jetsam on the greatest ocean on the globe. The first settlers must have been very few, for no substantial number of people are likely to have been washed up on shores over a thousand miles from the nearest land. Unless the settlers were 'exiles', and probably even then, there can have been few females, for women did not generally put to sea on fishing trips or expeditions of war. Sharp believes that some settlers may have come from the Cook Islands where, some traditions aver, the 'Fleet' put in on its way from Tahiti. Maori traditions may perpetuate the names of some of the canoes and their occupants, though there can have been no 'Fleet'. But the romantic reader may still find consolation in the thought that, after all, it is still not utterly impossible that some Polynesian seafarer, accidentally discovering New Zealand, might have found his way home to tell his tale.

The views of traditionalists are being further undermined by the work of linguists who are studying genuine Maori traditions as recorded a century or more ago. Much that now passes as tradition turns out to be a product of European scholarship of seventy years ago – interpretations, reconciliations of conflicting traditions achieved by omitting the marvellous elements in favour of the barely plausible. In particular there seems to be no traditional warrant for the assertion that Kupe discovered New Zealand in A.D. 925 and that Toi arrived in about 1150. Nor do early traditions speak clearly of a 'Fleet'. It is doubtful whether any Maori knew the 'tradition' about the discovery and settlement which is taught to most New Zealand school children until a European wrote it. If we content ourselves with the Maori traditions as they were first recorded, we find a mixture of unsifted fact and fable which contributes little to firm knowledge. Kupe lives on, but whether man or demigod, discoverer or post-settlement explorer, no one can say.

At present it seems likely that more than one group of Polynesians settled in New Zealand. Their landings may have been early in its human history, or separated by centuries. The unique Maori culture may have resulted from the amalgamation and evolution, over a millennium, of elements from different parts of Eastern Polynesia. But speculation must be cautious in view of the rapid growth of prehistorical studies.

Once the moa became extinct the moa-hunters and Maoris must have had a hard time in many parts of *Aotearoa*, 'the land of the long white cloud', as they came to call their home. It had a good soil, but in comparison with tropical Polynesia little food was to be had for the picking. There were berries. Fern-root, the rhizome of bracken, which could be dried and stored, and its starch made into cakes, became a staple food. Forest birds, shell-fish and fish were exceedingly varied and plentiful. They were the chief source of protein. There were no native land mammals except for a bat. The Maoris ate the dog and the rat, which they had brought with them. In addition, as Sir Peter Buck (Te Rangi Hiroa), the most famous Polynesian scholar, dryly remarked, 'Human flesh was eaten when procurable.'

The Maoris thrived and multiplied partly because they introduced certain food plants to New Zealand, especially the *kumara* (the sweet potato), the *taro*, and the yam. They grew their crops beyond the 44° south latitude in Canterbury, nearer to the South Pole than any other people in pre-Columbian times. For several months of the year their life was organized round the planting, weeding and storing of their crops. It was their custom to shift their cultivations from time to time, so the burning and clearing of new ground must have been a laborious and lengthy task.

The Maoris knew nothing of working metals, which were, in any case, scarce in New Zealand. They had no artificial source of power, no working animals, no means of transportation except canoes or walking. Yet, with bone and stone implements, and man-power, they evolved an impressive culture, in many respects the most highly-developed in Polynesia.

The reader must look in museums, in *The Coming of the Maori*, by Sir Peter Buck, or in other books by New Zealand scholars, to learn of the techniques by which the Maoris plaited and wove flax into baskets, cloaks, and skirts; of how they made adzes and axes of stone, fish-hooks and needles of bone; of their musical instruments and their ornaments; their methods of constructing their great wooden meeting-houses and their canoes. Most of these things were less efficient or harder to make than similar articles brought by the Europeans, and have almost ceased to be produced, but in one respect the material culture of the Maori was not inferior to that of the Europeans. In some of their crafts the Maoris produced objects not yet surpassed in beauty of design or decoration by the works of their successors. They excelled at carving: in wood, on their war-canoes, their ornate meeting-houses, their boxes and tattooing funnels; and in stone. Perhaps their most beautiful products were the short clubs and the personal ornaments they carved from a translucent nephrite, a type of jade known locally as greenstone. To acquire it they even crossed the Southern Alps to reach the west coast of the South Island – the Maori name for which was *Te Wai Pounamu*, the Water of Jade.

In Maori carving a conventionalized human figure was the chief motif. Their patterns, whether for painting on rafters or tattooing on men's faces, thighs and buttocks and on women's lips and chin, were predominantly curvilinear. They were based on various forms of scroll, crescent and double spiral, quite unlike those in general use in Polynesia. It appears either that the Polynesians brought a rectilinear art to New Zealand, and that their curvilinear patterns were therefore a local development, or that the latter patterns survived in New Zealand after they had almost ceased to be used farther north.

Over the centuries the Maoris multiplied and spread out until the whole island was divided up among a number of tribes, each tracing its origin to occupants of one of the original canoes: in the far north the Ngapuhi; to the south of present-day Auckland, the Ngatihaua, the Ngatimaniapoto and a group of tribes usually called the Waikato; in Taranaki, the Atiawa, Taranaki and Ngatiruanui; on the east coast the Ngatiporou and the Arawa confederation; and others too numerous to list. There were very few Maori inhabitants of the colder South Island, though the moa-hunters seem to have lived there in numbers.

The tribe was an extended kinship organization made up of *hapu*, sub-tribes and *whanau*, family groups larger than the European family. A Maori, belonging to each of these three groups, was a member of a community in a sense in which his individualistic European successor is not. The greater part of life was a communal experience. Most activities were shared and were performed for the sake of the community. Land, by far the most important form of property, belonged to the tribe, though the sub-tribe, the family and the individual had hereditary rights of usufruct.

Within each tribe the population was further divided into slaves, who were mostly prisoners of war, *tutua* or commoners, and the numerous class of chiefs, *rangatira*. At the head of the tribe there was a paramount chief, the *ariki*. Chieftainship, with its prerogatives of leadership and power, was hereditary, but a weak chief would find himself superseded, in the effective exercise of authority, by a more able rival. The chiefs were not entirely despotic, for they could not ignore public opinion as expressed at tribal meetings by subordinate chiefs. Nevertheless they possessed considerable power by virtue of the *mana* (a word meaning something more than 'prestige') which resulted from exalted descent and past achievements. The person of the chief was to some extent *tapu* (sacred); high chiefs were regarded with considerable awe and even dread.

The Maoris lived in a world dangerous and hostile. To modern New Zealanders it would seem that the gods and demons were close and uncomfortable neighbours. Many of the spirits inhabiting animate and inanimate nature had considerable powers for evil. But man was not defenceless. His priests possessed knowledge of witchcraft and magic which could be turned against invisible foes. Above all he could call the spirits of his ancestors and the gods, who were often identical, to his aid. When the mischievous Maui was stealing the fire of Mahuika, the fire goddess, she set the land and the seas and the forest on fire, but he was able to call on his ancestors, the gods Tawhiri and Whatitiri, who sent down torrential rain to save him. Fortunately, before all her fires were extinguished, the goddess threw a few sparks into the *kaikomako* tree from which mankind was able to make fire by rubbing two sticks together.

It is probable that many aspects of Maori religion have been forgotten by the Maoris and were never accurately written down or even understood by Europeans. Few of the early missionaries, who made a determined onslaught upon heathenism, were concerned to record for posterity what they were so busy destroying. Existing accounts of Maori religious beliefs are full of internal contradiction, but the indications are that these beliefs were not fundamentally different from those familiar in many other parts of the world. Maori religious tradition had its Flood. As in the Mesopotamian theogony, there was the Maori legend of the separation of the earth and sky. In the former case that feat was attributed to Enlil, the god of Winds who, in the popular Maori legend, under the name of Tawhiri, departed with his father, the sky. But such parallels, though innumerable, are of little or no significance except as a prompt to idle speculation.

The Maoris had vast numbers of gods. First there were the sons of Rangi and Papa, the 'departmental' deities, like Tane, the god of trees and birds; Tu, the god of war; Rongo, the god of peace and agriculture; or Tangaroa, the sea-god. Then there were gods who belonged exclusively to a tribe. Others were worshipped only by individual families. In addition there were deified ancestors and semi-divine heroes of mythology like Maui. There is no convincing evidence that the Maoris recognized a supreme god. An early missionary, Richard Taylor, who studied Maori mythology, wrote flatly that 'the natives had no knowledge of a Supreme Being'. Io, who has been assigned this role, seems to have been a post-Christian accretion.

The Maoris believed in an after-life, though not one in which reward or punishment was given for conduct in this world. After death, the spirit travelled to the north of New Zealand, where it drank from a stream called the Water-of-the-Underworld and then journeyed to Cape Te Reinga, one of the most northerly points. There it climbed down the roots of an ancient *pohutukawa*, a tree which in the summer is covered with fine, blood-red flowers, plunged into the great Ocean of Kiwa, and departed to the spirit world which was supposed to lie in the direction of Hawaiki.

The ministers of religion were the *tohunga*, who were usually chiefs, though they did not form a hereditary or distinct caste. The superior kind of priest received an arduous training in a *whare wananga*, a house of learning. He was not only supposed to possess powers of communicating with the gods and interpreting their will, but he was also the scholar, the living repository of knowledge and tribal history. The Maoris had no written language, but they were trained from childhood to marvellous feats of memory, especially in connexion with the tribal genealogies.

At the other end of the scale from the aristocratic priest was the sorcerer, the mere medium, who was allegedly 'possessed' by a god. In between these extremes were several grades of *tohunga* who were what we should call experts, whether in carving, tattooing, building canoes, or in other specialized skills.

The higher class of *tohunga* had many functions. They could recite the *karakia* (prayers, incantations, spells) with greater efficacy than the layman. In battle the *tohunga* would pluck the heart from the 'first fish', the first enemy killed, and offer it to the tribal war god – a rite which recalls the Aztec sacrifice. The *tohunga* conducted all sorts of rituals in connexion with war, birth, sickness, burial and other important occasions. Above all the *tohunga* could make and unmake *tapu*. '*Tapu*', like its anglicized form 'taboo', meant 'holy', 'prohibited', 'consecrated', or 'set apart as accursed'. It was one of the most useful of Maori concepts – and one of the widest application. Every chief was to some extent *tapu*, in which respect *tapu* served the political function of sustaining tribal authority. Furthermore, this personal *tapu* extended, in a lesser form, to the personal property of the chiefs, to their clothes, ornaments, or weapons. To steal such property, or to break the law of *tapu* in other respects, made the offender liable to mysterious but dreadful punishment at the hands of the evil spirits who caused sickness. Thus *tapu* not only constituted the law of property but also penalized the transgressor. The Maori tribe had no police force, but *tapu* inspired such terror that voluntary lawbreaking must have been rare. *Tapu* also protected burial grounds, cultivation grounds, provided a powerful sanction for the observation of etiquette, and served a hundred other social purposes besides its association with holy places and religious rites.

In his book *Old New Zealand*, Judge F. E. Maning, who in his younger days had been a 'Pakeha Maori' (that is a white man living with and more or less as the Maoris), in 1863 related how once he became *tapu* through accidentally touching a skull. He observed that this kind of *tapu* was like the 'uncleanness' of old Jewish law. His friends and servants fled and no one would come near him. He was not permitted to enter a house or to touch food. The unfortunate who became *tapu* was expected either to eat off the ground or to be fed by another person, lest his hands contaminate the food. After he began to fear that his excommunication would be indefinite, Maning was rescued by a famous *tohunga*, 'an old, grave, stolid-looking savage, with one eye, the other having been knocked out long ago in a fight before he turned parson'. He came up 'grumbling a perfectly unintelligible *karakia* or incantation'; fed Maning some sweet potato; made him change his clothes; and proceeded to destroy all the pots, crockery and cutlery in the kitchen in which Maning was discovered. Even then, although he was purified, Maning found that for years the servants kept at a safe distance for fear that he might 'retain some tinge of the dreadful infection'.

Religion pervaded the life of the Maoris; yet they do not seem to have been what we should regard as a religious people. There is something informal about their religious practices. They had no organized priesthood and their rituals were quite simple, lacking the complicated ceremonial found in many other lands. Whereas in some parts of Polynesia, the temples were elaborate buildings, in New Zealand they were mere shrines, secluded spots marked by stones or posts. Among the Maoris the *marae*, a word which elsewhere in Polynesia meant temple, was the plaza which lay before the meeting-house and was the focus of village life. Most important of all, the *marae* was the place where men of influence made their speeches.

Debate and war were the great excitements of the Maori public; and the greater of these was war. There was no finer way of acquiring *mana* than by seeking it, if not yet in the cannon's mouth, at least in the most dangerous position in the front of a phalanx. The Maoris were a military people and fighting was a highly-developed art. It had its rituals, its prayers, its dances, its traditions, its seasons. There can have been few people in the world who took as great delight in fighting or in stories of bloody deeds, treachery and heroism.

They went to war for such a catalogue of reasons that at no time was an aggressive tribe or *hapu* likely to be short of a pretext. Revenge for past defeat, for injury, even for insult, was a common motive. They fought, too, over land. As the population grew, North Island tribal boundaries became clearly defined and caused as much tension as those of European states.

The Maoris gave careful attention to training the young man in the use of weapons, spears, clubs or throwing sticks – they do not seem to have used the bow and arrow. They specialized in hand-to-hand fighting. Their favourite tactics were the ambush and surprise attacks. Their chief defence was the fortified hill-top village, the *pa*, which was capable of offering effective resistance to weapons much more formidable than those of the Maori. The intricate combinations of buildings, terraces, trenches and scarps, the stockades of tree trunks, lashed together with creepers and crowning either a terrace or the parapet of a ditch, made the *pa* extremely difficult to storm. Even when the outer wall was breached, the enemy found each inner terrace or house a fortress still to be taken. Many of the hills of northern New Zealand, carved with the great encircling terraces of ancient *pa*, remain as a memorial to forgotten enmities.

It does not seem, from the observations of explorers, that the Maoris normally lived in their *pa*: rather they retired to them in time of danger. Most of them apparently lived in small villages or hamlets. The explorers saw large houses, twenty or so feet long, and numerous huts. The more substantial, finished structures were sometimes taken to be chiefs' houses. Captain Cook, however, concluded that they were family houses. He thought that 'in the summer season . . . many of them live dispers'd up and down in little temporary hutts'. If so, they had already invented the 'bach', 'crib' or cottage which lines the modern seashore.

In many areas, especially to the south where agriculture was difficult, many Maoris led a more or less nomadic existence in search of food. In 1773 none of the people remained whom Cook had encountered in Queen Charlotte Sound three years before and none of the new inhabitants had heard of him. Settled life, the *pa*, and possibly warfare, were more characteristic of the warmer north.

The Maoris can never have been very numerous, though no one knows their numbers before the coming of the white man or for long after. Cook, who saw only coastal regions, supposed that there were 100,000. A fairer guess might be 200,000, though some estimates are more than twice as high again.

In numbers as in other respects, the Maoris were the greatest of Polynesian peoples. Their most notable achievement was to have found a way of living and thriving in a new country in an unaccustomed climate. But their epic lacked a Homer, and though many of their deeds are sketched in chant or song, most are not to be found among the scholar's facts, however vivid they may be to the historical imagination.

PART ONE

MAORI AND SETTLER
1642–1870

NORTH ISLAND
Showing several Maori Tribal Districts
and Early Settlements.
(About 1838)

Te Moananui a Kiwa

Whangaroa
Waimate
Bay of Islands
Kororareka
Waitangi
Ngapuhi
Hokianga

Kaipara

Ngati Whatua
Manukau

Waitemata

Waikato   Ngati Haua
Ngati Maniapoto

Waipa R.
Waikato R.
Ngati Awa
Te Arawa
Ngati Porou

Waitara R.
Taupo
Atiawa   Ngati Tuwharetoa
Taranaki   TE IKA
Ngati Ruanui
A MAUI

Ngati Kahungungu

Ngati Toa

Ngati Tahu
TE WAI
POUNAMU

Scale of Miles

0   50   100   150

I: AUSTRALIAN COLONY

Nothing is more evident than that New Zealand must, at no
distant period, form an integral and productive part of the
immense Australian empire.

Sydney Gazette, 1831

AFTER the spread of the Polynesians, none of the main tides of
world history reached New Zealand for a very long time. The
great religions, Hinduism, Buddhism and Catholicism, swept
down from Europe or India past Malaya and broke up in the
Indonesian archipelago. For centuries the Polynesians kept
their myriad islands to themselves, but they could not permanently hide such treasures from the curious European. While
the first immigrants were hunting the moa in New Zealand,
the feudality of Europe was embarking on the crusades; it was
not much later that Marco Polo reached the China seas, and his
countrymen heard of the fabulous province of 'Beach', which
supposedly lay to the south. The expansion of Europe had
begun. Before it ended, in our own time, the greater part of the
world, including the scattered islands of the Pacific, was to be
seized by an insatiable civilization, greedy for spices or for
realms of gold; for land, mere novelty, or for souls. Magellan
sailed the ocean which Balboa had first scanned from that peak
in Darien, and in the late sixteenth century Mendaña discovered some northern Polynesian islands. Soon *Te Ika a Maui*
and *Te Wai Pounamu*, the largest of the Polynesian islands,
were once more fished up from the depths of the south. The
new discoverer was a Dutch seaman, Abel Janszoon Tasman,
who was looking for something more marvellous and hoped he
had found it.

In the early seventeenth century the extent of the African,
American and European continents was roughly known, but
it was believed by many seamen and scholars that an unknown
continent, of which the partially explored northern coast of
Australia might be one limit, must stretch across the Pacific
between South Africa and South America. The existence of
this *Terra Australis Incognita* was argued on several grounds
supposedly scientific; but the chief reason why so many be-

lieved in it was that they hoped it was there. Perhaps the Dutch or the English could discover the place called 'Beach', a land richer than the Spaniard's continent. Drake had already sought it. Now, in 1642, Tasman was sent from Batavia 'for the discovery and exploration of the supposed rich southern and eastern land'. Should he fall in with civilized folk, his instructions from the Governor-General and Councillors of the Dutch East Indies enjoined that he should try 'to find out what commodities their country yields, likewise inquiring after gold and silver, whether the latter are by them held in high esteem; making them believe that you are by no means eager for precious metals, so as to leave them ignorant of the value of the same.'

On 13 December, the crews of the *Heemskerck* and the *Zeehaen* sighted 'a large, high-lying land'. It was part of the west coast of the South Island of New Zealand. A few days later, in Golden Bay (which Tasman named Murderers' Bay) they were visited by two 'praus' full of men who called out 'in a rough, hollow voice' and blew on an instrument which sounded like a Moorish trumpet (it would have been a shell trumpet, which was used, for instance, to announce visitors). Next day Tasman had a closer view of these men. Their colour seemed between yellow and brown and they wore their hair on the top of the head and decorated it with a large white feather. They wore mats or 'cotton stuffs' and paddled their double canoes at considerable speed. A cock boat was sent out to make friends but one of the canoes rammed it. In this first encounter between Maori and European, four Dutchmen were killed. Despite musket-shot and gunfire from the ships, the aggressors escaped to the shore.

Tasman charted part of the west coast of the country, which he called Staten Landt, hoping that the Staten Landt which had been discovered by one of his countrymen off Tierra del Fuego might stretch so far; but he did not linger long on this inhospitable shore. The Governor-General and Councillors were disappointed. True, Tasman had discovered Van Diemen's Land (now Tasmania) and Staten Landt (which was soon renamed Nieuw Zeeland, after the Dutch province, when the original Staten Landt was found to be an island); but 'in point of fact no treasures or matters of great profit' had been found. Nieuw Zeeland was left to its savage inhabitants for another century, though its existence was recorded in a few charts and books.

The next captain to sight the islands was James Cook, a labourer's son who rose from his apprenticeship in coal shipping to become the greatest seaman and navigator of his day and to explore perhaps more of the earth's surface than any man before him. He was sent by the Royal Society and the Admiralty to visit Tahiti in order to observe a transit of Venus. Thereafter he was instructed to search for the legendary southern continent. If this search were unsuccessful, finally he was to explore the coast of New Zealand. He failed only in the second impossible task, but he had the satisfaction at least of feeling that his circumnavigation of New Zealand meant 'the total demolition of our aerial fabrick called Continent'. On this occasion, in 1769, he established that New Zealand was not that fabulous land; three years later he proved that, apart from Australia, the southern continent did not exist at all.

Seldom can an expedition have added more to knowledge than Cook's first Pacific voyage. The *Endeavour* carried two distinguished botanists, Joseph Banks and Daniel Solander, whose observations and collections gave the first glimpse of a new world to European scientists.

New Zealand has been so long separate from other land that it is sometimes regarded as forming a distinct botanical region: as much as three-quarters of its flora is unique. It must, moreover, have been isolated before the appearance of mammals. In the New Zealand ecology, birds have come to occupy many of the positions held elsewhere by mammals. For instance, in the absence of competition from mammals, several species of flightless birds have developed. One is the *Notornis* which, as the moa once did, grazes on the grasslands; another, the kiwi, forages in the bush.

Geography as well as botany and zoology gained from the expedition. Apart from two obvious errors, Cook's chart of New Zealand was superb, especially in view of the fact that he relied on lunar observation to determine longitude. His charts revealed to the world a country a thousand miles long, extending over thirteen degrees of latitude, about the size of Italy or Great Britain. It lies at the centre of the water hemisphere, almost as remote as possible from the land masses of the globe. It is nearly 1,300 miles (as far as is London by air from Malta, or Paris from Moscow) from the east coast of Australia; 6,000 miles from the Asian or American continent; and twice as far from Great Britain. The southern island has a mountainous backbone, rising to over 12,000 feet, which was Tasman's first glimpse of the country; the northern island is extremely rugged. The climate is sub-tropical in the north, sub-temperate in the south, as befits a land lying at the antipodes of Gibraltar and Portugal.

The information which the expedition collected about the Maoris was a great stimulus, not only to the romantic, but soon to the missionary and the ethnologist, who were often the same person.

At Tahiti Cook took on board Tupaia, a chieftain and the principal priest of the local religion, who picked up a little English and whose presence enabled the British to communicate more easily with the Maoris. What restlessness, what curiosity, what courage, one wonders, could have led him to entrust himself to these strange white men who, only two years before, had first visited his island in their great ships?

With the Maoris, Cook's relations were at first as unfortunate as Tasman's. Several initial encounters resulted in the death of natives, following what the Europeans interpreted as hostile actions on their part. Eventually, however, Cook 'learned how to manage them without taking away their lives' and came to think of them as 'a brave, warlike people, with sentiments void of treachery'.

To picture how these undreamed-of strangers must have appeared to the Maori, we must imagine what our reactions would be if we suffered a Martian invasion. According to one Maori chief, Te Horeta Taniwha, who as a small boy was present when Cook came to Mercury Bay, the Maoris at first thought the white men were goblins and their ship a god. Eighty years later the old man recalled their astonishment when one of the goblins pointed a walking-stick at a shag and, amidst thunder and lightning, the bird fell down dead. 'There was one supreme man in that ship. We knew that he was the lord of the whole by his perfect gentlemanly and noble demeanour.' This chief goblin gave the little boy a nail which he long kept with great care as a tool and a god.

Many other explorers followed Cook before the end of the century. De Surville arrived two months after Cook and before he had left. His unnecessarily brutal treatment of the Maoris was followed by the massacre of his countryman, Marion du Fresne, three years later. George Vancouver, D'Entrecastaux, and the Italian Malaspina who led a Spanish expedition, came later. And so New Zealand became part of a world greater than the Polynesian. Cook had praised the country, remarking on the quantity of excellent timber and the native flax, noting the fertility of the soil. He had fancied that were it 'settled by an Industrus people they would very soon be supply'd not only with the necessarys but many of the luxuries of life'. It seemed to him that the natives were too much divided among themselves to unite in opposing settlers. It could not be long before the islands and their inhabitants would be drawn into the net of Europe's commerce and the grip of its power.

In the European history of New Zealand, trade came second, close in the wake of the first navigators. Trading and whaling vessels calling at New Zealand ports kidnapped Maoris, or signed them on as crew. A prison chaplain, who encountered these tattooed seamen at Sydney, determined to save their people from paganism and exploitation: thus industry and commerce brought the missionaries. Mission and trade led to a residence which became settlement; and the flag followed the settler.

The chief source of almost all these enterprises was Sydney, so that it might be said that for some thirty years before 1840 New Zealand was the colony of a convict settlement; but such a remark, while not devoid of truth, misses the dynamic of this Australian expansion. Almost from its foundations in 1788 the settlement at Port Jackson refused to remain a prison. No sooner had the first Governor left than there sprang up among the officials, who were soon joined by other free settlers and emancipated convicts, a group of men, aggressive and far from scrupulous, who began trading and farming on their own account. By means of speculative ventures, and through the unpaid services of 'assigned' convict labourers, they eventually formed a prosperous middle class. So the convict establishment, born of poverty and hatred, gave birth to wealth and hope.

It was this trading class which first took an interest in the profits which might be made in New Zealand; it would, therefore, be true to say that the story of early European enterprise in New Zealand is substantially the tale of an Australian frontier.

In 1792 a vessel from Sydney left a gang of sealers at Dusky Sound, a fiord on the south-west coast of the South Island. At about the same time a few whaling vessels began to fish for the cachalot or sperm whale in New Zealand waters. The *Fancy*, from India and Sydney, spent three months in the Hauraki Gulf in 1794-5 collecting a cargo of spars. It was soon followed by other vessels. But such enterprise was restricted by the monopoly of the East India Company, which forbade private British vessels to trade, or indeed to sail, between the Cape of Good Hope and the Horn. The early British whaling or trading ventures in New Zealand were either licensed by the Company or illegal. Originally intended to stimulate British enterprise, this monopoly had become an anachronism, effectively checking any rapid expansion of British trade while offering no hindrance to foreign commerce. In the last years of the century it was slowly whittled away by the British Government under pressure from whaling, sealing, and other interests.

After 1800 British, American and French whalers began to fish regularly off the coast. They often called at the Bay of Islands or other harbours in order to refit and to trade with the Maoris. A Sydney firm in 1803 sent a schooner to Dusky Sound to resume the hunt for seals and soon the most southerly sounds and islands were the scene of a sad but profitable slaughter. The sealing vessels, American and Australian, would leave a gang at some promising spot; the shore party would establish a rough camp of tents, flax-walled huts, or mere upturned boats, on these desolate shores; for a period of months or even years the sealers would lead a harsh and precarious existence until their ship returned to collect the skins and oil and to drop supplies. Only too often their ships did not return, and the starving survivors had to await rescue by some passing vessel. Some of these gangs, finding a spot favoured by the great herds of seals, were remarkably successful. In 1806 one American vessel brought a cargo of 60,000 skins to Port Jackson; in one week in 1810, presumably at the height of the season, cargoes worth over £100,000 were landed there. But the sealers were too efficient: the indiscriminate slaughter of bulls, cows, and pups alike rapidly led to the virtual extermination of the mainland herds of seals. After 1810 most of the gangs of sealers moved off to the Campbell and Macquarie islands. Those who remained continued sealing as a sideline to trading in flax and timber, thus preventing the seals from re-establishing themselves in large numbers.

In the first decade of the nineteenth century the coastal tribes of Maoris were brought into regular contact with Europeans. Maoris helped to cut timber for spars, to drag the great trunks down to sea or river and to load them on to the ships. They sailed in the whalers as crew. A few, not always voluntarily, visited Norfolk Island, New South Wales and even England. New vegetables such as the potato, and new animals, especially the pig, were introduced into New Zealand. Gradually, mainly at the Bay of Islands, a busy trade sprang up. From the Europeans the Maoris chiefly wanted nails, which could be used for chisels, fish-hooks, axes, and other iron tools superior to their own. They also delighted in acquiring red things, paint or cloth. Red was their favourite colour for decoration and was also used to mark *tapu* objects. In exchange they provided women and food, including potatoes.

At this time the Maoris had their first opportunity to observe closely the ways of civilization. Needless to say, since the people they met (including a very few sealers, deserters or escaped convicts who settled down with them) were generally of the most brutalized or degraded sort, what they saw was rarely edifying. Visiting seamen infringed Maori law in innumerable ways – defied the *tapu*, stole the crops, filched weapons or mats for sale as 'curiosities' and kidnapped men or women without scruple.

Relations between the two peoples soon deteriorated into what New Zealand's first historian, Dr A. S. Thomson, in the *Story of New Zealand* (1859), called 'a war of races'. In the South Island about 1810, after a few years of friendly intercourse, the Maoris began to attack isolated sealing gangs and boats' crews. In 1809 a Maori who was working his passage back to New Zealand induced his tribe to revenge the insults and ill-treatment he had suffered. Almost everyone on board the *Boyd*, which brought him home to Whangaroa, was killed and eaten. And the same fate befell the crew of another ship wrecked off Cape Brett. For the next few years shipping kept away from the northern ports. New Zealand had acquired the reputation of being one of the most dangerous places in the Pacific.

The Saint Augustine of New Zealand was the Reverend Samuel Marsden, who had been born the son of a blacksmith, educated by an evangelical society in Yorkshire, and induced by Wilberforce himself to cut short his studies at Cambridge in order to attempt the thankless task of carrying the gospel to his expatriated countrymen in New South Wales. He was a man of sturdy physique, character and views. While chaplain to the convict settlement he acted as a superintendent of public works, where his flock sweated on the chain gang, and employed 'assigned' convicts on his large and prosperous farm. As a magistrate he had the doubtful distinction of earning – in Botany Bay – a reputation for the frequency with which he ordered the lash. Like so many other evangelicals, he seems to have reserved his pity rather for the 'poor benighted heathen' (his own phrase) abroad than for the heathen poor among his fellow citizens.

Despite his numerous, exacting duties, for many years Marsden entertained a further ambition: to start a mission in New Zealand. The chaplain's views on missionary work were in keeping with his practical abilities. The heathen, he believed, could not be converted unless they were also raised in the scale of civilization. They should be taught the arts and handicrafts of Europe as well as the gospels. When the missionary landed in a new field, if he held the cross in his right hand, the axe should be in his left. He thought that the first missionaries should be a few 'mechanics'. As it happened, when the Church Missionary Society agreed to launch the new mission it proved impossible to find any ordained ministers anxious to embark on so hazardous a venture. The humble men who came forward were admirably suited to test Marsden's views, views which were shared by many other evangelicals. The first three missionaries whom he took to New Zealand were William Hall, a carpenter, John King, a shoe-maker, who also knew something of rope-making, and Thomas Kendall, a school teacher. Most of their immediate successors were also 'hardy mechanics'.

On Christmas day, 1814, the gospel was preached on New Zealand soil for the first time. Marsden's text was from the gospel of St Luke: 'Behold I bring you good tidings of great joy.' He then returned to New South Wales and left his disciples at the Bay of Islands to a task even more discouraging than his own.

Those who had undertaken to convert the Maori were untrained as evangelists, unpractised in the disciplines of clerical life which might have enabled them to withstand the ardours and resist the temptations of life in a pagan land. The early missionaries bickered incessantly and bitterly among themselves. Within twenty years three had to be dismissed, one for adultery, one for drunkenness, and one 'for a crime worse than either'. The first of these, Thomas Kendall, a tragic, Faustian figure, rendered considerable service to his faith despite his fall. He was a man whose great imaginative vision was not matched by the intellectual discipline or the powers of expression that might have enabled him to complete his chosen task, which was nothing less than to understand and interpret the Maori world. Perhaps no one in his day, when the concepts of modern social anthropology were either unknown or repugnant to religious sensibilities, could have succeeded.

Kendall saw that if the Maoris were to be converted it was

necessary not only to speak their language, but to study their own religion and customs: only then could Christianity be explained to them in terms they could comprehend. In much of his conduct arrogant, he yet differed from many of his successors in approaching his task in this humble spirit. But he was too weak to stand intellectually quite alone in a savage world full of what were, to a naïve and puritanical young man, concepts at once fascinating and terrifying. In a sense he was converted by those he had come to save. As he wrote himself: 'I have been so poisoned with the apparent sublimity of their ideas, that I have been almost completely turned from a Christian to a Heathen.' Marsden's account was that by 'prying into the obscene mysteries of the natives in order to ascertain their notions of the Supreme Being, etc., his own mind was polluted; his natural Corruptions excited, & his vile Passions inflamed, by which means he fell into their vices'. Unaccustomed to a society frank in sexual matters, to a religion in which 'midwifery' (in Kendall's evasive term) was so intermingled with theology, or to women who did not regard virginity as sacrosanct, Kendall began sleeping with a Maori girl. He did, however, succeed in 1815 in publishing a small Maori dictionary, *The New Zealander's First Book*. In 1820 he took two famous chiefs, Hongi and Waikato, to England, and there helped Professor Lee, a remarkable linguist at Cambridge, to produce a more accurate orthography of the Maori language.

On the whole the Maoris protected and up to a point respected the missionaries. Some of them were willing to learn European methods of agriculture or to send their children to be fed and instructed in the mission schools. But the missionaries failed completely in their main aim. It was nine years before the first Maori was baptized – a girl about to marry a European; eleven before the next and death-bed conversion. No substantial progress was made until the eighteen-thirties. The Maoris showed no inclination to heed the message of the gospel. It was not, said the great chief Hongi, suitable for warriors.

This was the period which an historian has appropriately called 'the Maori domination'. Maori culture was as dominant over European as the Maoris were over local European settlers.

The Maoris were not converted to European civilization or its religion. They made use of European goods, but for Maori purposes. A nail would be flattened for a chisel. Red cloth was pulled to pieces to weave into cloaks. European blankets were used as cloaks. Soon muskets were in demand to pursue the traditional objectives of Maori society. The Maoris were still completely confident in the merit and rightness of their own culture.

While the Anglican mission was struggling to find its feet, traders and 'southseamen' slowly established a friendly inter-course with the Maoris. During the eighteen-twenties the economic frontiers of the Australian colonies were rapidly expanding. The first bank opened its doors in Sydney in 1817. British capital poured in to finance the squatters' illegal west-ward movement on to Crown lands. Eastwards the trading vessels probed the New Zealand market. The influence of commerce spread to all but the most inaccessible regions, providing a varied scene of Australian and Maori enterprise.

In the eighteen-twenties a considerable trade grew up in New Zealand flax. Sydney firms sent agents to barter with the Maoris for the dressed fibre, which was used to make rope. In many coastal districts, especially in the North Island, tribes were hard at work cutting and scraping flax to exchange for European goods, especially guns. This trade was worth £26,000 in 1831, when it began to decline, partly because the market weakened, partly because the Maori demand for European goods was not yet insatiable. Having collected what they considered enough guns, many tribes stopped work and turned to the more interesting task of repaying old debts.

The trade in kauri, a pine which rises sixty and sometimes eighty feet before the first branch, was also worth several thousands of pounds a year to Sydney firms. The depots of their agents formed busy little settlements on a number of northern harbours and bays. At Hokianga there was even a shipyard where several small vessels were built in the late eighteen-twenties.

In the same period a new whaling industry led to the setting-up of twenty or thirty shore establishments, most of them in the South Island. From these stations the men went out in their

absurdly small boats to hunt the 'right' or black whale. In the
'off' season they built boats, fished, farmed and raised half-
caste families.

The scene of the greatest activity was the Bay of Islands,
which became the centre of a substantial general trade. Whaling and trading vessels began to call in ever-increasing numbers: ships from Sydney, French ships, British ships, New
England whalers from Sag Harbour, Salem or Nantucket,
which had outstripped their competitors, and local vessels, the
New Zealander or the *Tokirau*. By the eighteen-thirties there
were as many as a hundred-and-fifty ships a year calling at the
Bay. The local Maoris and settlers grew prosperous by vic-
tualling ships. Resident traders also collected Maori produce,
such as potatoes and maize, from along the coast, and exported
it to Sydney.

To give some idea of the extent of the New Zealand trade,
two figures may be mentioned. The cargoes of the American
ships which called at the Bay of Islands in 1839 were estimated
to be worth $U.S.1,636,335. According to the records of the New
South Wales Government, in the same year goods worth
£95,173 were exported to New Zealand and produce to the
value of £71,707 was imported from the same source. If this
was New Zealand's first trade deficit it was not its last, but the
suggestion has been made that the discrepancy between these
figures was due to ships sailing from Sydney to England using
goods loaded in Sydney to purchase cargoes of New Zealand
timber for the English market.

During the eighteen-twenties and even more so in the thirties, as a result of increasing contacts with Europeans, the
northern Maoris came to feel the weight of western civilization
pressing on their lives. Their community began to pass through
a moral and technological revolution more comprehensive and
more painful than contemporary industrialization in Europe.
Old customs, everyday habits of eating or dress, eventually
traditional beliefs, were abandoned or altered, not always for
the better. In some places the tribal structure itself was totter-
ing.

By the end of the thirties almost all the Bay of Islands Maoris
wore European clothing. Men and women generally smoked

pipes. The Maoris had known no alcoholic beverages, but now many of them had acquired what often proved a deadly taste. Potatoes had replaced fernroot as a staple food. The Maoris grew and ate wheat, corn and a variety of European vegetables. But far more significant changes had occurred which had reduced the total Maori population by perhaps two-fifths.

The main cause of depopulation was undoubtedly the introduction of new diseases to which the Maoris had no resistance. The Maoris appear to have been a relatively healthy people, despite their various skin complaints and a rare form of leprosy. They were long protected by isolation from the arrival of new viruses. But the Europeans brought an armament of disease. There are traditions of eighteenth-century epidemics, resulting from contact with explorers, and many records of early nineteenth-century outbreaks of whooping cough, some form of influenza, smallpox, measles and what were probably typhoid and cholera. Europeans also introduced prostitution – eventually on an extensive scale at the Bay of Islands. Venereal diseases became extremely common, taking their toll in lives and fertility.

And the Maoris slaughtered themselves. By 1820 the Bay of Islands Maoris had decided that 'the great god of the white man' was the *pu*, the gun. He was the first new god to make converts. By about 1815 they were carried away with desire for guns. Even the early missionaries were forced to take part in the abominable trade in muskets. They had to trade in order to live, and for some time muskets were the only European product for which there was a keen Maori demand. In the twenties there was a huge increase in the area of cultivations at the Bay of Islands, evidently to produce food for trade – the Maoris had entered not a money but a musket economy. When they got enough guns, they set off to even old scores. Because of the ramifications of kinship, each new death involved further tribes in the demands of *utu*: murder spread out like waves from a stone dropped in the pool of tribal society. Europe came to Aotearoa like nothing so much as the plague.

By 1819 the Maoris at the Bay of Islands had several hundred *pu* and the prized *tupara* (double-barrelled musket). They were regarded with terror for hundreds of miles. In 1821 Hongi returned to New Zealand from his visit to England with Kendall. In Sydney the chief exchanged all the presents he received in London for three hundred muskets. Then, dressed, it is said, in a coat of mail which George IV had given him, he proceeded to terrorize his ancient enemies. Near modern Auckland he killed a thousand men; another thousand at the Thames; as many more of the Waikato tribes; and perhaps twice as many of Te Arawa died on an island in Lake Rotorua.

The Waikato tribes recovered and attacked those near Kawhia and in Taranaki. Warriors from Taranaki, Kawhia and elsewhere, led by a formidable Ngatitoa chief called Te Rauparaha, ravaged Cook Strait and invaded the South Island. In the twenties and early thirties these savage civil wars led to heavy casualties and cannibal feasts unprecedented in pre-European battles fought with stone-age weapons. It is estimated that about forty thousand people were slaughtered. It has taken until the present day for the Maori people to reach anything like their former numbers. A further effect, the disorganization of the tribal structure and the confusion of land titles due to conquest and tribal migrations, produced a difficult situation for European administrators after 1840.

Ideas were as destructive as bullets. The traders gave the Maoris the means of self-destruction: the missionaries set out to change the constitution of Maori life.

In 1823 the Anglican missionaries found a leader in an ex-naval lieutenant, Henry Williams, who introduced order and discipline into their efforts. They turned away from Marsden's views, being unable to see that 'an Axe was the best Missionary', and concentrated on teaching the gospel. In the circumstances they were justified, for so far civilization in New Zealand had meant guns rather than ploughs; but in the eighteen-forties and -fifties they returned to a broader and, in peaceful times, more practical educational policy, which combined agricultural and religious instruction.

The Anglican was joined by a Wesleyan mission in 1822. By 1830, having established firm beach-heads at the Bay of Islands and Hokianga respectively, they were able to launch an offensive towards the south. Victory was rapid and overwhelming. By 1840 perhaps half the Maoris of the Bay of Islands were at least nominally converts to Christianity. Farther south there were a thousand baptized and ten thousand regular churchgoers. Within a few years probably a majority of Maoris had been converted. Sometimes a tribe would follow its chief into the new religion. Christian doctrine spread far ahead of the missionaries as converts – notably ex-slaves – carried the word of the Europeans even to the most distant tribes.

The Wesleyans and Anglicans at first worked in friendly rivalry, but religious harmony was disrupted by the arrival of a French Catholic mission in 1838. The islands soon rang with doctrinal disputation and mutual accusations of unfair tactics in the competition in conversion. A Roman Catholic priest and a lay millwright were said to have worked their way up the Wanganui river, staying long enough at each village to build a mill, convert the inhabitants and teach them that the Church of England was adulterous. Anglicans sniffed at the lay baptism practised by Wesleyan missionaries; both accused the Catholics of pandering to superstition by making a liberal dispensation of crucifixes, medallions, and images, thus 'withholding the second Commandment', and of being too tolerant of bigamy, tattooing or other Maori 'vices'.

The Maoris greatly enjoyed the theological controversy, which became as heated amongst themselves as amongst their pastors. When one European traveller arrived at a village to beg lodgings for the night he found the tribe divided between two factions, one of which had secured possession of the gate. Before he was allowed to enter he was asked to what church he belonged. His discreet reply, 'To the true church', satisfied both parties, and a feast was prepared. When in 1843 the Anglican Bishop Selwyn asked Te Heu Heu, a famous chief at Taupo, why he refused to become a Christian, he stretched out three fingers and replied, 'I have come to the cross-roads, and I see three ways – the English, the Wesleyan, and the Roman. Each teacher says his own way is the best. I am sitting down, and doubting which guide I shall follow.' He dallied too long. Before he had made up his mind he, his wives and many of his followers were buried by a landslide.

The missionary did not merely aim at converting the Maoris to Christianity. To him many Maori customs seemed as abominable as the superstitions; Christianity seemed synonymous with western European manners as well as morals. The evangelical spirit which induced the Englishman to become a missionary, also led him to emphasize, in his teaching, his own puritanical code. The Reverend Richard Taylor, an Anglican missionary, related how he reformed an old man called Ake who insisted on maintaining the custom of working nude in the cultivations.

I repeatedly spoke to him but in vain. One day, however, when I was going over the river to the town with my wife and daughter, I saw old Ake in his usual state. I ran on before and bid him go into a house and put on his mat; he refused, I said he should, he declared he would not, I pushed, he resisted, at last I saw there was no alternative but force, so I put my arms around him and fairly pushed him into a house, to the great amusement of the natives who stood by. He was conquered, but I dearly paid for the victory; Ake's skin had been anointed with red ochre and oil, which, I found to my cost, had completely destroyed my best black coat. Ake never attempted to go about naked again.

Why was it that, in the eighteen-thirties, the Maoris were for the first time willing to listen to the missionaries' message? Their society was being undermined and their confidence with it. Increasingly they were unable to cope, by traditional means, with the new complexities of life. For instance a new problem had arisen by the end of the thirties. The Bay of Islands Maoris had sold half their land for European goods. A missionary suggested that they should make an agreement to sell no more and in 1839 they did try to establish a 'confederacy' for this purpose. But there were deeper problems which led to bewilderment or apathy. Their *tohunga* could not cure the new diseases: sometimes the missionary could. The missionary was impervious to the powers of their *atua* (god) and of *makutu* (witchcraft). Maoris grew careless of *tapu* – sometimes intentionally defied it without ill effect. Above all there was the feeling, openly expressed, that the Maoris were dying out. The *ngarara*, lizard of death, was gnawing at the heart of the people. They began to wonder whether it was not the European *atua* who was punishing them. He must be propitiated. First of all at the Bay of Islands, then elsewhere, losing faith in their own gods and culture, they turned in hope or despair to the Europeans for guidance.

It is clear that one of the important causes of the Maori conversion was the spread of literacy among the Maoris. They found learning to read and write their own language enormously exciting, and all they could read in it was the Bible and other religious works.

At the same time as the Maoris began to be converted in numbers there appeared at the Bay of Islands a 'resistance cult' which might be regarded as an effort by Maoris to meet their new situation in their own way. In about 1833 the Serpent of the Book of Genesis, called *Nakahi* (Nahash) by the Maoris, appeared in a vision to a Maori and commanded that he be worshipped. The Maori, Te Atua Wera (the Red God or Fiery God), founded a new religion, *Papahurihia* (one who relates wonders). It rejected the European God yet contained Christian elements including heaven – an abundant and amorous paradise. There was a strong note of millenarianism – an expectation of the arrival of great treasures. There were Hebraic elements, including the appointment of Saturday as the Sabbath. The missionaries had implanted the idea that the Maoris were descended from the Lost Tribes of Israel and the followers of the new god came to be called *Hurai* (Jews). There was also a stratum of Maori religion. *Nakahi* was associated with the Maori lizard *ngarara*. The god *Nakahi* appeared at night and was worshipped round a flag pole. His priest seems to have practised ventriloquism and other tricks to add to the mystification. This cult survived until at least the end of the century at Hokianga.

During the eighteen-thirties Christianity and exhaustion called a halt to the tribal wars. Missionaries induced many tribes to forgo their claims for revenge. But in other respects the missions hastened the decay of tribal society. The chief source of tribal law and authority, of tribal cohesion, had been Maori religion, but once the old gods died their commandments had no sanction. The chief was no longer *tapu*; his *mana*, his power and prestige, suffered accordingly. Christian chiefs put aside their extra wives, gave up killing and cannibalism, freed their slaves, only to find that the ex-slave – and often the younger generation – no longer fearing the chief, would not obey him. The Maoris were no longer fully members of their old society nor of the new European one. By 1840 they inhabited a disordered world.

By 1838 there were about two thousand Europeans living in New Zealand. Five or six hundred of them had settled round the Bay of Islands, where Kororareka had become a busy little town. A good many visitors or residents have left us portraits of the early settlement, few of them very flattering.

The only bright spot which Charles Darwin could discern when he visited the Bay of Islands in 1835 was the mission station at Waimate:

At length we reached Waimate; after having passed over so many miles of an uninhabited useless country, the sudden appearance of an English farm house and its well dressed fields, placed there as if by an enchanter's wand, was exceedingly pleasing. ... At Waimate there are three large houses, where the Missionary gentlemen, M[ess]rs: Williams, Davies and Clarke, reside; near to these are the huts of the native labourers. On an adjoining slope fine crops of barley and wheat in full ear, and others of potatoes and of clover, were standing; but I cannot attempt to describe all I saw; there were large gardens, with every fruit and vegetable which England produces, and many belonging to a warmer clime. I may instance asparagus, kidney beans, cucumbers, rhubarb, apples and pears, figs, peaches, apricots, grapes, olives, gooseberries, currants, hops, gorse for fences, and English oaks! and many different kinds of flowers. Around the farm yard were stables, a threshing barn with its winnowing machine, a blacksmith's forge, and on the ground, ploughshares and other tools; in the middle was that happy mixture of pigs and poultry which may be seen so comfortably lying together in every English farm yard. At the distance of a few hundred yards, where the water of a little rill has been dammed up into a pool, a large and substantial water-mill had been erected. All this is very surprising when it is considered that five years ago, nothing but the fern here flourished. Moreover native workmanship, taught by the Missionaries, has effected this change: – the lesson of the Missionary is the enchanter's wand. The house has been built, the windows framed, the fields ploughed, even the trees grafted by the New Zealander. At the mill a New Zealander may be seen powdered white with flour, like his brother miller in England.

For the rest Darwin found New Zealand 'not a pleasant place; amongst the natives there is absent the charming simplicity which is found at Tahiti; and of the English the greater part are the very refuse of Society'. In the eighteen-twenties the debauchery natural to a whaling port took place mainly on board visiting ships. In the thirties it moved to numerous 'grogeries' ashore. 'The Beach', as Kororareka was called, was not that fabled 'Beach' which the explorers had sought: the dissolute men known as 'the beachcombers' found no gold nuggets; they made a living by preying on seamen in one way or another. J. R. Clendon, the first United States Consul (appointed in 1838), reported to Washington that some of them got a livelihood 'by decoying seamen from their ships and shipping them at an enormous advance onboard of any other vessel that may have been in like manner distressed'.

According to F. E. Maning, the 'pakeha-Maori' who was mentioned earlier, the 'beachcombers' were 'a sort of nest of English, Irish, Scotch, Dutch, French and American runaways from South Sea whalers, with whom were congregated certain other individuals of the pakeha race, whose manner of arrival in the country was not clearly accounted for, and to enquire into which was, as I found afterwards, considered extremely impolite. ... They lived in a half savage state, or to speak correctly, in a savage-and-a-half state, being greater savages by far than the natives themselves.' Regarding the origins of most of the northern population J. D. Lang, the senior Presbyterian minister in New South Wales, was more blunt. In 1839 he wrote that 'with a few honourable exceptions, it consists of the veriest refuse of civilized society – of runaway sailors, of runaway convicts, of convicts who have served out their term of bondage in one or other of the two penal colonies, of fraudulent debtors who have escaped from their creditors in Sydney or Hobart Town, and of needy adventurers from the two colonies, almost equally unprincipled.'

Kororareka had some sober citizens. There was a British Resident and an American Consul. There was a doctor. There were several sawyers, a blacksmith and other tradesmen who found plenty of work repairing ships. A number of merchants, such as Gilbert Mair, J. R. Clendon and J. S. Polack, who had their warehouses at Kororareka or in the vicinity, engaged in general trade. They victualled or repaired ships, owned their own small vessels, which traded along the coast, and exported local produce. By 1840 they formed a thriving little business community. In 1839 a land company and a bank (which commenced business in 1840) were both floated at Kororareka.

Some of the missionaries, if not as prosperous as the merchants, had excellent prospects. Twelve of them were said to have eighty-four children – and the Church Missionary Society had authorized the expenditure of £50 from its funds on land as a provision for the maintenance of each child. No modern system of social security will ever rival this. Since land was to be bought for a few axes and blankets, fifty pounds would purchase a large farm, while a large family was security for an estate. When the early land purchases were investigated in the eighteen-forties, several Anglican missionaries claimed ten or twenty thousand acres.

The rise of a middle class indicated that settlement had been successfully established and gave promise that it would be permanent; but it did not please everyone. The Reverend J. D. Lang feared that, unless the British Government intervened, these land dealings with the Maoris would 'elevate the family of the Fairbairns, of Mount Fairbairn, or the Polacks of Polack Hall, to the rank and dignity of an illiterate, narrow-minded, purse-proud, heartless colonial aristocracy'. 'Fairbairn' was a Church Missionary Society catechist, W. T. Fairburn, who had bought a large area of land; Polack was a Jewish merchant, far from illiterate – he left us three verbose volumes. Neither was to realize their critic's fears.

Just as Australian historians long minimized the role of convict transportation in Australian colonization, so New Zealand writers have traditionally made light of the importance or influence of commerce and settlement before 1840. Scholarship has thus followed public opinion, for in both countries the settlers who arrived after 1840, the year when New Zealand was annexed by Great Britain and when transportation to New South Wales was abolished, preferred to forget most of their hardy but not always respectable precursors. Nevertheless, the first traders and settlers played an important role in New Zealand history. They established the first colonies; as we shall see in the following chapter, they were largely responsible for the annexation of the country; their influence upon the Maoris helped to determine the future course of racial relations. The export of timber, corn and other 'primary produce' marked the effective beginnings of the modern New Zealand economy. It is difficult to judge what lasting effect the earliest pioneers may have had on the European community. Elsewhere they were suddenly swamped by organized settlement, but in the north of the North Island, which became the Auckland Province, and has almost continuously had the largest European population, as well as the bulk of the Maori population, there was no abrupt break in the continuity of settlement. There, one may suppose, the settlers of pre-British and 'Alsatian' days helped to establish the 'levelling' attitude which was to become characteristic of the New Zealand community.

More significant than any direct influence which the first European residents may have had on their successors was the fact that the conditions which moulded the character of pre-1840 settlement also helped to shape the destiny of the later colonies. For this reason, much of the future history of the country was foreshadowed in the earliest northern settlement. Kororareka was a Pacific port. It also possessed many of the characteristics of a frontier town, though, because of its unique environment, it differed from the home towns of the Australians or Americans, settlers or seamen, who played the chief part in its foundation. It was, in particular, given a special character by the presence, not of Australian aborigines or Red Indians, but of Maoris. New Zealand was to remain, for many years, part of the Pacific frontier. The mission farms, upon whose astonishingly English appearance Darwin remarked, also seem to cast a long shadow across the history of New Zealand.

II: BRAVE NEW WORLD

Honourable members will scarcely believe now the kind of fervour which existed in Great Britain in the time of my youth to found a New World differing greatly from the Old World.

SIR GEORGE GREY, speaking in the House of Representatives, 1890

As a country without civilized law and order, New Zealand posed a difficult problem for the governments whose citizens most frequently traded there. In 1838 the United States appointed a local trader, J. R. Clendon, as Consul at the Bay of Islands, but long before then the Governments of New South Wales and the United Kingdom had been concerned both to protect British subjects from Maori savagery and, in an age increasingly humane, to protect the Maoris from European riff-raff. But how could either objective be achieved?

The commissions of early Australian Governors gave them vague powers of representing the Crown in adjacent islands. It was assumed in Sydney, though this was stretching the meaning of 'adjacent' a long way, that the Governors had some sort of jurisdiction in New Zealand. After the *Boyd* massacre, ships leaving Sydney to trade in the South Seas were required to deposit a bond of £1,000 as security for good behaviour; and Kendall, the missionary, was appointed as a Justice of the Peace. Neither of these measures was effective in restraining the behaviour of British subjects in New Zealand; both were probably illegal.

After the Napoleonic wars, during which the Australian Governors had largely been left to their own devices, the British authorities tried a new approach. It was provided that British subjects could be tried in British colonial courts for major crimes committed in New Zealand or other islands subject neither to Great Britain nor any civilized power. Because of legal difficulties, such as that of obtaining witnesses to distant crimes, these acts proved practically unenforceable. In the famous case of Captain Stewart and the brig *Elizabeth*, when Governor Darling of New South Wales tried to enforce the law, the Crown law officers neglected to obey his order to prosecute. In 1830, in return for a cargo of flax, Stewart had transported Te Rauparaha and a war party down to Akaroa, where, with his help, they had massacred the population of a *pa*. Stewart had then taken them back to the North Island with their baskets of human flesh.

This atrocity led Darling to press his earlier recommendation that a British Resident should be appointed in New Zealand. In 1833 James Busby was sent over from Sydney. He was instructed to apprehend escaped convicts and to send them back for trial, to encourage trade, to assist settlers, to keep on good terms with missionaries and Maoris, and to urge the chiefs to keep law and order: but he was given neither the magisterial powers nor the armed force which might have enabled him to carry out such tasks. Instead of granting him extra-territorial jurisdiction, which would have required prior treaties with the chiefs, the British Government, not eager to incur more responsibility than it could avoid, left him 'a functionary without any apparent function', 'a man-of-war without guns'.

Busby proved unable to influence the chiefs, or to keep on speaking terms with the missionaries and settlers, or even to maintain an official appearance of dignity. No one in New Zealand took the Residency seriously except Busby, a pompous young man, who felt cut out to play some important role in life, but found himself cast as the central figure in a solemn farce. However, in view of the false position in which he had been placed by the remissness of the authorities, it is a mistake to attribute his failure chiefly to his personal faults. It was inconceivable that he should succeed.

If Kendall awaits his Marlowe or Goethe, Busby (and his superiors) deserve the attention of a Ben Jonson, or perhaps of a Gilbert and Sullivan. In one passage of glorious foolery in the Resident's career a rival momentarily stole the show. In 1835 Busby heard from a person called Baron Charles Philip Hippolytus de Thierry who styled himself 'sovereign chief of New Zealand, King of Nukuheva'. De Thierry was the English-born son of a French *émigré* family; his delusions of grandeur were worthy of a Bourbon. When Hongi was in England, de Thierry, through the agency of the missionary

Kendall, had arranged to purchase a large estate at Hokianga. Now he wrote to the Resident announcing that he was preparing to land in his demesne. He also communicated with the missionaries, telling them that he was, at that moment, about to cut the Panama Canal, which was to remain New Zealand property for fifty years. Busby feared that there was foreign method in his madness, and prepared to resist his onslaught by inducing thirty-five chiefs to sign a Declaration of Independence. They declared that they were the heads of a sovereign state to be known as the 'United Tribes of New Zealand' and announced that they would meet annually in congress to consider the welfare of their realm.

The Governor of New South Wales called this constitution 'a paper pellet fired off at Baron de Thierry', but in fact Busby was firing a big diplomatic gun at a cardboard silhouette. The Foreign Office had already recognized Pomare of Tahiti as the ruler of an independent state and was later to recognize sovereigns in other islands. The tribal communities of the Pacific bore little resemblance to the sovereign state of international law; but the acknowledgement of native sovereignty was a polite fiction which enabled the Foreign Office to disclaim, as far as possible, responsibility for the actions of British subjects in the area. The attribution of sovereignty to the Maori chiefs (a doctrine which had the great merit of admitting the Maoris' rights to their country) remained the basis of British policy in New Zealand until 1840. Busby's action, 'silly and unauthorized' as it may have been, was taken seriously in London. Lord Glenelg, another humourless official, approved of it because, for some reason, he felt that the sovereignty of the Baron could not fail to lead to the extermination of the aborigines. For his part, de Thierry, though 'an Englishman at heart', believed that he must save the Maoris from the degradation and destruction which would follow in the wake of the British Crown.

The Baron promised to found a kingdom with free trade and all modern freedoms including free medicine; to give 'occasional bounties' to the chiefs; and to grant to six respectable settlers the boon of forming a *curia regis* to advise him on the first Wednesday of every month; but his feudal dream, the first and most exotic of a long line of Utopias to be built in New Zealand's cloud-land, was soon dissolved. Once he landed in 1837 his retinue, enlisted from the dregs of Sydney, deserted him; his money was quickly dissipated; and for a time he was forced to live on Maori charity.

By the late eighteen-thirties Australian 'imperialism' was rapidly drawing New Zealand from the Polynesian into the British share of the world. Enterprising speculators, foreseeing that circumstances must soon dictate British annexation, hastened to stake their claims. The 'land-sharks' grew fat. Sydney trading houses sent over agents with blank 'Deeds of Feoffment' and supplies of 'trade' to tempt the Maoris into selling their land. Huge areas were, so it was alleged, purchased for a few muskets, blankets or duck trousers. W. C. Wentworth, 'the Australian patriot', took time off from the struggle for self-government to join a syndicate which 'bought' the entire South Island and Stewart Island for a few hundred pounds. At this time a long drought, falling wool prices and stringent credit due to the withdrawal of British capital, were causing a serious crisis in the Australian pastoral industry. Squatters or would-be squatters began to turn to New Zealand in search of land where they might prosper, temporarily free from licence fees and variable taxes on their flocks. Almost every ship crossing the Tasman Sea brought land-hungry passengers from New South Wales.

Respectable settlers, missionaries, Sydney and London merchants and shipping interests, the New South Wales Government – all demanded that the British Government act to control the alarming situation in New Zealand. In 1837 two hundred missionaries and settlers had petitioned William IV to afford them protection. The British Resident, whose life had been endangered by a Maori attack on his home, needed protection as much as anyone else. In 1836 some of the Bay of Islands settlers, already growing tired of life in a state of nature in which, as F. E. Maning wrote, 'everyone did as he liked, except when his neighbours would not let him (the more shame for them)' had drawn up an 'original contract' in the manner approved by generations of political philosophers. They did not go so far as to set up a state, but they formed a temperance society – an institution which, for nearly a century, seemed to many New Zealanders almost as important. This particular society, the first of a long series, apparently met only once. To introduce the blessing of sobriety among the inhabitants of Kororareka must have appeared an impossible task. The town continued as wild as ever – though less sinful than the neighbouring *pa* of Pomare. In 1837 there was a gun battle on the beach between J. S. Polack, the Jewish merchant, and a grog seller called Ben Turner. Turner was wounded, but Polack retreated to London for a few years. The continual disorder was bad for trade. In 1838 some of the residents took a further step towards a political society by forming a vigilance committee, the Kororareka Association, for the preservation of persons, property, and especially of propertied persons. Each member was required to arm himself with a musket and bayonet, a brace of pistols, a cutlass, and thirty rounds of ball cartridge. The Association introduced a penal code to deal with theft, non-payment of rent, enticing seamen to desert, and other misdemeanours. The punishments, which were suitably vigorous, included the stripping or tarring and feathering of culprits. This rough-and-ready justice seems to have had some effect in making Kororareka safer for the more respectable citizens, but it made no pretence of impartiality. One man was tarred and feathered for coming over from Sydney to collect a debt from a leader of the Association.

Hokianga also had its temperance society. In 1835, at his own instigation, Captain Thomas McDonnell, a local trader, was appointed a second British Resident (without salary), thus doubling the application of impotent authority. He took the lead in setting up a society which forbade the sale of liquor. Ships were searched and quantities of grog poured into the harbour. But though he helped to reduce the consumption of alcohol, he was scarcely more capable of keeping order than Busby.

New Zealand cried out for British intervention: the Colonial Office could no longer turn a deaf ear. By 1835 Lord Glenelg had reluctantly been forced to recognize that something more was required. He was considering the possibility of investing the Residents with effective jurisdiction.

Some historians have dignified British policy at this time with the label 'minimum intervention', and concluded that this policy was abandoned in 1839 and 1840. In fact the British Government hardly wavered in its determination to do as little as possible. To the last it continued to ask itself the question, how little is enough? Meanwhile, throughout the thirties, British subjects in New Zealand increasingly involved the Government in responsibilities which, however unwelcome, it could not entirely fail to acknowledge, until complete annexation could not be avoided.

A good many writers, at the time and since, have seen something reprehensible or odd in the Government's attitude; but it does not now seem difficult to understand. New Zealand offered little scope for investment and a very limited market, but had its value been far greater the need for annexation would not have been obvious. While Great Britain was the leading industrial, maritime and commercial power, British trade, so it seemed to many economists, politicians and business men, should be able to take care of itself in any market without the help of British sovereignty or tariffs, or of more than an occasional salutary call by a man-of-war. For many years the free traders had been multiplying and spreading their opinion that colonies were of little intrinsic value, while they involved great administrative expense and unnecessary wars. This was an argument very convincing to the overworked Colonial Office which, during the late thirties, was faced with revolt in Canada, wars in South Africa, turmoil in the West Indies. In a hundred places traders and missionaries were making embarrassing demands for official action of one sort or another. It is not surprising that harassed officials should have been reluctant to administer half the globe.

How little was enough? In 1837 James Busby offered his answer. He thought it was useless to pass an Act of Parliament giving him power to control British subjects. What was wanted was 'a paramount authority', backed by adequate force. He proposed that the chiefs who signed his Articles of Confederation, in 1835, should now sign a treaty giving Great Britain the power to administer the affairs of New Zealand in trust for its inhabitants. Thus the country would remain a sovereign

Maori state under British protection. The chiefs would meet periodically in a Congress, which would serve to school them in the duties of government, but they should have no real power outside their own districts. 'In theory and ostensibly, the Government would be that of the Confederated Chiefs, but in reality it must necessarily be that of the Representative of the protecting power.' In reality, in other words, the ruler of the country would be James Busby. He thought that British troops would be needed to strengthen his authority and that of the chiefs, but that this would not be an expensive establishment because, he held, 'one hundred English soldiers would be an overmatch for the united forces of the whole Islands' – though, in his opinion, there was small chance of even two tribes uniting to oppose them.

There were to be doctors and school teachers, a Maori newspaper, Maori police to enforce a simple code of laws, and a small European council to advise the Resident. The whole scheme was to cost a mere £1,000 a year.

In stressing the uselessness of conferring on the Resident further powers which he was powerless to exercise, and in asserting that his authority must be backed by force, Busby was right, but his plan was full of the absurdities which seemed to mar everything he touched. No one could believe that so ambitious a project would be so cheap. Had Busby's knowledge of the Maoris been less superficial, or had he travelled south of the Bay of Islands, his estimate of their fighting skill might have been less fatuous. Had he pursued further the line of reasoning which led him to suppose that, because of the incessant tribal wars, the Maori tribes would never combine, he might have seen how far-fetched was the notion that the chiefs might travel safely to a Maori parliament or co-operate should they meet.

To Governor Bourke of New South Wales the defects of the plan were obvious; instead he recommended the more modest proposals of William Hobson, the captain of H.M.S. *Rattlesnake*, whom he had sent to protect the settlers at the Bay of Islands during a Maori war in 1837. Hobson suggested that the British Government should negotiate treaties with some of the chiefs to acquire jurisdiction within restricted areas which should be purchased from the native owners. He

called these British enclaves 'Factories', after the early establishments of trading companies in India. The 'Heads of
Factories' were to be magistrates and consuls accredited to the
United Chiefs of New Zealand. In this way British subjects
could be controlled and the Maoris could be introduced to
civilized government.

It seems unlikely that Hobson's plan would have proved
adequate, for the settlers were already very scattered, but it was
a sensible one. It is worth noting that for twenty years after
New Zealand was annexed, the Government had little or no
effective jurisdiction outside the coastal settlements. To the
Colonial Office, Hobson's proposal held out hope of continuing
to limit official commitments. In 1838 it seemed, to one official
at least, to provide 'all that was essential for the present'. But
by that time the situation facing the British authorities was
rapidly changing. They had now to take into account not only
conditions and opinions in the antipodes, but also, to a much
greater extent than before, opinion in Great Britain. New
Zealand affairs had become the subject of a loud and bitter
public agitation. The Government was under strong pressure
from two influential and well-organized groups: on the one
hand the 'colonial reformers', on the other the missionary and
humanitarian societies. British idealism, as well as Australian
and American commerce, was taking a hand in shaping the
future of New Zealand.

Although his name did not appear among those of the eminent members of its Committee, the New Zealand Association,
which was formed in 1837, was, like many other colonizing
associations and companies, a product of the fertile brain and
untiring intrigue of Edward Gibbon Wakefield. Wakefield has
been credited, even by reputable historians, with the chief, if
not the sole responsibility for the annexation of New Zealand.
Many New Zealanders have believed that their original colonies
were planted much as he planned, and that the European social
pattern in New Zealand was formed on the model he provided.
For those who wish to understand New Zealand, a glance at
Wakefield's dreams and schemes is indispensable.

Wakefield was the back-room boy of the 'colonial reformers', a group of writers and politicians, of whom Lord Durham was the most eminent, who endeavoured in the eighteen-thirties and -forties to invigorate British colonial policy and to encourage the foundation of new settlements. At a time when free traders, not admitting that trade and finance formed imperial frontiers of their own, regarded territorial empire with scepticism or hostility, the 'colonial reformers' did a great deal to maintain a thoughtful interest in colonial questions.

Wakefield wrote of 'the Art of Colonization' and hoped to make it an objective and experimental science, much as Bentham and the 'philosophic radicals', on whose teachings he was brought up, hoped to discover a science of politics. But though his economic and political theories derived in part from the doctrines of the utilitarians, he was in many respects an old-fashioned mercantilist. At home he sensed the threat of revolution in the unemployment, low wages and grim living conditions which afflicted the poor. The rich were alarmed by radical political movements and hungry mobs, while they were uneasy about the stern competition for existence amongst themselves. Respectable occupations and secure or high interest rates were alike scarce. Wakefield believed that England could ease her discontents by exporting large numbers of the discontented. Thus would 'relief be obtained from excessive numbers', while wages would rise as a result of the diminution of the labour force. The colonies would offer valuable markets and high profit on the investment of surplus capital.

It is fair to suppose that Wakefield's first – though not his final – thought was for England, for when he wrote *A Letter from Sydney* in 1829 he knew the colonies only from books or hearsay; but he intended to benefit the colonies as well as the motherland. He hoped to reform existing settlements and to found better ones. In Canada or Australia, he believed, so much Crown land had been given away or sold cheaply that everyone could become his own landlord. The population was scattered like so many Daniel Boones along a barbarous frontier. Consequently labour was scarce and there was little to attract the gentleman capitalist who disliked becoming his own labourer. In these circumstances there had appeared in each settlement 'a new people', a term charged with so much disgust, as Wakefield used it, that his attitude presents an interesting problem for a future biographer. 'What are the ideas that we mean to express by the words a *New People*?' he asked.

We mean, it strikes me, a people like what the Canadians will be, and the United States' Americans are – a people who, though they continually increase in number, make no progress in the art of living; who, in respect to wealth, knowledge, skill, taste, and whatever belongs to civilization, have degenerated from their ancestors; who are precluded from acquiring wealth except by the labour of slaves; whose education, though universal, stops before the age of puberty, and thus becomes, if not an evil, at least a dangerous thing instead of the greatest good; who, ever on the move, are unable to bring anything to perfection; whose opinions are only violent and false prejudices, the necessary fruit of ignorance; whose character is a compound of vanity, bigotry, obstinacy, and hatred most comprehensive, including whatever does not meet their own pinched notions of right; and who delight in a forced equality, not equality before the law only, but equality against nature and truth; an equality which, to keep the balance always even, rewards the mean rather than the great, and gives more honour to the vile than to the noble. . . . We mean, in two words, a people who become rotten before they are ripe.

Whether equality can be forced, whether a universal elementary education could be dangerous, whether these judgements were just, are of course matters of opinion; but Wakefield believed that he had accurately diagnosed the colonial condition and that he knew of an operation which would put it right. If a 'sufficient price' were placed on all colonial lands, the dispersal of population would be prevented. Labourers would be forced to concentrate in the vicinity of employment and capitalist employers would then be willing to purchase land and settle in the colonies. The sale of land would provide a government revenue and a fund for the immigration of further supplies of labourers – a simple and useful idea which, in the writings of Wakefield, who had not originated it, became the focus of a mystique of colonization. The 'sufficient price' was to be 'sufficient' to prevent labourers from immediately becoming landowners, but sometimes Wakefield imagined that it would also provide the fares for the required number of labourers, so that there would be a self-regulating relationship between land sales and immigration.

How long thrifty labourers should be kept from becoming landowners; whether a price could be found which would prevent them from becoming landowners too soon, while not being too high to deter capitalists from buying land, and yet providing fares for the labourers needed on newly purchased estates – these were unanswerable problems. The 'sufficient price' was never to be tried in practice because it was impracticable. The valuable parts of Wakefield's theory were that land should be sold, that the proceeds should be used to develop public works and to assist needy people to migrate, and that such migrants should be carefully selected in accordance with their age and occupation and with a regard to balancing the sexes in the colonies.

The ideal colony of Wakefield's 'gorgeous fancy' (a phrase applied to him by *The Times*) was to be an agricultural settlement. He had little understanding of the squatters who, lost in a vast interior, were already laying the foundations of Australian wealth. But if he did not consider that pastoralism might suit the new colonies he hoped to establish, the omission was due to disapproval as much as ignorance. Sheep meant scattered shepherds and could not provide a suitable means of subsistence for the closely-knit society he desired. In Wakefield's Utopia, land policy would control the expansion of the frontier and regulate class relationships. There would be higher wages than in England, which would induce the 'mechanic' to migrate and which would, in time, enable the 'industrious and thrifty' among the workmen to become 'Masters of servants'. There would be room for a leisured and wealthy class of landowners – 'persons of cultivation and refinement'. In contrast to what another writer called 'the great democratical movement' of population from Great Britain to North America, future colonization would be a 'systematic colonization'. Neither the transportation of convicts nor the 'shovelling out' of paupers should threaten the colony's standards of civilization or contaminate its selected stock. The new colonial society would consist of a vertical section of English society, excluding the lowest stratum. It would form, not a 'new people', but an 'extension' of an old, retaining its virtues, but eliminating its poverty and overcrowding. The colonists, being as civilized as their relatives in Great Britain, would be equally entitled to a voice in the framing of their own laws. Wakefield, whose radicalism stopped short of universal suffrage, hoped that, as in England, a property qualification would temper the popular vote.

In some respects such views, originally formulated before the Reform Bill of 1832, were very radical; but Wakefield's central aim, the preservation of the existing social and economic structure, was essentially a conservative one. It was also, in another sense, reactionary. In picturing the future colonial community, he looked back to a legendary past, to the squire surrounded by his contented, cap-tipping yokels, in the good old days before industrialism and new ideas had upset the rural harmony.

Much in Wakefield's career and thought can be connected with a few biographical facts. He came of a Quaker and radical family, but his philanthropical and philosophical bent was at every point crossed by his perverse and unstable character. After his successful runaway marriage with one heiress had terminated with her death in child-birth, he was imprisoned for abducting a second. While serving three years in Newgate, where he doubtless heard much intimate detail about the transportation system, he became interested in convictism and colonization. Because he was thereafter unacceptable in polite society, he was forced to work underground. Not a profound thinker, and unable to act as a public figure, he became a great publicist, with a genius for talking people into doing for him what he was debarred from doing himself, a sort of intellectual confidence man, adroit, resilient, yet regarded with unalterable suspicion by those out of range of his persuasive voice and the fascination of his personality.

Colonization was a noble work, but it had formidable antagonists, not merely lethargy, scepticism, and *laissez-faire*, but the high-minded force of humanitarianism itself. When, in 1837, the distinguished committee of the New Zealand Association, which included Lord Durham, the radical Sir William Molesworth and several other Members of Parliament, announced its plans to launch a large emigration to New Zealand, there was an immediate outcry from the equally eminent leaders of the Anglican and Wesleyan missionary societies. The Association's plans, they noted, said precious little about the welfare of the Maoris; there was, it was true, a proposal that a small proportion of the land sold to the Association by the Maoris should be reserved for the perpetual use of chiefly families, but there was nothing to convince them that systematic colonization would not hinder if not cancel out the work of the missionaries.

English humanitarianism, like systematic colonization, was partly of Quaker stock. The Quakers, in the United States and in England, had in the eighteenth century been the first religious group to oppose the institution of slavery and to take an active interest in the welfare of the afflicted and the poor. Their charitable purposes received powerful support from the evangelical revival, led by Wesley and Whitefield, in protest against the easygoing ways of the Church of England in the eighteenth century. Religious enthusiasm gradually became respectable; Bible Christianity took the offensive. In the eighties and nineties the formation of the British missionary societies and the Society for the Abolition of the Slave Trade bore witness to the great change in the temper of English religion. The leading evangelicals, often bankers, brewers or merchants, were frequently strangely blind to the sufferings of the factory workers – George Eliot was not unfair in her acid definition of a philanthropist as a man whose charity increased directly as the square of the distance – but armed with their doctrine of the brotherhood of man, the English middle class at least set out to free the slave and save the heathen. On their banner this text was inscribed: 'God hath created of one blood all nations of men.'

By 1833 within the British Empire the slave trade had been abolished and slaves had become free subjects. The evangelicals, the missionaries, the 'Saints' were at the zenith of their influence. They now turned their attention to the more positive but more difficult task of civilizing primitive peoples within the Empire and without. For this purpose the Aborigines Protection Society and a Society for the Civilization of

Africa by means of the gospel and commerce were formed. A Committee of the House of Commons was appointed to consider the best methods of improving the condition of the aborigines. Its Report, issued in the same year that the New Zealand Association was formed, emphasized that all past colonization had for non-European peoples been a calamity involving oppression or even extermination.

Needless to say, holding such views, the majority of the humanitarians looked forward to a future for New Zealand very different from Wakefield's anticipations. Dandeson Coates, the Lay Secretary of the Church Missionary Society, took the lead in attacking the proposals of the New Zealand Association. He wished to restrict official British interference in New Zealand as much as possible, in the hope of keeping the country a missionary preserve. He proposed, like Busby and Hobson, that the independence of the 'Native Authorities' in New Zealand should be recognized by the British Government. He urged the appointment of consular agents having the power to arrest and try British offenders; and that Great Britain should take New Zealand under its 'protection'. But 'the curse of colonization', which would aggravate, not alleviate the evils existing in New Zealand, by multiplying the number of British settlers, must not be encouraged. So long as New Zealand remained Maori territory, he thought that any Europeans there could do little harm because they lived on sufferance, with no government to back them up and perhaps to oppress the Maoris in the event of trouble. In the immediate future, the Lay Secretary thought, the missionaries would act as the 'coadjutors' of the British consuls; ultimately, when the mission had achieved its purposes, New Zealand would be a Christian Maori state. More than one historian has suspected that Coates secretly dreamed that it would be a theocracy.

Most of the missionaries in the field agreed with Coates. Marsden, like Henry Williams, had longed for 'the blessings of established government and administration'. They wanted British 'protection'; they might even have welcomed annexation; but they were strongly opposed to extensive colonization. There were, however, a few missionaries who looked more favourably than did Coates on their fellow-countrymen and who felt that sober and honest settlers might help to intro-duce the Maoris to civilized ways. This was Wakefield's asser-tion, and there was also one optimistic group of humanitarians in London, the Aborigines Protection Society, willing to accept his word. The Society believed that 'Christianity could be harmonized with colonization' and looked forward in New Zealand to the 'amalgamation' of two races, in occupations, class structure, civilization, and religion, if not in blood.

There was, in fact, little reason why anyone should suppose that extensive settlement would be a blessing for the Maoris; past colonial history offered every reason for supposing the contrary. In suggesting that one of his aims was to civilize the Maori, Wakefield was merely seeking to conciliate evangelical opinion. His real opinion was more nearly expressed in a later New Zealand Company dispatch which remarked that 'If the advantage of the Natives were alone to be consulted it would be better, perhaps, that they should remain forever the savages that they are.'

Fundamentally, Wakefield regarded New Zealand as a white man's country; Coates urged that the highest purpose of British power was to benefit the Maori. From 1840 until 1860 there was in New Zealand a political struggle to decide which view should prevail. The interests and wishes of the Maoris were gradually lost sight of; there followed a long war which established the settlers as the dominant race and led to the oppression of the Maoris. But there was the third opinion about New Zealand, that of Hobson and Busby – an opinion shared by the Aborigines Protection Society. They saw that the future of New Zealand, whatever Dandeson Coates or Wakefield might wish, was that of a 'plural society'. Colonization could not be stopped – that was the flaw in Coates's argument – but on the other hand the Maoris could not be ignored. New Zea-land was to be the home of white and brown men. The prob-lem of government was to reconcile their interests.

Despite the lobbying of colonizers and philanthropists, both protesting their 'pure and disinterested zeal' – the first to found a colony without cost to the taxpayer; the second to establish a new civilized state without harm to the Maoris – the Govern-ment could not be expected to join whole-heartedly in either idealistic scheme. It was chiefly concerned to solve the urgent problem of lawlessness in New Zealand. However, it attempted to reconcile the ambitions of both bodies. Lord Glenelg, the Secretary of State for the Colonies, and James Stephen, the permanent Under-Secretary, had become convinced that some form of British intervention was essential because colonization, already begun, must inevitably continue. Stephen was persuaded that the two thousand settlers would, if they were unchecked, exterminate the Maoris. From 1837 to 1839 the two officials and their assistants were engaged in thinking out a policy which would protect the Maoris and introduce some law and order in New Zealand. Provided that these aims could be achieved, they were not at first unsympathetic to the wishes of the New Zealand Association.

The Association wanted a royal charter and broad powers to govern the projected colony on the model of seventeenth-century companies in North America. Such a proposal was not unwelcome to Glenelg, providing that the Government should have some power of veto over the Association's measures, for it would leave the responsibility and cost of government to an intermediary body. Late in 1837 he entered into negotiations with Lord Durham. Glenelg conceded Wakefield's argument that the alternatives were 'between a Colonization, desultory, without Law, and fatal to the Natives, and a Colonization organized and salutary'. He was prepared to grant a charter on certain conditions, the chief of which was that the Association should form itself into a joint stock company, with adequate subscribed capital, and thus demonstrate its ability to bear the initial costs of colonizing.

Many of the members of the Committee of the Association refused to agree. Their interest in the project arose, they protested, from a sense of public duty, not a desire for private profit. Furthermore, some of the would-be colonizers were becoming impatient with what they regarded as the suspicious opposition of the Colonial Office, and especially of James Stephen, whom they called 'Mr Mother Country' and accused of ruling the empire according to the dictates of the missionary party.

Their abuse was quite unfair. Stephen disliked and distrusted Wakefield, who returned his feelings. But though, like Glenelg, he was an officer of the Church Missionary Society, he did not, as the colonizers alleged, defer uncritically to Dandeson Coates. Providing that Maori interests were protected, he was prepared to go some way to meet their wishes. On two occasions in 1839 he recommended to his superior that they should be given a charter to colonize parts of New Zealand.

Once the Association declined his conditions, Glenelg came to the conclusion that the best alternative was to adopt the recommendations of Captain Hobson who, in December 1838, was offered the appointment of British Consul in New Zealand. Glenelg's intention, which he outlined in a minute written in February 1839, was not to encourage any 'extended system of colonization' but to establish a regular form of government, and for that purpose to acquire, by cession from the chiefs, sovereignty over those parts of New Zealand where the British were settled. Before he could get cabinet approval, however, he was forced to resign, and there followed some months of indecision under his successor, Lord Normanby.

In the meantime the would-be colonizers did not give up their project but dissolved their Association and, deprived of some of their most influential leaders, formed the New Zealand Company, which now demanded its promised charter. This time Stephen detected a popish plot in the fact that several Catholics were among the list of directors of the Company. The colonizers were again rebuffed. They decided to act on their own initiative. In May 1839 a preliminary expedition, led by one of Wakefield's brothers, Colonel William Wakefield, sailed in the *Tory* to purchase land in New Zealand and prepare a site for the first settlement.

Wakefield and his associates ever afterwards asserted that by secretly, and without permission, dispatching the *Tory*, they forced the British Government to annex New Zealand, thus narrowly forestalling the French. Their claim introduces an appropriate element of drama into the story; but it must, unfortunately, be largely discounted by the historian. The French had from the time of de Surville's visit, shortly after Cook, taken a considerable scientific interest in New Zealand. French whalers had been almost as numerous as the British in

New Zealand waters. The Catholic mission provided another link with France. Some French officials, business men and politicians wanted France to annex the country, but the Government of Louis Philippe took only a languid interest in the idea. In December 1839 it agreed to help a small company, the Nanto-Bordelaise Company, which intended to establish a settlement on Banks' Peninsula. But there is no evidence of an official intention of annexation. As we shall see in the next chapter, if indeed there was an Anglo-French race to possess New Zealand, there was only one starter.

The allegation that the New Zealand Company forced the British Government's hand is equally exaggerated. As we have seen, Lord Glenelg had determined to acquire sovereignty over at least part of New Zealand months before the *Tory* sailed. This policy had been suggested by Hobson; and the considerations which led to its adoption arose from conditions in New Zealand. In 1839 (as in 1833, when Busby had been appointed) British policy was a belated response to circumstances in New Zealand and to the initiative of the New South Wales Government. New Zealand would have become British had the New Zealand Company never existed. This is not to say, however, that the Company had no influence on policy. It may be that the constant hue and cry in *The Times*, in the *Spectator* and in Parliament forced the Colonial Office to act with a greater sense of urgency – though it is difficult to believe that its indecision could have been further prolonged. The immediate effect of the Company's precipitate action was to cause Stephen and his superiors to give up all idea of co-operating with the colonizers. The most important effect was to extend the Colonial Office's views on the minimum degree of intervention which could possibly be effective in New Zealand affairs.

It seems not unlikely that the reason for the colonizers' haste in dispatching the *Tory* was not to force the Government to intervene in New Zealand, but because they knew that it was going to intervene. The Company was aware that the Government was preparing to regulate the affairs of New Zealand by some means or other, and in particular, that it meant to control the purchase of Maori lands by Europeans.

This would restrict the Company's activities, and might put it out of business altogether if the cost of land in New Zealand rose considerably. The colonizers had to raise their initial capital on the security of the profits expected from their land dealings; and land sales were to be the source of their emigration fund. Thus, though Wakefield may have feared that Great Britain might not forestall the French, he certainly wanted the Company to forestall Great Britain.

In August 1839 Hobson was, at last, issued with his instructions. He was sent to New Zealand to treat with the Maoris for the recognition of the Queen's sovereign authority 'over the whole or any parts of those islands which they may be willing to place under Her Majesty's dominion'. In addition he was given permission, at his discretion, to annex the South Island by right of discovery; a 'right', it may be added, which the British no more than the Dutch could claim so long after the event.

That the authorities were now prepared to contemplate annexing the entire country was largely a result of the Company's proceedings. But the Government accepted this possibility most unwillingly. It considered itself to be 'embarking on a measure essentially unjust, and but too certainly fraught with calamity to a numerous and inoffensive people', but it felt compelled by circumstances beyond its control to act in order to avert or at least to mitigate the 'process of War and Spoliation, under which uncivilized Tribes have invariably disappeared as often as they have been brought into the immediate vicinity of Emigrants from the Nations of Christendom'.

Such parts of New Zealand as Hobson might annex were to become a dependency of New South Wales, a further indication that the authorities saw New Zealand as a problem arising from Australian expansion. Hobson was strictly enjoined to deal fairly with the Maoris, to appoint a Protector to guard their welfare once his government was established, to guarantee their rights to the land and, in order to prevent European purchasers from defrauding them, to provide that all European land titles must derive from a Crown grant.

These instructions marked a new and a noble beginning in

British colonial policy. The history of New Zealand was to be distinguished from that of earlier settlement colonies; the fate of the Maoris was to differ from that of the American Indian, the Bantu, the Australian or Tasmanian aborigine; for the new colony was being launched in an evangelical age. Imperialism and humanitarianism would henceforth march together. Even the Colonial Office, without much conviction, hoped that New Zealand would be the scene of a Utopian experiment.

III: THE FOUNDATIONS
OF THE STATE

Without plenty of Government the settlement of a waste country is barbarous and miserable work.

E. G. WAKEFIELD

THE first 'colony' of New Zealand Company settlers reached Port Nicholson late in January 1840. A few days later Captain Hobson, with his little entourage of civil servants transferred from New South Wales to the prospective government of New Zealand, arrived at the Bay of Islands. These two events marked the beginning of a struggle between settlers and Governor which was to continue, with little intermission, for thirty years; and the inception of a rivalry between north and south (terms with more than a geographic significance) which was to become a permanent feature of New Zealand life. What was more important, they also marked the transfer to New Zealand of the argument between humanitarians and 'systematic colonizers'. The theories of both parties were now to be put to the test.

On 5 February several hundred Maoris gathered at Waitangi – the Waters of Lamentation – to discuss the greatest question which ever came before a Maori assembly. The debate in the marquee which was erected on the lawn in front of the British Residency was no academic contest of wit; no organized parties made the result a foregone conclusion. Had the majority refused to accept him, Hobson could not have annexed the country.

Many powerful chiefs longed to return to the golden Polynesian age before white sails had divided their unchanging horizons. They had no need, they argued, for blankets or bread; flax matting and fern-root had satisfied their ancestors. Furthermore, they were afraid that if the Governor stayed, chiefly dignity would be overthrown and they would be as low as worms. Already much land had been sold to the missionary or trader. Their own past improvidence with their chief possession now seemed, in Maori eyes, to accuse the European. Soon, one chief foretold, the Maoris would 'be reduced to the condition of slaves, and be obliged to break stones for the road'. Some of them feared a worse fate, for they had heard of the Tasmanian aborigines.

In the end these conservatives were defeated. Tamati Waka Nene, one of the greatest chiefs of the Ngapuhi tribe, won the day when he called on necessity and hope to put down nostalgia and fear. It was too late to turn the white man away. They should, he said, have told the grog-seller to depart a generation ago. British colonization had begun and British authority must follow, but to him it held out the promise of better days. Christianity, trade, tribal peace were blessings for which he would exchange the pagan past or the anarchic present. He called to Hobson:

remain for us a father, a judge, a peacemaker. You must not allow us to become slaves. You must preserve our customs, and never permit our lands to be wrested from us.... Stay then, our friend, our father, our Governor.

On 6 February some fifty chiefs signed the Treaty of Wai-tangi. Missionaries and officials then carried it about the country and, after much further discussion, over five hundred Maoris, mostly chiefs, added their marks. The chiefs of the Arawa, the Ngatihaua, the Ngatimaniapoto and many other tribes either were not asked to sign or, like Te Wherowhero, the great leader of the Waikato, refused to sign away their power. What those who signed or those who refused may have understood by the treaty, it is difficult to say. By the first article the chiefs ceded their sovereignty to the Queen. In return the Queen guaranteed the Maoris in the possession of the lands, forests, fisheries and other property which, collectively or individually, they possessed. The chiefs yielded to the Queen the sole right of purchasing their lands. Finally the chiefs were given the rights and privileges of British subjects. One chief interpreted the treaty as meaning that 'the shadow of the land goes to Queen Victoria, but the substance remains with us'. An Under-Secretary in the Colonial Office, reading these words, feared that the Maoris would discover that they had parted with a not insubstantial shadow.

It is improbable that Captain Hobson was aware of the fact that the Treaty of Waitangi had no standing in international law; but though he was no lawyer, he seemed determined that the country should become as firmly British as his ingenuity could make it. He had been given two commissions; one appointing him Consul, the other, Lieutenant-Governor over any territory which might be acquired for Great Britain in New Zealand. The intention of the British Government was plainly that, in his capacity as Consul, he should negotiate with the Maoris for the recognition of British sovereignty, and should then take office as Lieutenant-Governor over such parts of the country as they should cede. On arriving at the Bay of Islands, however, and before the negotiations at Waitangi, he declared himself Lieutenant-Governor. His intention was, presumably, to assert his authority over British subjects in the vicinity, but his procedure was anomalous, for he had proclaimed himself Lieutenant-Governor of a British colony that did not, as yet, exist.

After the transactions at Waitangi, while Maori signatures were being collected throughout the country, he learned that the New Zealand Company settlers were making their own laws, and had already had a man imprisoned. He thought it imperative to put a stop to these proceedings, which he regarded as treasonable; so without waiting to hear from his agents whether the Maoris in the Cook Strait region and the South Island had signed the treaty, on 21 May he proclaimed British sovereignty over the whole country, the North Island on the ground of cession by the Maoris, the South Island by right of discovery. Although he had been authorized, if he saw fit, to ignore the few Maoris inhabiting the South Island, it is difficult to see what justification there was for doing so.

That Hobson felt something was lacking in this procedure was suggested in July when a French corvette arrived in the Bay of Islands. Knowing of the French plans for a settlement on Banks' Peninsula, and suspecting that to be the destination of the French vessel, he instructed the captain of a British brig, H.M.S. *Britomart*, to hurry there in order to consolidate British claims by establishing effective occupation. The British flag had been hoisted when the French gunboat, followed immediately by a ship bringing a handful of French colonists, arrived at Akaroa. There was, however, no 'race' to Akaroa, for the French captain had no intention of contesting the British claims.

New Zealand was at last British, by discovery, occupation, cession and – the definitive act – by virtue of Hobson's proclamation of 21 May. The islands were technically part of New South Wales for a year, and thereafter a separate colony. Though the acquisition of sovereignty had been altogether a curious business, nevertheless British policy proceeded from an assumption which was unquestionably as just as it was unusual. The Government accepted that the country, or at least the populous North Island, belonged to its native inhabitants, and neither ignored their rights nor attempted to qualify their dominion out of existence by appealing to international law.

The Treaty of Waitangi was intended to lay a basis for a just society in which two races, far apart in civilization, could live together in amity. It merited the symbolic significance which it came to assume in the minds of both peoples. At the time, however, though almost everyone concerned received some satisfaction, it pleased no one entirely. The British Government had been forced to accept more responsibility than it wanted; the treaty (and official proclamations invalidating land purchases unless confirmed by the Crown) prevented unrestricted settlement by the New Zealand Company; and the missionaries had lost their preserve. But at least Wakefield could derive some satisfaction from the fact that New Zealand was British, while James Stephen and Dandeson Coates could hope that, under a humanitarian government, Maori interests might not be entirely overlooked.

No Delphic oracle was needed to prophesy the history of the first few years of regular settlement and government in New Zealand. Anyone in the Colonial Office, anyone who had read the history of colonization in America or Australia, could imagine something of the native and land troubles, the shortage of capital, the confusion in the Civil Service, the unpopularity of the governors, and the settlers' demands for self-government. Despite lofty talk of systematic colonization and British law and order, for some years after 1840 New Zealand exhibited a scene of anarchy more varied than before. Where cultures met or colonies were planted it was always so. What distinguished the situation in New Zealand from that in earlier days in Australia was the numerical supremacy of the Maoris, their proximity and their formidable fighting prowess. The European towns for a decade or more were mere encampments on the fringe of Polynesia; the settlers held their land on the doubtful tenure of Maori sufferance. Consequently a solution of the problems arising from the contact of the two cultures was a necessity upon which, for both races, all progress attended.

Almost all of the more serious difficulties of the settlers and their government were related to – if they did not derive from – the fundamental problem of racial relations. But, though they were dependent on the Maoris even for food, the New Zealand Company settlers were blind to this reality or reluctant to face it. For instance, when Governor Hobson decided, in 1840, to place his capital on the Waitemata Harbour and not at Port Nicholson, the Company settlers were indignant. They maintained that the site should be decided on geographical grounds alone and that a glance at the map was sufficient to reveal the superior claims of their own town. But Auckland was central in another sense. It lay between the two chief European settlements at Kororareka and Port Nicholson (where Wellington was to be built), and between the two areas with the densest Maori population, the Waikato and surrounding districts, and the country to the north of Auckland. It was a good choice for the site of a capital for the kind of New Zealand society which Hobson envisaged: a bi-racial community. This was the natural anticipation of such persons as Hobson and his successor, Robert FitzRoy, who had visited the country in the days before British sovereignty. In his book *Poenamo*, Dr Logan Campbell relates how, on his arrival in 1840 at the Waitemata Harbour (where Auckland was soon to be established), he realized that, since the Maoris would long be 'the dominant race', his fortunes rested with them. For a time he went to live with a neighbouring tribe, where he served his apprenticeship in the new land by helping to hollow out a canoe, and came to love his hosts. But to the Company settlers, as to Edward Gibbon Wakefield, the man who inspired their migration, New Zealand's destiny was to provide a home for British migrants. There was no

room, except perhaps on the periphery of their vision, for
Maoris. It was many years before they would admit that the
success of their settlements depended on their ability to live
with the native New Zealanders.

Even the government finances were largely derived, in one
way or another, from the Maoris. For many years the settlers
were poor and could not be expected to pay much in taxation.
The British Government, in the face of all its past experience
of colonies, persisted in hoping that Wakefield was to be trusted
at least in his promise that systematic colonization would pay
for itself. The Treasury waited until the colony was bankrupt
before giving grudging aid. At first Hobson was hopeful that the
re-sale of Crown land, purchased from the Maoris, would
provide a large revenue. When sales failed to come up to
expectations he tried to rely on customs revenues, which
largely fell on the Maoris; but it was impossible to stop smug-
gling; and the cost of collecting the duties on such a long coast-
line absorbed a large part of the paltry revenues gained.
Eventually he had to discount bills drawn on the British Treasury, at exorbitant interest, with an Australian bank; and the
Treasury had reluctantly to pay them. When he died in 1842,
worn out by his task, his successor, Robert FitzRoy, against
instructions, issued government debentures which he declared
legal tender. Needless to say this bad paper currency drove
out good sovereigns.

FitzRoy found himself in an impossible situation and succeeded in making it worse. The Maoris at the Bay of Islands
were rapidly becoming discontented with the new order. One
of their chief complaints was that the levy of customs was driving away shipping and hence their long-established trade. In
1844 FitzRoy abolished the customs duty and substituted for
it a property tax, thus leading the world, he boasted, in putting
into practice the 'true and beautiful' theory of free trade. In
later years New Zealand was to prove rather fond of claiming
for itself world leadership, but in this case it proved a costly
mistake, for it led to a rapid drop in revenue. FitzRoy also
proceeded to extend the free trade principle to land dealings,
and thus to destroy the sole potential source of substantial
revenue which remained.

Old settlers greatly resented the Crown monopoly of purchasing Maori lands, which excluded them from a speculation bound to be profitable as immigration increased. Since the impoverished Government was unable to buy much land for re-sale to settlers, newcomers sometimes joined in the protests of the would-be speculators. Furthermore, some of the Maoris were disgusted with the Crown pre-emption, both because of the few purchases made and because the Government, which relied on the profits from land sales for part of its revenue, paid much less for their land than they could have obtained on an open market. FitzRoy bowed to what he called 'popular feeling', though it seems in reality to have been merely the noisy agitation of a minority. Early in 1844 he waived the Crown right of pre-emption and allowed individual settlers to purchase land from the Maoris on payment of a tax of ten shillings an acre to the Government. A few months later he reduced the tax to a penny.

The political question that most interested the settlers was land policy, which, since the Maoris owned most of the land, was in practice a branch of native policy. The English authorities, briefed by the humanitarians, were well aware of the vital importance of land in the relations between European settlers and the native inhabitants of colonies. Consequently they had both guaranteed the Maoris in their landed possessions and declared that no European land claims would be recognized until they had been investigated and confirmed by a Crown grant. Hobson and his successors instituted a scrutiny of pre-Waitangi land claims, whether of missionaries, settlers, or Sydney speculators, to determine to what extent purchases had been fair. The investigations went on interminably and kept old settlers in a constant state of litigation and apoplexy.

A lawyer, William Spain, was sent from London to decide the validity of the New Zealand Company purchases. After holding court for three years he found that only a small proportion of the 20,000,000 acres to which the Company laid claim had been fairly purchased by its agent, Colonel Wakefield. Wherever Spain went Maoris challenged the Company's title. In founding its first settlement at Wellington, the Company had acted more like a group of anxious speculators than determined idealists. Not only did the Company recruit settlers before it possessed a site, but it sold in advance the land it hoped Colonel Wakefield would buy and dispatched the first settlers without waiting to hear whether he had been successful. The settlers, who had arrived to find their land unsurveyed, now learned from Spain that much of it still belonged to the Maoris. In the end Spain succeeded in smoothing the settlers' path; but it took time. The delay was disastrous for many settlers, who had to waste their capital in the town instead of getting on to their farms. That the investigations were necessary, however, may be seen from the fact that at every one of the New Zealand Company sites, within a few years of the settlers' arrival, there was either fighting, or the threat of war with the Maoris over the Company's disputed land purchases.

In Wellington the Maoris, who denied having sold several of their villages which stood on the site intended for the town, tried to stop the survey. Two years after the second Company settlement, Nelson, was established in 1841, there was a serious incident (termed by the settlers the 'Wairau massacre') when Captain Arthur Wakefield and several other Europeans were killed while attempting to arrest two turbulent chiefs, Te Rauparaha and Te Rangihaeata, ostensibly for burning surveyors' huts, but in reality for resisting the survey of land which the Maoris denied having sold. In this case FitzRoy rightly concluded that the settlers were in the wrong. While condemning the murders, he refused to take action against the murderers. Whether it would have been wiser to have demanded *utu* (payment, revenge), as the Maoris expected, in order to teach the chiefs that they could no longer act as they had in the tribal wars of the twenties and thirties, has been debated ever since. Certainly Octavius Hadfield, the Anglican missionary at Otaki and one who knew and understood the Maoris as well as any European, believed that 'a sufficient demonstration' of military strength was necessary to impress these arrogant chiefs with the realities of British power. Perhaps the Governor was wiser, however, in fearing that the small forces at his disposal might create the wrong impression.

At New Plymouth, in Taranaki, where the Plymouth

Company, an offshoot of the New Zealand Company, established a settlement in 1841, the two races hovered on the brink of war for almost twenty years. Spain had reported that the Taranaki purchase, alone of Colonel Wakefield's claims, had been fair and had awarded the settlers 60,000 acres. Taranaki was almost unpopulated because in the twenties, after many of the local Maoris had migrated to Otaki and Cook's Strait, the Waikato tribes had killed or enslaved almost all the rest. It seemed to Spain that a large area could be granted to the Company without injury to Maori interests, but he ignored the absentee owners who had received none of Wakefield's paltry payment. After 1840 sections of the local tribes, many freed from slavery in the Waikato, began to drift back. Atiawa tribesmen, returning to the vicinity of New Plymouth and finding Europeans on their land, intimidated the 'out-settlers' and obstructed surveyors. FitzRoy ordered a fresh investigation of the Company's title, and decided to set aside Commissioner Spain's award. Instead he purchased from the Maoris 3,500 acres round the town. Once again he was justified, for the Company title had been most defective and Spain's award could only have been given effect by force. The settlers, however, saw nothing except that the Governor had thrown away most of their best land, the coastal strip northwards from New Plymouth to beyond the Waitara River.

The facts of the situation throughout New Zealand justified the views of the British Government, the first governors, and the old settlers on the paramount importance of racial relations. For some years, however, the local Government was conspicuously unsuccessful in its attempts to keep on good terms with the Maoris. There was, it is true, a Protectorate Department, which had been set up by Hobson, but it was not the Maoris who most needed protection. In any case that Department, hampered by lack of funds and poorly staffed, was able to do very little. It investigated a few crimes, spent a few pounds on medicine for the Maoris, and for a time acted as the government agency for the purchase of Maori land. The Chief Protector, George Clarke, an indolent and ineffectual man, who had been a missionary and before that a gunsmith, at least protested vigorously and successfully against this incongruous conjunction of tasks; to guard the Maoris' interests and to separate them from their lands.

The helplessness of the Department, and of FitzRoy's Government, may be judged from the fact that Clarke was reduced to measures such as the publication in the *Maori Gazette* of a notice prohibiting tribal warfare. The British Government, which had come to New Zealand to keep law and order and to benefit the Maoris, was able to do neither. Moreover, unable to keep the peace, it was in no position to go to war. Apart from the disputes in the New Zealand Company settlements, there was fighting among the Maoris in several districts. Since he had only a hundred troops in the colony, and for some time refused to carry out his instructions to form a militia because he believed that the settlers were not to be trusted with arms, so great was their antagonism to the Maoris, there was little FitzRoy could do but watch. On the one occasion when he could not avoid taking action, he was conspicuously unsuccessful.

British annexation and the foundation of Auckland had left Kororareka an historic relic. Customs duties discouraged whalers from calling, while much of the remaining trade, like the population, was attracted to the capital. The population fell by half in four years. There was a rapid decline in the northern Maoris' earnings from trade, so that they became increasingly disgruntled with the Government which had largely caused their poverty. They complained of the almost complete cessation of land sales; some of them complained, too, that the settlers had their best land. In 1844 Hone Heke, a nephew of the infamous old savage Hongi Hika, and the first Maori to sign the Treaty of Waitangi, showed what he thought of British sovereignty by cutting down its symbol, the flagstaff at Kororareka, and then sacking and burning the township.

Hone Heke had many complaints but he was not very clear about the aim of his revolt. Perhaps inspired by French and American settlers, he had certain republican aspirations; but though he saw himself as a national leader, he acted only as the unruly chief of part of the Ngapuhi tribe. About a thousand Maoris, under Heke and Kawiti, took arms against the British. Fortunately for the settlers most of the tribe remained neutral or, under Tamati Waka Nene, came to the aid of the Government. Even so the British forces, reinforced from Sydney, suffered several defeats through underestimating their foe. In one action, after artillery had failed to breach the heavy timber stockade round Heke's *pa*, a mixed force of red-coats, marines, sailors and volunteers was sent in to make a frontal attack. As the British advanced in close formation, the regulation twenty-three inches apart, they were mown down by concealed fire.

For over a year, while the 'Far North' was in an uproar, FitzRoy acted in the most vacillating way, hesitating to fight lest a general uprising should result, yet alarming the rebels by talking of confiscating land as a punishment; and obstinately insisting on putting up the flagstaff each time that the Maoris as obstinately cut it down. Much of his difficulty was a result of the parsimony of the British Treasury, but he seemed incapable of using effectively what resources he possessed. As W. P. Morrell has judiciously remarked, although 'a case may be made out for most of FitzRoy's acts, taken separately . . . taken together they lead irresistibly to the conclusion that he was totally lacking in the essential qualities of cool judgement, resolution, and consistency of purpose.' It was obvious, even to himself, that he had to go. In the dispatch in which he announced his reduction of the land purchase tax to a penny an acre (an act which, he remarked, must seem 'startling and unauthorized'), he added, unnecessarily, that he would not be surprised if he were immediately superseded.

The main trouble was not his disobedience or his vacillation, but the fact that he was a fanatical humanitarian – he had, indeed, been recommended for the governorship by Dandeson Coates of the Church Missionary Society. FitzRoy made no effort to conceal his hostility to the settlers, whom he regarded, in the event of trouble, as invariably in the wrong. This attitude did not endear him to the Europeans, nor assist him in his task, which was not merely to guard Maori welfare, but to govern both races, and to endeavour to mediate between their demands. To ignore the settlers' interests was as unrealistic as to disregard the Maoris' power.

The increased rate of settlement brought about by the New

Zealand Company and British annexation had made conditions more anarchic than before, but so far British government had made little impression. The North Island was in an uproar. The Government was bankrupt. Disputed land titles and obstreperous Maoris held up the progress of European farming. The flourishing trade of earlier days had been checked. But, in 1845, when things were at their worst, into this scene of disorder there stepped a man who, in retrospect, seems a Caesar in the provinces. With a few strokes, subtly conceived, boldly executed, he ordered the chaos. When he left in 1853 it seems, as we look back over a century, that New Zealand life had begun to follow a clear pattern, and that of Grey's devising. This is, of course, in part, a romantic illusion. Governor George Grey did not regulate the colony's affairs on his own. He was, however, one of the most outstanding personalities in New Zealand political history; he was the only able governor sent out while governors possessed any considerable influence; and the shape of New Zealand life in the nineteenth century owed more to him than to any other individual.

Grey was such a strange mixture of man and superman that his career has had a never-failing fascination for posterity. He had only a nodding acquaintance with truth and in his dispatches home the facts he mentioned, carefully selected and artfully presented, usually managed to convey what impression he wished. The editor of an Auckland newspaper, the *Southern Cross*, thought that Grey must live in daily terror of 'the apparition of a misstatement starting up in his path. His morning prayer must be that of Falstaff at Shrewsbury – "Would it were bed-time, Hal, and all were well".' Grey did not, however, so much lie as fail to tell the truth; and despite a further reputation for enjoying his pleasures, he was no Falstaff. The genial Governor was a lonely, secretive man who, as he grew older, found it more and more impossible to get on with his equals or superiors and who, as a party politician, later in the century, compensated for the absence of wife and friend by seeking, through his skill as a popular orator, the approval of the masses. He was a man of the widest interests in the humanities and natural science, and of considerable intellectual force; an efficient if despotic leader; a ruthless foe who would stoop to petty victories; and altogether what his arch-enemy, William Fox, called him: 'the great dictator, the great pro-consul, the great Maori-tamer'.

To tame the rebels did not prove as difficult as had been expected. Kawiti was driven out of his *pa*, the Bat's Nest – Ruapekapeka – and made peace. Heke was left alone, but he fought no more. Grey then turned his attention to the Cook Strait area where there had been a Maori attack on European outposts in the Hutt Valley. He suspected that Te Rauparaha, if not behind this disturbance, was busy plotting further trouble. Grey took him by surprise, arrested him, and held him in illegal custody for eighteen months. The bloody Te Rauparaha's *mana* fell as the Governor's rose. Te Rangihaeata was obliged to retreat and eventually to make peace. Then, apart from a Maori attack on the town of Wanganui, an off-shoot of Wellington, in 1847, the fighting between Maori and pakeha was, for the time being, at an end.

As a measure fundamental to any effective government control throughout the North Island, Grey restored the Crown monopoly of purchasing Maori land, which was maintained until 1862 despite the opposition of speculators. This system was open to severe criticism. The Government bought huge areas of land for sixpence or a shilling an acre and sold it to the settlers for ten shillings or a pound; this was robbing the Maoris ostensibly in order to save them from being swindled by settlers. In fact it was increasingly unnecessary to protect the Maoris from the 'land-shark', for they were shrewd traders, well aware of the monetary value of land. They were also aware, though there were surprisingly few complaints, that the Government paid them much less than they might have obtained by free enterprise. However, the Crown monopoly served a number of purposes which justified its continuance. Above all, land dealings were under some degree of control. When a government agent was negotiating a purchase, the tribe concerned was usually very agitated. It was quite impossible to allow hundreds of private individuals simultaneously to go about seeking land. Free trade would have kept the whole Maori population in a perpetual state of excitement. Moreover, Maori customary tenure was exceedingly complicated.

Purchasing land was too tricky and dangerous a business to be left to individuals. Under government regulation, a proper investigation of titles could be made, and thus disputes over whether lands had been fairly purchased could be minimized.

Under Grey a method of negotiating land purchases was developed which was nicely grafted on to Maori custom and which for some years worked well and fairly. As we have seen, the Maoris had no private property in land, nor, in pre-European days, any system of alienating tribal land. The Europeans found that the consent of the individuals using a piece of land, the chiefs of their sub-tribe, and of the tribe itself, was necessary before a purchase could be made. In practice, during Grey's governorship, Land Purchase Commissioners would seek the approval of a tribal meeting at which the ownership, boundaries and price would be discussed. Large numbers of owners used to sign the deed of sale. In theory the Government did not solicit offers of land, but in practice all the age-old tricks of the huckster or politician were employed by its agents. In 1859 – after Grey had left – to give but one example, the Commissioner of Crown Lands in Taranaki went with Robert Parris, the local land purchase agent, to visit 'Raumoa's widow'. He wrote afterwards,

Parris commenced blubbering at some distance and he rubbed noses [the Maori equivalent of kissing] with the widow and the three or four other withered old things there. It was worth the trip to see the profile of Parris' mug as he was getting up steam. I had intended to joke him on the subject but he was so cursed dismal on the road back that I couldn't venture on it. I suppose he had a 'motive' for it, or thought he had, which is the same thing – some hopes of land in that direction.

Such practices were unavoidable, and did no great harm so long as Grey kept a firm hand on the reins.

Large areas of land were purchased in the North Island. Almost the entire South Island was bought in a few huge 'blocks'. Only in Taranaki was Grey unsuccessful in securing enough land to meet the urgent requirements of the settlers. He had been instructed by the Colonial Office, which disapproved of FitzRoy's reversal of Spain's award, to put the settlers in possession of the original 60,000 acres should this be at all possible. At first he had some success. In 1847–8 over 27,000 acres were purchased near New Plymouth. Almost immediately, however, the situation was made much more difficult by the return to Taranaki, in 1848, of five hundred Maoris who had been living for about twenty-five years in exile in the Wellington district. Grey tried first to prevent their return, and then to induce their chief, Wiremu Kingi (William King), to settle to the north of the Waitara river, leaving the southern bank for the settlers. Kingi declared: ' I will not give up my land till I am first dragged by the hair and put in gaol'; and he insisted on settling on the south bank, within the limits of Spain's award. Thereafter, like the great majority of the Taranaki Maoris, he declined to sell any of his ancestral land.

When these Maoris returned to Taranaki, Grey remarked gloomily that now 'no land at all would be obtained, without a war.' When he visited Taranaki in 1850 Kingi's younger brother Matiu (Matthew) and another chief, both of whom had quarrelled with Kingi, offered to sell land on the Waitara, but the Governor was too cautious to accept this kind of offer against the will of the tribe. As the New Zealand Company agent, who was present on this occasion, wrote: 'His Excellency avoided the explicit answer the friendly natives had a right to anticipate, and the meeting terminated unsatisfactorily.' In an almost identical situation, nine years later, another governor was to give the answer the settlers longed to hear.

As immigration fell to a trickle, because of the native troubles, the general poverty, and the shortage of land, the settlers naturally became obsessed with the need for land. Their political representatives and the press carried out to the full the policy advocated by a correspondent in the *Taranaki Herald*:

We should haunt His Excellency night and day – every post should carry messages to him – every hour should whisper the same tidings – his midnight dreams should be of the one thing requisite – 'Taranaki wants more land!'

The Government did manage in the fifties to buy three more blocks of land in Taranaki, though not on the Waitara; but the Taranaki settlers still had much less land than those in the other settlements, and very little good land. The sight of the rich coastal strip lying vacant, covered with weeds, while they were obliged to undertake the expensive and heart-breaking task of clearing the heavily timbered and mountainous interior, excited their envy and anger. As the *Taranaki Herald* remarked in 1855, more judiciously than usual:

> The feeling generated in the mind of the actual settler, who is compelled to go miles back into the forest because he cannot obtain land, is one extremely unfavourable to continued peaceable relations with the Natives; and with the growth of European population, and the increased pressure for land, this feeling will become more bitter.

Grey failed to find a solution to Taranaki's difficulties; but elsewhere, as the Under-Secretary of State for the Colonies wrote, his presence seemed to have 'thrown a kind of sunshine' over the settlements. The British authorities gave him their confidence, more troops and more liberal grants of money. He was able to restore the currency as well as to provide land and to keep law and order. After their initial difficulties, the settlements began to thrive. New colonies, on Wakefield's model, were founded in Otago, in 1848, and in Canterbury, in 1850. Immigration increased rapidly; import and export statistics and land sales revenues all testify to a general prosperity.

Grey's purchases from the Maoris had provided ample scope for the expansion of most of the settlements, but he wanted to ensure that poor men could share in their prosperity. All his life, it is said because of his youthful experience in Ireland, Grey was antagonistic to landlordism. Considering that the price of land in the Wakefield settlements (£1 an acre in Wellington, £2 in Otago, £3 in Canterbury), and the current price of £1 an acre for Crown land, were too high, in 1853 he passed an ordinance lowering the price of Crown land to ten shillings an acre, or five shillings for poor land. Though this permitted needy men to buy a few acres, as he intended, its chief effect was to enable rich men to buy up large areas. In Canterbury and elsewhere it helped to create a class of rich pastoralists. Speculators, who had no intention of farming, acquired choice land and sat tight waiting for prices to rise. Nevertheless, the ordinance assisted the progress of the settlements at the time. It exemplified Adam Smith's dictum (as opposed to Wakefield's theory) that plenty of cheap land was one secret of colonial prosperity.

In certain respects at least, the Maoris were thriving too. They owned most of the coastal shipping in the North Island, grew a large proportion of the food sold locally and exported considerable quantities of potatoes, wheat, and other foodstuffs to Australia. In the Waikato alone in 1853 they owned ten water-mills, worth £2,700, while eight more were being erected, and they had thousands of acres planted in wheat. A chief seemed to be speaking the simple and final truth when he declared: 'We have abandoned our old ways. The rule now is kindness to the orphan (charity), peace, and agricultural pursuits.' At the Waitara, Wiremu Kingi was reported, in 1855, to speak in the same vein: 'Peace is good, and cultivation is good; he does not wish to live in strife; his only war is cultivation – as much as the Europeans can consume.'

Grey did everything he could to encourage Maori agriculture. He made them private and public loans (which they almost invariably repaid) for the purchase of ploughs, mills or small vessels. And throughout his governorship he laboured to establish other measures calculated to improve the condition of the Maori people and to 'elevate' them in the scale of civilization. This was the only attempt at all systematic which was made to civilize (that is, to Europeanize) the Maoris. Judged by the humanitarian ideals of the time it was an enlightened attempt.

Grey subsidized mission schools, and encouraged the missionaries to start new ones. Several co-educational Industrial Boarding Schools were established in which the pupils received instruction in carpentry and agriculture, or sewing, as well as in arithmetic, English, and Maori. In 1852 some seven hundred Maoris were attending government-subsidized schools. In four of the North Island towns he built hospitals where Maoris received free treatment. Several Resident Magistrates were appointed to introduce the tribes to European law and legal procedure, while a few chiefs were given small salaries to assist the magistrates as assessors. Maoris were employed on public works and at other tasks, with a similar intention of encouraging them to accept European society.

In the early eighteen-fifties Grey was confident that he had established a basis for 'peaceful co-existence', indeed that the two races were well on their way to the humanitarian goal of 'amalgamation'. The Maoris seemed to be adapting themselves happily to the politics of the sovereign state and to the economy of the market-place. He reported to the Secretary of State that 'both races already form one harmonious community, connected together by commercial and agricultural pursuits, professing the same faith, resorting to the same Courts of Justice, joining in the same public sports, standing mutually and indifferently to each other in the relation of landlord and tenant, and thus insensibly forming one people.'

Though there were grounds for optimism, this was going too far. Most of the Maoris continued to live in their tribal communities, under what remained of their own laws. Most of them derived little benefit from the schools, while they saw no doctors, magistrates or any government officers except the ubiquitous land purchase agents. Though their social structure was subject to great pressure and was rapidly changing, the main European influences came from traders, missionaries and ordinary settlers. The effects of Grey's civilizing measures were very superficial and were confined, in general, to the vicinity of the settlements, where the Maoris were, in any case, subject to the strongest European influence. The Government did not direct the main changes which were occurring in the Maori community, though this was not very apparent until after Grey had left.

In one respect Grey's government of the Maoris was a wonderful success. He recognized that the Treaty of Waitangi was not merely 'a praiseworthy device for amusing and pacifying savages', as the New Zealand Company supposed: government by Maori consent was a necessity. He tried to make the state an impartial third party, which would stand outside racial competition, and reconcile conflicting interests. While he was present, the ideal was to some extent realized. His enormous prestige among the Maoris enabled him to deal with situations which would have defeated lesser men, though even then there were difficulties (in Taranaki for instance) which he could not solve. But it was a personal success. It was typical of him that he not only watched over the details of administration but also formulated the principles of Maori policy. He abolished the Protectorate Department, and dispersed its officers, but made little attempt to train other Civil Servants to administer Maori affairs. The Department had been a rudimentary administrative body with no policy: Grey provided a policy with no permanent administrative machinery to maintain it.

Apart from the unlikelihood of his successor's possessing the qualities that sustained Grey's benevolent despotism, and the fact that there was no government department which might give continuity to his Maori policy, there was another reason why his system was unlikely to continue without great modification. It was plain that, sooner or later, the settlers would be granted self-governing institutions. Here Grey was in a dilemma. Democratic by conviction, he was authoritarian by temperament. For this reason, and because it was doubtful whether popular European rule was compatible with an impartial regard for Maori interests, his attitude towards the introduction of self-government was ambivalent. Unable to disapprove of the principle, he yet hoped to postpone its application.

In 1846, under pressure from the directors of the New Zealand Company, Earl Grey dispatched a most intricate constitution which would have set up a pyramid of representative institutions, from municipal councils to two provincial assemblies to a general assembly, entailing plenty of elections, direct and indirect – all for fourteen thousand settlers. When the 'paper constitution' reached New Zealand the town of Wanganui was in imminent danger of destruction by rebels: indeed, Grey later alleged, rather for dramatic effect than in strict truth, that when he received it he was standing on the beach near Wanganui watching a skirmish between two parties of Maoris. Certainly the circumstances made plain the dangers of giving the European minority the power to rule the Maori majority. On the Governor's representation, the introduction of·the constitution was postponed.

For the next five years the settlers of the southern provinces fought what seemed to them a desperate struggle against the

Governor, whom they regarded as a local representative of the Tsar Alexander's Holy Alliance, to get their constitution. In fact they were shadow-boxing. The chief architect of the New Zealand constitution of 1852 was Governor Grey himself. He had differed from the settlers on little more than the question of timing.

The 1852 constitution was extremely democratic, more so than those then in force in the Australian colonies. The six Provincial Councils, the House of Representatives and the Superintendents of the Provinces were all elective, though the members of the Legislative Council (the Upper House) were nominated for life by the Governor. There was a low property qualification, which effectively excluded almost all the Maoris, because they did not possess individual landed property.

No one regarded a unitary state as feasible, for the several settlements were so isolated that government from one centre was virtually impossible. Communications between settlements were often worse than those of individual settlements with Australia. At times neighbouring Provinces heard no news of each other for many months at a time. It took Otago members over two months by sea to reach Auckland for the first session of the General Assembly. There was good reason, then, for decentralized institutions. The constitution provided for a formal division of authority: certain powers, such as those over customs, coinage, justice and Crown lands, were reserved for the General Assembly. The residual powers left to the Provinces ample scope for legislation and administration. But there was no doubt where final authority lay. Any laws passed by the central Parliament superseded provincial ordinances repugnant to them. Moreover Parliament had the power to constitute new provinces or to revise the powers of the provincial councils. In 1857 Parliament was given power to amend large sections of the constitution, so that the provinces could be abolished by a mere majority of a body in which they had no representation.

The sum of £7,000 was reserved on the civil list to be expended on Maori welfare. The Crown right of pre-emption over Maori land was retained in the Governor's hands. The constitution did not give the Governor, as Grey had urged, the power to continue his control of native policy as a whole (though Grey's successor, Gore Browne, was in fact to retain this authority); but it permitted him to declare native districts within which the authority of the colonial government would not operate. The 'rights of aborigines' had not, then, been overlooked, but it was clear that the new freedom would be more European in complexion than the old despotism.

Having salvaged the ship of state in 1845 and 1846, kept her in dry dock from 1847 to 1852, and now relaunched her completely refitted, Grey departed for the governorship at Cape Town, rather relieved, one would guess, not to have to take command during the next voyage.

Already some of the structural features of modern New Zealand life had been erected. The Americans and French had been driven off and a British century had begun. The establishment of parliamentary institutions, the search for a means of living peacefully with the Maoris, the desire to make land available to all, were to remain important elements in the country's history. The idea of the state as a just arbitrator was to have a recurrent appeal: half a century after Grey's first governorship it was to be called in to mediate in the class war. It is not entirely fanciful to see in Grey's government one of the sources of the 'welfare state' in New Zealand. In his day the state did little to benefit the poor. Governmental humanitarianism began with the 'uncivilized', not with the 'underprivileged'. But Grey's schools and hospitals mark the beginning of a tradition of benevolent state activity. Maori policy accustomed the settlers to the idea of government welfare services, while the building of government roads – and, later, railroads – made public ownership familiar. Thousands of settlers, it should be added, came to the country only with the aid of colonizing companies or, later, of provincial governments. If we examine the social or economic development of the settlements it becomes equally plain that, in many respects, the character of New Zealand society was formed in its infancy.

IV: THE PIONEERS

Now, while I am convinced that society in such a colony as
New Zealand must daily Americanize, I am also persuaded
that the New Zealander will retain more of the Briton than
any other colonist.

THOMAS CHOLMONDELEY, *Ultima Thule*, 1854

OF the six Provinces set up under the 1852 constitution, five
were Wakefield settlements. Two of these, Wellington and
Nelson, were founded by the New Zealand Company. Most of
the original settlers came from London or near-by counties.
The colonization of Taranaki, initially with folk from Devon
and Cornwall, was begun by a subsidiary body, the Plymouth
Company, which was soon absorbed by the parent organization.

Although in 1840 the New Zealand Company at last received
official recognition, a royal charter, and a Crown grant of four
acres in New Zealand for every pound sterling it had expended
on colonizing, it languished after these initial efforts. In 1845,
following further acrimonious disputes with the Colonial
Office, the Company was given a large government loan on the
security of its lands, but even this assistance could not save it.
In 1850 it was forced to surrender its charter. A few years later
the New Zealand Government paid to the shareholders their
original capital and a small dividend.

Colonization had proved a poor business proposition, for
the demands on the Company's cash had been immediate,
while its antipodean acres were of only prospective value.
Nevertheless, the work of colonizing on 'systematic' principles
was continued by two new associations which founded Otago
in 1848 and Canterbury in 1850. Both were inspired by Wakefield, that indefatigable, indomitable, insufferable schemer, who
managed to sell to the Church of England and to the Free
Church of Scotland the idea of establishing denominational
colonies. Though without religious enthusiasm himself, as one
of his biographers has remarked, to get his plans adopted 'he
would have transplanted the Grand Lama of Tibet with all his
praying-wheels, and did actually nibble at the Chief Rabbi.'

The original promoter of the Otago scheme, George Rennie, aimed at a more broadly-based settlement. He hoped that, through the promotion of emigration in general, it might be possible 'to save the institutions of England from being swept away in an uncontrollable rebellion of the stomach' – an argument in favour of colonization which had also been advanced by Wakefield. But he was himself swept away by a revolution of the spirit, at the time of the disruption of the Presbyterian Church. He was supplanted by two members of the schismatic Free Kirk: Captain William Cargill, a battered old soldier from the Peninsular War, and the Reverend Thomas Burns, a censorious old bigot who was a nephew of the poet. Supported by the Association of the Lay Members of the Free Church, these two decided to plant a Free Church settlement where 'piety, rectitude and industry' would feel at home, and where the inhabitants as a body would form 'a vigilant moral police'. The pioneers of Otago sailed in the wake of the *Mayflower*.

Two hundred miles to the north of Dunedin, the new Geneva, the Canterbury Association established its colony two years later. The Association consisted of a most distinguished collection of archbishops, dukes, earls, bishops, lords. Its driving spirit was a High Church Tory, or rather, Peelite, John Robert Godley, an exceedingly able convert to Wakefield's as well as Pusey's doctrines. With the Canterbury pioneers, whom Wakefield described as 'not merely a nice, but a choice society of English people', Godley hoped to found a colony which (when he pictured it 'in the colours of a Utopia') he saw as English, Anglo-Catholic, and conservative.

Were these experiments in 'systematic' colonization successful? Did Wakefield's formula, when tested, produce the results he predicted? He did, of course, succeed in helping to establish five colonies in New Zealand, as well as South Australia, which was a feat remarkable and surely unequalled. He also had the satisfaction of seeing some of his suggestions incorporated in British colonial policy. The sale of Crown land became a standard practice. In the Wakefield settlements it was sold at a high, though not, in Wakefield's sense, a 'sufficient', price. The employment of land revenues as an immigration fund proved a practical way of diverting to the distant southern colonies part of the stream of migration which tended naturally to flow across the Atlantic.

The efforts made by the colonizing associations to select suitable migrants undoubtedly influenced the composition of the original population of the Wakefield colonies, though a certain number of the aged and infirm, of rogues and paupers, managed to slip by the scrutiny of the emigration agents. The disciples of Wakefield did succeed in establishing, in Otago and Canterbury, colonies with a denominational bias, though neither was ever as exclusive as their founders had intended them to be. The Wakefield companies also achieved their aim of founding colonies with a reasonable balance of sexes and with a youthful population. As C. E. Carrington has pointed out, many of the better-known figures in New Zealand a century ago, men no doubt pictured by school children as bearded ancients, were young men. In 1850, Godley and J. E. Fitz-Gerald, two fathers of Canterbury, were thirty-six and thirty-two respectively. Archdeacon Octavius Hadfield was thirty-six and Selwyn, nine years a Bishop, forty-one. Grey, nine years a Governor, and William Fox, a New Zealand Company agent and future Premier, were both thirty-eight.

In these important respects Wakefield's system offered useful practical hints for colonizers. On the whole, however, it failed to work. The experiments in New Zealand produced colonies – but not 'Wakefield' colonies. It proved impossible to regulate either the expansion of the frontier or the form of class structure by means of a price upon land.

'Agriculture', as the writer of many a handbook for immigrants advised, 'did not pay'. Until later in the nineteenth century the only form of farming which was really profitable was to run sheep. Consequently the New Zealand frontier, like the Australian, was in most Provinces a 'big man's frontier'. The sheep farmer needed considerable initial capital, not to buy land, which he leased illegally from the Maoris or legally from the provincial governments, but to buy sheep, and, if he were not the original run-holder, to purchase the 'goodwill' of a sheep run. Samuel Butler, who came out in 1860 to take up a run, found that 1,000 ewes cost him £1,250. (Four years later he returned to England after doubling the £4,000 advanced by his father.) It was generally agreed that a man needed from £1,500 to £2,000 to establish himself as a sheep farmer, or 'squatter', as the pastoralists were often called, the term having become respectable and acquired a connotation of wealth, rather than of illegality, as in earlier days in America or Australia.

All of the districts where the Wakefieldians had established their settlements, with the exception of Taranaki, were pre-eminently suitable for sheep. Christchurch, for instance, was on the edge of the immense, tussock-covered Canterbury plains. But most of the 'capitalists' (few of whom had, in any case, more than a modest fortune), misled by English experience and Wakefield's dogma, had sunk their capital in land. They lacked the money to purchase a flock as well as the experience to manage it. Some of the 'capitalists' turned to sheep; but many of the early pastoralists in the Wairarapa and Wairau districts, in Southland and Otago, were Australians. Even the Canterbury Association, almost as soon as its settlement was founded, had to let in the 'shagroons', as the Australian stock-men were called.

The run-holder bore little resemblance to Wakefield's ideal gentleman farmer. He was certainly not leisured. He often led a semi-barbarous existence for many years living in rough huts and eating mutton and damper. Moreover, he employed very little labour in proportion to the extent of his land holding. Soon after the initial settlement, Wellington, Nelson, Canterbury and Otago presented the spectacle, not of the 'concentration' which Wakefield desired, but of the widest dispersion, as the flocks and their owners and shepherds spread up the valleys and across the plains.

Agriculture largely fell into the hands of those who were meant to be agricultural or general labourers. The immediate cause was the limited number of employers of labour. In Nelson, for instance, three-quarters of the proprietors, the owners of most of the land sold, were absentees. It was impossible to prevent labourers from becoming landowners, or at least land-users, when landowning employers were so few. In the long run, however, agriculture remained the province of poor men for substantial economic reasons, the chief of which was that no extensive market lay near enough to make it very profitable. The costs of farming on the English model were, moreover, prohibitive. It cost several pounds an acre to clear heavy bush or fern, while, after an initial period of unemployment in the forties, wages were much higher than in Great Britain. In agriculture the Maoris, who competed directly with the settlers, enjoyed considerable advantages. They owned most of the good land in the North Island. They farmed communally, and thus had no labour costs. Until the eighteen-sixties they probably produced the greater part of the food crops consumed in New Zealand or exported to Australia.

In these circumstances, the small farm of a few acres, worked by the owner, or lessee, and his family, became the characteristic unit of European agriculture, market gardening and dairying. Sometimes the family would live off their land; more often, perhaps, the men would supplement their income by casual labouring, and by other means, such as buying a team of bullocks and contracting to plough for neighbouring farmers. According to Sir George Grey the majority of the population consisted of these small landed proprietors.

The land holdings in actual occupation tended to be of two sorts. There were very large sheep stations and very small family farms. Neither met the essential requirement of Wakefield's system by providing employment for a large class of labourers. And there was another important aspect of land tenure which upset the mechanism of 'systematic' colonization. Many settlers, townsmen in England, inclined to cling to the small towns in the colony, engaging in trading of one sort or another. Almost to a man, the members of this middle class indulged in speculative land dealing. Naturally the volume of land sales bore little relation to the expansion of farming and gave no indication at all, as the Wakefield theory postulated, of the demand for labour.

Since the economy was so different from Wakefield's anticipation, the social structure could scarcely correspond to his desires; but even the original groups of settlers did not remotely resemble a cross-section of English society. Except in Otago, where most of the founding fathers were indigent tradesmen or labourers, there was, it is true, a high proportion of people of comfortable means. On board the Company ships the cabin passengers, who paid their own fares, and who called themselves 'colonists', while referring to the assisted passengers down below as 'emigrants', amounted to twelve or fourteen per cent of the total passengers. They formed almost a quarter of the settlers in the first eight ships of the Canterbury Association. But by no means all of these 'colonists' stayed. It has been estimated, for example, that by 1848 only eighty-five of the original four hundred and thirty-six remained in Wellington. A similar exodus, often back to England, occurred in the other settlements. There is no reason to suppose that there was a higher proportion of people of educated middle-class background in New Zealand than in South Australia, Victoria – or Connecticut where, we are told, there were in the seventeenth century proportionally as many university graduates as in England.

While, in the Wakefield colonies, gentlemen employers were rare, the workmen were, in any case, unwilling to accept an inferior status. From the start they not only became landowners, but formed 'combinations' to raise wages and reduce hours of work. John Robert Godley thought that within eight years the Wellington and Nelson settlers had become 'bitter, abusive, disloyal, democratic, in short, colonial'. He wondered how long it would take his followers in Canterbury to become Chartists. Another active member of the Canterbury Association, a future Premier, Henry Sewell, was shocked to find, on the day he landed in Canterbury in 1853, that the settlers were 'mightily republican'. He observed that the fashion of servants was 'to speak of their fellow-servants and labourers as "Mr" and "Mrs" but of gentlefolks by their surnames only'. The settlers were already coming to resemble Wakefield's anathema, 'a new people', not least in their 'delight in a forced equality'. A visiting Frenchman thought insolence (which commonly accompanies inverted snobbery) was *à la mode* in New Zealand as was familiarity in America.

The Otago poet, John Barr of Craigielee, wrote in the fifties,

> When to New Zealand first I cam,
>   Poor and duddy, poor and duddy,
> When to New Zealand first I cam,

It was a happy day, sirs.
For I was fed on parritch thin,
My taes they stickit thro' my shoon,
I ruggit at the pouken pin,
 But couldna mak it pay, sirs.

In Scotland he strove 'to please a paper lord' and 'wasna worth a steever'; but all that was altered now.

Nae mair the laird comes for his rent,
 For his rent, for his rent,
Nae mair the laird comes for his rent,
 When I hae nocht to pay, sirs.
Nae mair he'll tak me aff the loom,
Wi' hanging lip and pouches toom,
To touch my hat, and boo to him,
 The like was never kent, sirs.

Now the beef was 'tumbling in the pat' and he was 'baith fat and fu', sirs'.

At my door cheeks there's bread and cheese.
I work or no', just as I please,
I'm fairly settled at my ease,
 And that's the way o't noo, sirs.

And an Englishwoman observed that

The look and bearing of the immigrants appear to alter soon after they reach the colony. Some people object to the independence of their manner, but I do not; on the contrary I like to see the upright gait, the well-fed, healthy look, the decent clothes (even if no one touches his hat to you), instead of the half-starved, depressed appearance, and too often cringing servility of the mass of our English population.

Many Wakefield 'colonists' were, of course, less tolerant or understanding; for Wakefield had fostered the idea, which rapidly became a myth, that New Zealand was a colony which, if not quite uncolonial, was at least created as nearly in the image of the motherland as could be expected. The first Bishop-designate of Canterbury, an individual singularly silly, though not alone in his delusions, came out under the impression that he was going to a colony fit for the quality, not one 'where slang will be substituted for conversation . . . where men drink and do not dress for dinner'. He stayed for no longer than a month.

There were, of course, classes, in the sense of rich and poor. In each settlement small cliques usually ran all public functions from balls to race meetings. They also managed to control political life. But there was little of the forms or trappings of the English class system.

In 1859 Governor Gore Browne, Grey's successor, wrote:

In fact society in a Colony, though divided into sets which refuse to associate with each other, is chiefly remarkable for the absence of any order which is an object of respect: – a fact racily expressed in a vulgar saying that 'every man is not only as good as his neighbour, but a great deal better.'

In settlements intended to preserve British class relations, the most striking phenomenon, among the great majority of the population, was a reaction against them. There was nothing surprising about this attitude, for it had existed in a good many other English colonies. The British colonial tradition was reasserting itself, despite the plans of the new colonizers. Thomas Cholmondeley, an original Canterbury settler, and one of the gentry who returned to England, believed that the New Zealanders would 'daily Americanize', but, to him, the qualities which Englishmen regarded as 'American' were, in fact, the characteristics of the British colonist:

The American is essentially a colonist, and his ways and doings express a habit of life, rough and ready, free and daring, generous but dangerous, of infinite suppleness, dexterity, and resource. He cannot be equalled for contrivance. . . .

If most of the settlers in Wakefield's colonies had rejected his ideals, and were unashamedly 'colonial' in their attitudes, most of the others had never had any other pretensions. In the eighteen-forties 'the great promoter' gave a considerable boost to migration to New Zealand, but only during that decade did the 'Wakefield' settlers constitute a majority. Only about 15,000 settlers were brought to New Zealand in the ships of the companies and associations which tried to apply Wakefield's principles.* In 1854, a year after the last of these organizations, the Canterbury Association, had ceased to function, the European population of New Zealand was about 32,500. There were nearly 12,000 in Auckland, the first unsystematic colony, and only 20,000 in the five planned settlements. To see these figures in a useful perspective, it is worth recalling that in 1863, during the Otago gold-rush, 35,000 immigrants arrived, mostly from Australia, in an unpremeditated mob.

Provincial governments took over from the Wakefield organizations the task of colonizing. Most of them continued to use land revenues to pay the fares of immigrants, but the screening process was quite perfunctory. Most of the New Zealand immigrants had not been 'selected'. The attempt to establish a new type of colony was no more than an important episode in the history of migration to New Zealand. In comparison with the great random stream of migration, the contribution of the Wakefield companies was a mere trickle.

New Zealand was settled in a hundred ways. Some towns were 'military settlements', garrison towns. Some were laid out and sold by entrepreneurs. Others were established by a group of compatriots, such as the Highlanders who gathered at Waipu, or the Bohemians who founded Puhoi (the name of which, corrupted, is apparently the origin of the slang term 'the Boo-ay', a synonym for 'the out-backs'). Some towns grew up round Maori villages. The settlement of some districts began when a squatter drove in his sheep. And traders, missionaries,

* New Zealand Company	11,680
Plymouth Company	337
Otago Association	348
Canterbury Association	3,247
	15,612

The N.Z. Company figures are from the 27th Report of the Company, cited J. S. Marais, *The Colonization of New Zealand*, p. 208, and the Plymouth Company figures from Marais, p. 52, The Otago figures are from A. H. McLintock, *The History of Otago*, p. 235 and p. 274. He gives no figure for the third ship, the *Blundell*, but the passengers in this vessel, and in the *Victory*, as well as the Plymouth Company immigrants, may be included in the N. Z. Company figure. The Canterbury total is from an unpublished thesis, N. J. Northover 'The Control of Immigration into Canterbury, 1850–53' (Canterbury University).

whalers, gold-diggers, or dairy farmers were the pioneers in others.

The haphazard process had a long start on systematic colonization. Auckland, a typical settlement, was the heir to Kororareka. It was, the Wellington settlers mocked, not a colony but a 'proclamation town', created by the Lieutenant-Governor's decree on a site inhabited by a few Maoris, one Scotsman, and his partner. But despite such inauspicious beginnings, Auckland grew rapidly. Land speculators and labourers (many of them Irish) came from the Bay of Islands and Australia. The population was 2,000 by 1841. In 1842 a few hundred Scottish immigrants were brought out; a few more Scottish settlers retreated to Auckland from an unsuccessful settlement on a neighbouring harbour; ninety boys were sent out from Parkhurst Prison; 1,700 discharged soldiers were imported to found garrison settlements in the neighbourhood. Such were some of the first ingredients of the capital. Auckland was a garrison town, dominated by the presence of the Maoris and British troops, though its frontier quality was mitigated by the presence of the Government and its small groups of officials of cultivated tastes. Certainly its character was different from that of the other early settlements. In 1851 its population was thirty-one per cent Irish, as compared with two per cent in Wellington. Probably over half the population had come from Australia. William Fox, a Wellingtonian, thought it 'a mere section of the town of Sydney transplanted'.

It would be misleading to dwell further on the failure of Wakefield's plans: the character of the settlements represented a victory for the anonymous, common colonist. Why, after all, did the majority of immigrants come to New Zealand? In this, as in many other respects, the colonization of New Zealand was a by-product of industrialism, as had been true even in the days of Australian 'imperialism', for the poverty and crime which attended the foundation of the factory had given new vigour to the transportation system. Wakefield's theories had been intended as a cure for the ills of an industrialized England. The British annexation was also an indirect consequence of the industrial revolution, for the evangelical movement, which had prompted official interest in the Maoris, was in part a response to industrial evils and found its chief strength in the middle class. The slaves were freed the year after the industrial middle class was enfranchised. In 1840, and for sixty years thereafter, the British emigrants to New Zealand were fleeing from industrialism.

Not persecution or famine but poverty and the fear of poverty were the chief stimuli of migration – that poverty or dread which, especially in the 'hungry forties', haunted the millions who were receiving parish relief; who were unemployed or 'half-employed' in the factory towns or in the English countryside in its decline. The pioneers of New Zealand were not from the highest, nor were they usually from the most down-trodden sections of British society. They were people, who, while poor, while usually from the upper working class or the lower middle class – the 'anxious classes', Wakefield called them – had lost neither enterprise nor ambition.

Many of the well-to-do or better-educated settlers were driven to the end of the earth in pursuit of a dream, some new Jerusalem or brighter Albion, but, even for the middle class, unemployment or the rigours of competition were potent reasons for migration. And, among the more respectable families, poverty had scarcely less powerful allies. Whoever reads the innumerable letters surviving from the correspondence of the pioneers can scarcely fail to be struck by the frequency with which men of the middle class went to New Zealand into exile because of bigamy or bankruptcy, disappointment or disgrace.

The pioneers left failure or hardship, but not usually in despair. There was also hope. Many of them hoped for something for nothing. The Australian 'land-sharks' of the thirties, like the gold-diggers of the sixties, hoped to get rich quickly. New Zealand Company propaganda in England 'puffed' the colony in such a way as to give a quite misleading impression. Dr A. S. Thomson, writing in 1859, remarked that the Company settlers seemed to be bewitched: 'there was a feeling among them that they were moving with, and not away from, the civilized world'; some of them felt that 'migration was not a flight from starvation to exile but a short road to abundance and affluence'. Emigration was itself a 'spec'. The feverish speculation in land among members of the middle class, the incessant gambling in all sections of the community, were but outward signs of the universal devotion to the New World deity, Luck.

Other organizations published misleading advertisements. In the eighteen-sixties the Auckland Provincial Council, for instance, promised each immigrant a 'free farm' of forty acres. The word 'farm' must have conjured up in the mind of the Englishman or Scot something very different from the reality, which only too often turned out to be an inaccessible section of heavy bush or scrub; but the bait of free land lured thousands of migrants to Auckland. As one of the 'forty acre farmers' said in the House of Representatives thirty years later, he came out because he wanted 'a bit of land of his own'. Cheap – or free – land was a demographic magnet weaker only than gold.

The provision of free or assisted passages by the colonizing associations, the provincial, and later the central governments, must often, with restless individuals, have been the reason for migration as well as the means. No return tickets were issued.

What the average immigrant hoped for may be summed up quite simply as – a better life. He thought of it in terms of simple materialism, more comfort and money; but as Thomas Cholmondeley, that shrewd but sympathetic observer, exclaimed, 'Material, you may call it; behold, then, the material of a better world!' To achieve a higher standard of living – and of self-respect – the settlers felt that they must break away from the confines of class; but though they were filled with a pronounced dislike of their superiors, they showed little desire to pull them down. Their ambition was to equalize upwards. As Cholmondeley observed, 'the life of the poor working emigrant represents an incessant struggle to get into the middle class: he hates the individual; but he likes the position. The middle class is all in all in a colony . . .' The pioneers aimed at creating a society which was classless because everyone was middle class.

In a passage of rare honesty E. B. Fitton (who published his

New Zealand in 1856) passed the following judgement on New Zealand society of the time. It could scarcely be improved. 'No person who has ever enjoyed a life in England would, I think, profess to *prefer* a colonial life, if he were sufficiently independent to make a selection.' But, Fitton wrote, for those who could 'find no opening' at home, New Zealand was the best place. Few people picked up gold in the street; but by hard work and with luck it was possible to 'get on', to achieve an independence and a plain comfort which most of the immigrants had not known in Great Britain. One Taranaki workman, who secured the local agency for a Sydney boot polish, wrote in a letter: 'The labouring class is as well off here as the nobs are at home . . . . A person has a little chance to do something in this part of the world, and that is more than you can do at home.'

On the other hand, the cultivated or fashionable visitor, like Lord Lyttelton, one of the founders of Canterbury, had often to confess that he found life in the colony dull or 'unkempt'. Clothes, conversation, or accommodation were alike cut to the standards of utility. Samuel Butler remarked the conversation of the colonists to be monotonously 'horsy' and 'sheepy', though he appreciated a certain vigour in local expressions. The settlers, he learnt, said 'no fear' instead of 'certainly not'. They used many Australian or North American terms. A stream was known as a 'creek', forests or woods were merely 'bush', while the largest field could be a 'paddock'.

Clothes as well as speech were influenced by American or Australian fashion. The working settler commonly dressed in a blue woollen shirt or blouse, moleskin or cord trousers, boots, and the slouch felt hats known as 'rowdy' (that is, backwoodsmen's) hats. Butler called them 'exceedingly rowdy hats'.

By the fifties there were some fine large houses, mostly wooden, in each town, but many of the poorer people still lived in the tiny cottages built by the first settlers. These were constructed of wood, of cob (a mixture of clay and straw), or of 'wattle and daub', that is, a frame of saplings filled in with puddled clay. The roofs were of tussock, thatch, or wooden shingles. Sometimes the walls themselves consisted only of *raupo*, a plant resembling the bulrush, or even of reeds.

About a quarter of the early settlers were illiterate, while another fourteen per cent could read but not write. Few of their children received any formal education. In Nelson in 1843 only a quarter of the children under fourteen were going to school, and only a sixth of those in Wellington.

Among the literate members of the community one of the chief occupations was writing letters and pamphlets. The level of public debate in the newspapers and in pamphlets was very high indeed, in spite of the indulgence in personalities. Some of the colonial newspapers, such as the *Lyttelton Times* and the *Nelson Examiner*, achieved a most creditable standard, particularly in the editorials. The writing and publication of diaries might well be described as an industry. Most of the best New Zealand books were of this nature, being reminiscences or more or less personal accounts of life in the colony, such as E. J. Wakefield's vigorous and prejudiced *Adventure in New Zealand* (1845), F. E. Maning's *Old New Zealand* (1863), or J. E. Gorst's *The Maori King* (1864).

Each town had its bards. The best of them, John Barr, the Otago Burns, has been mentioned. In Canterbury the gentry established a tradition of writing verse, whether graceful tributes to the Avon, or vigorous political skits like those of Crosbie Ward. The poet with the greatest reputation was Alfred Domett, apparently because he was praised by his friend, Robert Browning. Anthologists still make implausible attempts to discover merit in his ramshackle and prolix epic poem, *Ranolf and Amohia*. Some of the artists were more successful than the rhymesters. Charles Heaphy and John Buchanan, two draughtsmen, produced some superb landscapes in watercolour.

For a decade or two, organized entertainment was comparatively rare. There were occasional balls. Regattas, ploughing matches or horse-races were held periodically, especially on the 'Anniversary Day' of the founding of each settlement. In the main centres there were small choral, literary or amateur theatrical societies. But, in entertainment as in other respects, since there were so few 'aids to life', great demands were made on individual character and effort. In their pleasures the mass of the male population were by no means bourgeois. The colonists were very partial to a mixture of brandy and ginger beer, which was known as a 'stone fence'. Governor FitzRoy reported that the Wellington beaches were so littered with broken bottles that it was dangerous to walk there. In 1847 William Fox, a Wellingtonian, was appalled to learn that in Auckland there was one conviction for drunkenness for every eight persons. Nor was the South Island more sober. In 1861 the 15,000 Canterbury settlers maintained half-a-dozen breweries, besides importing over three gallons of spirits, seven of beer, and nearly two gallons of wine per person. In Otago, too, the annual *per capita* consumption was three gallons of spirits. Contrary to a popular belief, drunkenness has become less rather than more common over the past century.* By modern standards, the colonial towns were riotous and often brutal places. The *Auckland Times* in 1845 complained that the police were in the habit of beating drunks with their staffs, tying their wrists with cords, and dragging them through the streets.

In a society in which the men tended to spend their leisure in pubs, grog shops, or gambling dens, it is scarcely possible to exaggerate the importance of the women as a civilizing influence. The excessive drinking explains the tremendous fervour and strength of the Women's Christian Temperance Union later in the century. To the women, drinking was the greatest of sins. 'Temperance' was the strongest moral – almost religious – movement of the century.

Of religion in general, it is more difficult to speak. There was a much greater interest in doctrinal argument then than today. The evangelical and puritanical Protestant churches were very active and vocal. But whether, as is often supposed, the general population was in any sense more religious is doubtful. In Auckland in the late forties only a quarter or less of the population attended church – rather less than in England. In Canterbury a settler remarked in 1863 that a labourer was almost never seen in church: churchgoers were 'mostly the upper and middle classes and women and children of the lower.'

There were, from the commencement of large-scale settle-

* By comparison the annual *per capita* consumption in New Zealand at the present time is 24·5 gallons of beer, 1·0 gallons of wine, 0·4 gallons of spirits.

ment, marked regional differences which provided the basis of the provincial rivalry and raillery which has ever since been a healthy feature of New Zealand life. There were social differences due to the different methods of settlement. Dunedin was more Scottish, Christchurch more English, Auckland more Australian, than most other towns. The Aucklanders were slower to develop a civic pride than the Wakefield settlers, and the muddy and unlit streets of the capital drew frequent comment from southerners.

Another regional distinction could be observed between the four pastoral Provinces, Wellington, Nelson, Canterbury and Otago, on the one hand, and on the other, Auckland and Taranaki, where small mixed farming was more usual. Ironically it was Auckland, not a Wakefield settlement, which in the forties and fifties was the chief agricultural Province.

There was a striking contrast between the North and South Islands. Until the gold-rushes, most of the settlers lived in the North Island. The presence of the large Maori population greatly affected, indeed often dominated, their lives. Auckland derived much of its wealth from Maori trade. Even the local shipbuilding industry existed, in the fifties, because of Maori demand. The Maoris built the roads, helped to clear the bush, assisted in fencing and harvesting. The history of the North Island was one of racial relations; the South Island story is of Europeans, their sheep, and their gold. While life in the northern Provinces was disrupted by the Maori troubles of the sixties, the southerners prospered.

Gold was discovered in Otago by Gabriel Read, an Australian with experience of the Californian and Victorian fields, in 1861. Within two years the population rose from 12,600 to some 60,000. Dunedin became the largest town in the country while, to the horror of the 'Old Identity', saloons, billiard rooms, gambling dens and dance halls sprang up to attract the gold of the 'New Iniquity'.

In Westland the diggers were the original pioneers. In the years 1865–7, 15,800 immigrants crossed from Australia to the new goldfield there. Thousands more came from Otago or from Nelson, where gold had been found on the Wakamarina. A large proportion of these men, too, were experienced men from the Australian diggings – during 1861–3 Otago received 64,000 Australian immigrants and only 8,600 from Britain. The West Coast was said to be an 'Australian community'. Its towns seemed for a century to retain something of the atmosphere of the frontier of gold – if only in their contempt for liquor licensing laws. To a lesser extent the same could be said of Thames and Coromandel, where later and less dramatic gold rushes occurred.

For some years gold was New Zealand's major export. Over a century it earned nearly $50 billion in export earnings – not a negligible contribution to a small economy. But its impact on New Zealand life was much less than in Victoria or Australia in general. The influx of diggers intensified egalitarian sentiment and a fondness for gambling. Anti-Chinese prejudice can be traced to the diggings. But, by and large, the influence of the gold rushes was stronger locally, in the relatively isolated districts of Westland and Thames and Coromandel, than in the life of the colony in general. Though there were hold-ups and brawls, the New Zealand goldfields were quickly brought under legal control and the diggers were relatively law-abiding. There was no Californian anarchy or Victorian revolt. The gold rushes have not lived on in the New Zealand imagination outside the gold Provinces. What they did do was to add to the variety of New Zealand life.

The rivalry between the settlements was often vituperative, especially over the question of immigration. Among the Wellington settlers, Hobson was called 'Captain Crimp' because, having insulted them by placing his capital in the north, he then sent a ship to entice some of the Wellington labourers to help in building Auckland. It frequently happened that when an immigrant ship called at one port, *en route* to another, patriotic citizens or 'short-handed' employers would induce passengers to disembark by doleful tales of the conditions awaiting them at their intended destination. The Aucklanders were the most notorious offenders, but in 1859, to the delight of southerners, there occurred an incident known as the 'Otago Raid'. The wily Scots, hearing of unemployment in the capital, carried off a hundred settlers 'from the mild, temperate and fruitful North, to the frigid, bleak and snowy South', which was, so the *Auckland Weekly Register* alleged, inhabited only by 'the Squatters of Otago, Lords of Wastes and Princes of Deserts'.

Regional or provincial divisions largely shaped the character of political life. The Provincial Councils met before Grey's departure, but no General Assembly met until May 1854, when the House of Representatives immediately became involved in an attempt to force Wynyard, the Administrator, to grant responsible government. As a result of this dispute, in which E. G. Wakefield played a last characteristic role, first demanding responsible government in public, but then, when three Members of the House of Representatives had been appointed to the Executive Council as a step towards full responsible government, privately opposing it while acting as unofficial adviser to the Administrator, the central Parliament did not get down to serious legislating until 1856. In the meantime the Provincial Councils had a flying start which they were to keep for twenty years.

The '1856 Compact', which settled the financial relations of the provincial and central governments, also helped to strengthen the independence of the Provinces. After provision was made for paying the New Zealand Company debt, and for establishing a fund for purchasing Maori lands, the revenue from land sales was handed over to the Provinces. The North Island had made a bad bargain, for the Provinces in the South Island possessed great areas ready for settlement, while most of the North Island was heavily wooded and was still in Maori possession. The South Island Provinces were enabled to advance with little regard for the interests of the country as a whole. Until late in the nineteenth century, however, most of the settlers thought of themselves as belonging to the colony of Otago or Wellington, not the colony of New Zealand.

The Provincial Councils and their Superintendents controlled immigration, education and public works. By an Act of 1858 they also secured power to dispose of waste lands and determine land policy. They carried on the task of colonization. Their measures affected the lives of the settlers far more closely than most of the acts of the General Assembly. In many spheres they experimented with legislation later to be adopted by the general government. In Otago, for instance, once the alluvial gold was worked out, there was, as in Australia after the gold-rushes, a demand for land for the ex-diggers. Otago played an important part in experimenting with a system of deferred payment which would enable the small man to purchase his own farm. The Provinces served as a training ground for the country's political leaders. The demand for cheap land in Otago led to the formation of the first radical political party in which Robert Stout and John McKenzie, Liberal leaders of later years, served their apprenticeship.

In the General Assembly, which met in Auckland until 1865, thereafter in Wellington, provincial jealousies exercised an influence which was usually decisive. It had, according to Sir David Monro, one of the first speakers of the House of Representatives, 'the character of a body compound of a number of squads pursuing local objects'. Frederick Weld, who was Premier in 1864–5, said that the main question which members asked him was 'What are you going to give us to take back home to our provinces?' Politics, said two other Premiers, J. E. Fitz-Gerald and Harry Atkinson, on separate occasions, were nothing more than 'a disgraceful scramble'–'a gigantic scramble'– for public money.

There were in the House of Representatives in the fifties, less clearly thereafter, two loose groups which were called 'Centralists' and 'Provincialists', but the labels do not appear to have been very meaningful. As in many British Crown Colonies, constitutional questions had to be solved first in order to determine within what framework economic or social problems should be tackled. To some extent, it is true, the Assembly was divided over the degree of authority to be given to the central and provincial governments respectively. Politicians from needy Provinces, such as E. W. Stafford from Nelson or C. W. Richmond from Taranaki, sought to improve the lot of their constituents by strengthening the General Assembly. But, in this sense, 'centralism' was merely an alternative method of satisfying provincial aspirations, one which survived long after the abolition of the Provinces.

In general the politics of the provincial period consisted of a confused competition of cliques which coalesced into so-called 'parties', or disintegrated, as expedient. There was in the country no firm basis for British-type political parties, no powerful vested interests, no popular radical movement. The clash of personalities was perhaps the most powerful source of political groupings. As in eighteenth-century England, the small population, the very small number of politicians, all more or less intimately acquainted with one another, meant that personal likings or antipathies tended to override other loyalties and to encourage the existence of a large number of 'independents' in Parliament. It seems likely that the personal rivalries of provincial politics were carried over into colonial politics, since a large proportion of members took part in local as well as central affairs. This circumstance may go a long way towards explaining the manner in which politicians voted in the General Assembly.

Though there were no modern parties, there is no doubt about the strength of partisan feeling. Until 1870 New Zealand's history was singularly troubled. The Colony's public business was debated by Victorian gentlemen with appalling ferocity. Wakefield once feelingly remarked that, in colonial politics, each man struck at his opponent's heart. To the reader of nineteenth-century parliamentary debates, the country's history must often seem an endless stream of well-phrased abuse.

To what extent the property franchise was in practice democratic is uncertain. Since all women and almost all Maoris were excluded, only a small proportion of the population appeared on the electoral rolls. Grey claimed, and some scholars have accepted his view, that most respectable, adult males were enfranchised. Plural voting, however, gave effective power to the property owners. It is indisputable that politics, as in Great Britain, remained the prerogative of the well-to-do. The mass of the settlers demanded not democracy but equality. Public affairs were controlled, in each settlement, and in the General Assembly, by small groups such as Captain Cargill's 'family clique' in Otago. Although some of the most influential leaders, like Julius Vogel and Frederick Whitaker, were exceptions, the country was ruled for much of the nineteenth

century by a handful of the 'gentry' from the 'Wakefield'
settlements. Most of them set a high standard of political honesty
and, apart from the too personal tone, of oratory. Many members of the colony's intelligentzia were also its political leaders.
But few possessed the political ability to match their intellect
or rhetoric with deeds. In comparison with later political
leaders, most of them were amateurs. E. W. Stafford, a man
with no obvious qualification except a conciliatory manner, was
Premier on several occasions for a total of a dozen years, while
giving always the impression of wishing to be elsewhere.
Alfred Saunders, Canterbury politician and historian, wrote
of F. E. Weld that 'He ... held his unattractive office as a
swallow sits in a smoky chimney, and gave both the Governor
and the House to understand that the slightest breath of dis-
approbation would drive him from [his] perch.' Modern
leaders, seldom so articulate or well read (though, certainly as
incorruptible) have been made of sterner stuff. As a group, the
founders of New Zealand parliamentary life were good, honest
gentlemen, who thought politics an unpleasant duty. It was in
political life, perhaps, that the visions of Wakefield or Godley
came nearest to realization.

V: THE MAORI KING

These lands will not be given by us into the Governor's and
your hands, lest we resemble the sea-birds which perch upon
a rock: when the tide flows the rock is covered by the sea, and
the birds take flight, for they have no resting place.

WIREMU KINGI to Donald McLean and Governor Gore Browne,
11 February 1859

IN April 1854, a month before the first Parliament met in
Auckland, a very different but scarcely less important gathering assembled at Manawapou, an obscure spot in southern
Taranaki. There the Ngatiruanui tribe had built a very large
meeting-house called *Taiporohenui*, a name which was supposed to come from ancestral Hawaiki, and meant 'the finish-
ing of the work'. The business which the conveners hoped to
bring to an end was colonization.

About a thousand Maoris from the tribes of southern Taranaki,
together with some from Wellington Province, met to discuss
the problems caused by the coming of Europe, and especially by
the steady loss of Maori land to the settlers. To open the proceedings a chief chanted a magical incantation to bring about
the fall of the Europeans; but the Ngatiruanui meant to achieve
that result by more direct means. They wanted to secure an
inter-tribal agreement to stop sales of land to the Taranaki
settlers south of their existing boundary at Tataraimaka. Some
hotheads went further and proposed that the white men should
be driven off lands which they had already purchased in
Taranaki. One chief, Paratene Te Kopara, held up a tomahawk
and cried, 'This is Okurukuru!' Matene Te Whiwhi, a Christian chief from Otaki, near Wellington, rose to ask, 'Was that
land paid for?' When told that it was, he said, 'It is wrong.
Leave that for your *pakeha* [white] kinsmen. But, as to land not
yet sold, retain that.' Then the hatchet, an as yet unbloodied
symbol of death to the settlers, was thrown away.

In later years the settlers came to believe that a conspiracy
was hatched against them at Manawapou; that the Maoris had
formed a 'land-league ... a *war league*, a league of blood and
death'. In fact, according to a missionary and a government

land purchase agent, who had early news of the meeting, no agreement was made. The gathering broke up after the visitors had eaten so much food that they left their hosts hungry as well as disappointed. A Maori spy, who 'represented' the land agent at the meeting, said it was all 'protruding tongues, contortions [a reference to a Maori dance], spears and guns', a hopeless muddle with 'not a chief to direct the proceedings'. Moreover, the Maoris spoke not of a 'land league' – a European term – but of *he tikanga pakeke*, an obstinate plan, or policy, to withhold land from the Europeans. Nevertheless, the Manawapou meeting was of considerable importance: it was the first of a series of great inter-tribal meetings which marked the rise of a Maori national movement and led, in 1858, to the election of a Maori king. Though there was peace between the two races, in the late eighteen-fifties they began to go along divergent political paths. The outcome, in 1860, was warfare on a much greater scale than before.

Beneath all the friendship between Maoris and settlers, underlying all their mutually advantageous relations, there lay the stubborn fact that they were rivals for the possession of the land. To some extent, as agriculturists, they competed directly for the good arable land; but in general the uses to which they put the land were incompatible. The two ways of life could not indefinitely co-exist. The Maoris cultivated small areas, while relying on the extensive forests for berry, bird and root; the settlers burned forest and fern, then planted grass-seed in the rich ashes. To the settlers, land was money; but to the Maoris it was life itself and more. It is impossible to exaggerate their love for their tribal lands, scene of a thousand ancestral deeds or ancient legends which were recounted endlessly and in loving detail in the houses of learning and on the village *marae* (plaza).

The most direct, most persistent, most urgent source of nationalist sentiment among the Maoris was the fact that they were losing much of their land by sale to the Government. Some of the influential chiefs in the eighteen-forties, such as Te Rauparaha, had opposed land sales, but in the next decade this attitude became much more general. As the settlements became firmly established and prosperous, the rate of immigration rose steeply, so that the demand for land increased proportionately. It increased, indeed, disproportionately. In Auckland, the land speculators, who had bought much of the available Crown lands, were asking such absurd prices that, while thousands of acres lay vacant, new immigrants urged the Government to buy more Maori land so that they could get it at the rate of five or ten shillings an acre laid down by Grey's ordinance of 1853.

The head of the Native Land Purchase Department, a shrewd and strong-willed Scot, Donald McLean, found himself under constant pressure to speed up the land purchase procedure. With Grey's strong hand no longer in control, complaints were heard that the Department was becoming less scrupulous about its methods. Formerly the consent of the tribe had been required for all purchases, but McLean now began, on occasion, to accept offers made by chiefs or small groups of owners. Where influential chiefs supported him, he could sometimes ignore claimants who declined to sell; but such methods, successful or not, caused much hostility and suspicion.

As the Maoris watched the white frontier encroaching on their soil, they grew increasingly uneasy about their future. The European rat, they told one another, had eaten up the Maori rat; the European dog had displaced the *kuri*. Would they, they asked, be next? Large numbers of Maoris tried to ensure that they would, in fact, have a future, by joining the anti-land-selling movement, which, they hoped, would stem the tide of settlement before their land, if not their race, was submerged for ever.

Some Maoris had a larger aim than to form anti-land-selling agreements. As early as 1847 Grey, remarking on the decline of the 'mutual jealousies and animosities' between the tribes and on the rise of 'a feeling of class or race', observed that many of the younger chiefs 'entertained the design . . . to set up some national government'. The first clear information we have of such an intention concerns two remarkable young chiefs, Tamihana Te Rauparaha, a son of the old savage, and Matene Te Whiwhi, who lived at Otaki. In 1839, after encountering an ex-slave who had been converted to Christianity, they travelled to the Bay of Islands to beg for a missionary, and carried back with them the young Octavius Hadfield. Under his guidance they became, in the estimation of Europeans, the most civilized of their race. They were to be met, tail-coats and all, at Governors' balls. In 1851 Tamihana Te Rauparaha achieved the height of respectable colonial ambition by visiting England, where he was presented to the Queen. Thirty-odd years before, Hongi had met George IV and had returned with his armour and a cargo of muskets. Tamihana came back with a weapon much more dangerous to the British Empire, the notion of forming a Maori kingdom. In 1853, accompanied by Matene, he set out from Otaki to carry to the tribes a mystical doctrine of Maori unity. Even Grey and Bishop Selwyn, encountering the young chiefs on their journey, failed to see where it would end.

The *kotahitanga* or 'unity' movement took shape at innumerable tribal or inter-tribal meetings, like that at Manawapou. The man who did most to mould it was a remarkable chief of the Ngatihaua tribe, Wiremu Tamihana, who earned the name of the 'king-maker'. John Gorst, the English politician and the author of *The Maori King* (1864), wrote of him that he had met many statesmen in the course of his long life 'but none superior in intellect and character to this Maori chief, whom most people would look upon as a savage.' In about 1855 Wiremu Tamihana had sought government assistance in bringing law and order to the Waikato. Rebuffed, he directed his considerable talents to securing the election of a king. After further meetings and negotiations he was successful in 1858.

The first Maori king was an ancient Waikato chief, Te Wherowhero, who chose the title of Potatau I. He had his flag, his council of state, his code of laws, a 'King's Resident Magistrate', police, and even a surveyor. The lawmaking, the trials, the interminable meetings and debates, provided his followers with a satisfying and exciting activity which invested their lives with new purpose.

The Kingites were not merely copying the settlers' political organization. Rather, European institutions were being grafted onto native foundations like the tribal *runanga* (assembly). As with most similar movements there was a conservative, even backward-looking strain in Maori nationalism. There was a revival of declining customs such as tattooing – Wiremu Tami-hana said he had searched the scriptures and found nothing against it. Some of the nationalists tried to induce their people to cease trading with the settlers and to abandon European agricultural techniques. The extreme Kingites were imitating European organization in the hope that it would enable them to bring European political and cultural dominance to an end. A favourite Kingite song expresses with great force this rejec-tion of Europe and antagonism to Europeans:

> Let the mad drunkards set off to Europe, to the dig-
>   gings, the sugar, flour, biscuit, tea consumers.
> That is all. New Zealand still possesses great power.
> The King shall encircle the whole island.

The 'diggings' referred to were the gold-fields of Australia, or perhaps Otago. Some Maoris even hoped to drive the Euro-peans into the sea.

Fortunately for the Europeans, many tribes did not share such aspirations; even within the King movement there was deep division between the moderates led by Wiremu Tamihana, and the anti-European extremists who followed Rewi, chief of the Ngatimaniapoto tribe. Traditional tribal rivalries, which had not been altogether reconciled by the doctrine of unity, were another source of division. The King reigned, but he did not rule his subjects, who included most of the Waikato and Taupo Maoris, some from Hawke's Bay and the eastern coastal region, and, within a year or two, the tribes of southern Taran-aki. In practice his kingdom was merely a loose federation of tribes, yet it represented a formidable opposition to the pur-poses of the settlers, for it was united by the resolution to sell no more land. The land of the Kingite chiefs was placed under the *mana* of the King; it was made *tapu*. Many Maoris who declined to do fealty to the King, such as Wiremu Kingi of Waitara, were at one with the King party on this issue. In Taranaki and on the East Coast there were sporadic Maori feuds, during the fifties, between the 'land sellers' and the 'land holders'; but it seems probable that the great majority of Maoris, south of Auckland, sympathized with the latter party.

Settlement was the cause of Maori nationalism and provided
it with an objective, to keep the land. The peace of God and
British law and order made nationalism possible by making it
safe for the Maoris to travel throughout the country. And
there was an even more fundamental sense, paradoxical as it
may sound, in which the Europeans created the Maori nation.
Before the arrival of strangers from overseas among the warring
tribes, the inhabitants of New Zealand were Atiawa or Ngapuhi
or Waikato. So far as is known, they had no name for their
race: the word *maori* meant 'normal'. They applied the term
to themselves only when, for the first time in their recollection,
they encountered another race.

The newcomers were of a different colour. From the highest
to the lowest these white men (*pakeha*) assumed their superiority to the Maori. The enlightened and evangelical saw their
superiority merely as one of civilization; but most of the settlers were unenlightened, never having felt the gentle touch of
humanitarianism. In their European cultural baggage they
brought a very different attitude towards the Maoris. They
called these brown folk, whom they regarded as dirty, degraded,
lazy, and immoral, 'blacks' or 'niggers'. They despised them;
but in many parts of the country they also feared and hated
them. There is no need, in an age which has seen so much of
racialism, to labour the point, but it is useful to recall the observation of J. E. Gorst, that men who are 'habitually told that
they emit a disagreeable smell, are not likely to feel a very strong
affection towards the race that smells them'. On the Maori
side, resentment and feelings of inferiority both fed the emotional
springs of aggressive racialism. The European, as the Maoris
saw him, was as unpleasant a figure as the settlers' stereotype
Maori. He was greedy, arrogant, lacking in courtesy, selfish
– in a word, 'individualistic'. He treated Maori women as
prostitutes and, being without natural decency, deserted his
half-caste children. He was, moreover, not half the warrior
that the Maori was: had not he been beaten by Hone Heke
and Te Rauparaha?

Some of the most intelligent of contemporary observers,
both politicians and missionaries, interpreted the King movement not as a reaction against European influence, but as a

consequence of the weakness of European political influence in Maori districts. The tribal system was falling into decline, they observed, but the Government was doing little to replace it with European political institutions. The King movement, in this view, was the creation of a people searching for law and order amidst the chaotic remnants of tribalism.

This explanation had much to recommend it. It saw the King movement, not as a 'childish game', as Governor Gore Browne called it, nor as a conspiracy, but as a brave attempt to meet the challenge of a changing world. There is no doubt that to some Kingite leaders, like Wiremu Tamihana, the aim was to introduce some effective system of law and order. He complained that the Government had made no attempt to stop the 'river of blood' which flowed from Maori land-feuds. Nevertheless, this explanation reveals a fundamental misunderstanding of nationalism, which is never as rational as many Victorian gentlemen supposed. Good government has nowhere proved a cure for nationalism. Judging by experience elsewhere, it seems probable that the effective government of Maori districts, since it would have meant more interference with Maori society, would have intensified the nationalist reaction. In the nineteen-twenties, by trying to incorporate the village institutions in its machinery of control, the New Zealand Government was to touch off a revolt in Samoa.

If such a view of Maori nationalism is accepted, it necessarily calls in question the whole basis of government native policy in New Zealand. Grey's policy had been to smooth over existing difficulties, while aiming at bringing racial friction to an end through the Europeanization of the Maoris. That the Maoris would eventually become brown Europeans had also been implicit in land policy, for, on this assumption, they would eventually need less land. Consequently, providing that purchases were fair and that adequate reserves were made, no harm was done if the settlers acquired a large proportion of the land.

Some degree of Europeanization was, of course, inevitable; but missionaries, politicians and governors alike tended to assume that the faster the application of Grey's Europeanizing policy, the better it would be for both races. They assumed, in other words, that the way to cure the 'Maori problem' was to administer larger and more frequent doses of what was causing it – European influence.

In a matter so speculative it is not possible to reach a firm conclusion, but it seems reasonable to suggest that, at that stage of inter-racial relations, exactly the opposite policy would have been better; that what was needed was to minimize the pressure of European society on the Maoris, a result which might have been achieved by some degree of segregation. The possibility of introducing such a policy had been envisaged in the 1846 constitution and in that of 1852, both of which made provision for the declaration of native districts within which the Maoris could live in accordance with their own laws and customs; but it had been ignored. To have adopted a policy of partial segregation would have meant a reversal of current ideas about the possible speed of amalgamation. Moreover, it would have been difficult to apply, for any Maori districts which might be set up were bound to include lands, such as the banks of the Waitara and Waikato rivers, which the settlers particularly coveted. A modification of this policy was tried, half-heartedly, in 1858; and in 1861, too late.

Apart from land purchase policy, the Government's native policy, which was restricted by a shortage of money and of qualified agents, did not cause Maori nationalism. The Government failed, indeed, to exert any appreciable influence on the rate or direction of change in the Maori community. It still seemed not impossible, however, that the authorities could establish friendly relations with the King movement, or even guide it. But, owing to the extraordinary disorganization in the administration of Maori affairs under Governor Gore Browne, no attempt was made to do either.

Colonel Thomas Gore Browne was a pleasant, well-meaning gentleman, straightforward, sincere and, in contrast to his predecessor, morally quite scrupulous. He had retired from the Indian army, and had come to New Zealand in 1855, after serving as Governor of St Helena, where, the *Dictionary of National Biography* tells us, he improved the water supply. He would have made an admirable, indeed a typical, governor of New Zealand fifty or a hundred years later. He was the centre of the social life of the capital, popular with the crowds, regular at church. He loved his musical evenings in Government House and the society of gentlemen politicians such as F. D. Bell. But it was his misfortune to be appointed at a time when governors possessed power as well as influence; and in a situation of great stress, which called for energy, impartiality and discernment, he possessed none of the requisite qualities.

The new Governor was instructed to introduce responsible government: that is, to choose ministers who were members of the House of Representatives, who enjoyed its support, and who should be responsible to it for their actions. There was no intention that this system, essentially the British cabinet system, should be applied to all departments of the administration. As in Canada, where responsible government had been introduced a few years previously, it was accepted that imperial (as opposed to domestic) affairs should still be controlled by the Governor on instructions from London. Gore Browne decided, as Grey had recommended, that Maori policy was an imperial responsibility. No such provision had been made in the constitution, though Maori land purchasing had been reserved to the Governor, but it seemed a reasonable decision. General native administration and land purchase were closely allied. Imperial troops would be needed to protect the settlers in the event of a Maori revolt, which was a strong argument for giving the imperial authorities the right to determine Maori policy. Moreover, Gore Browne shared the misgivings of the humanitarians about giving the settlers the right to govern the Maoris. They would be likely, he wrote privately to the Colonial Office, to take a 'one-sided view of native affairs'.

The Governor did not prove capable of exercising the power he had retained. He never learned to speak to the Maoris, nor could he mix with them happily. He never acquired more than a superficial knowledge of their customs. The day-to-day task of governing the Maoris on behalf of the Crown fell into the hands of Donald McLean, the Chief Land Purchase Commissioner, who also, at the first opportunity, appropriated the office of Native Secretary. This was a disastrous combination of functions which confirmed the Maori nationalists in their impression that the Government's Maori policy amounted to buying their land. Gore Browne left everything to his able and aggressive assistant. 'Pray push on your purchases if you find it practicable and let me know (at your leisure) what purchases you have made and where,' he wrote; and, on another occasion, 'You know how entirely I depend on you, and how ill I get on without you.'

The General Assembly was not entirely pleased with the Governor's control of native policy, nor at all happy about his delegation of authority to McLean. From 1856–60 the politicians conducted a campaign against the Governor and his assistant to secure as much influence over native policy as possible. The result was a stalemate in which each side tied the other down. The Assembly had the right to pass – or refuse to pass – legislation affecting the Maoris and to vote extra money for Maori policy. By a close scrutiny of native expenditure, it was able to restrict the efforts of the Native Department. When, in 1856, at McLean's instigation, the Governor asked for an increased grant in order to send more government agents into Maori districts, the Assembly refused. For his part, McLean was able to subvert ministerial policy simply by failing to carry it out.

In 1858 the ministry introduced a series of very important measures of Maori policy. One of these, avowedly an experiment, would have made it possible for Maori communal land holdings to be 'individualized', that is, divided up among the owners. It would then have been permissible for individual title-holders to sell direct to the settlers instead of to the Crown. This Act, which is worth noting because it summed up what the ministers, the settlers, and even the Governor were all coming to regard as a necessary change in land policy, was for various reasons disallowed by the Crown. A second Act was passed extending Grey's system of appointing magistrates in Maori districts. A third, the most important, was a response to the Maori King movement. On the advice of F. D. Fenton, the Native Secretary who had been ousted by McLean, the ministers tried to introduce a system of 'indirect rule' in the Waikato. The Governor-in-Council was empowered to pass regulations for Maori districts on the recommendation of the Maori tribal

assemblies. It was intended to seek the co-operation of the
Maoris and to give them a direct share in formulating the law;
it was hoped that it would be possible slowly to guide them into
the British political and legal system. This policy, which arose
from the view that the King movement was a result of the
Government's failure to govern the Maoris, represented a
compromise between complete segregation and rapid Europeanization. It was the most promising policy conceived in
the colonial period. But, though the Governor as well as the
ministers favoured it, it was not carried out.

Donald McLean believed that the best policy was to ignore
the King movement. He had seen the Maoris make many
unsuccessful attempts to form 'land leagues'. They lacked, he
considered, the necessary powers of combination. If they were
left to their own quarrels, in his judgement this new league
would collapse too. Unfortunately he converted the Governor
to his opinion. 'Hoping rather than believing' that his assistant
was right, Gore Browne adopted his policy of 'supreme indif-
ference' and 'salutary neglect'.

Despite the reasonableness of the Governor's decision to
reserve the control of Maori affairs to himself, it was a mistake.
Had the settlers' elected representatives been constitutionally
responsible for Maori policy – and for the cost of any rebellion
which might occur – they would have been forced to devote
more serious attention to Maori affairs. The consequence of
the division of legislative and executive powers was that nothing was done to extend Grey's measures, to apply new ones,
or to come to terms with the Kingites.

While the Government lay paralysed, the situation in the
North Island grew rapidly more dangerous. A deterioration in
racial relations became apparent in 1854: the year after Grey's
departure, the year that Maori feuds began in Taranaki, the
year of the first General Assembly and the first great inter-
tribal anti-land-selling meeting. The European Parliament and
the Maori King became the foci for the discontents of *pakeha*
and Maori. The creation of separate political organizations
brought the conflict of interests between the races more clearly
into the open. The growing Maori resistance to land sales

coincided with a greatly increased demand by the settlers. The 1858 census revealed that the Europeans at last outnumbered the Maoris, a fact whose significance escaped neither race.

There was a growing feeling that war was scarcely to be avoided. In March 1859, for example, Henry Sewell wrote in his diary that unless some new system of land purchase were introduced, the end was certain: the settlers, outnumbering the Maoris, would not suffer their progress to be checked by an inferior race. They would, if necessary, take the land; the Maoris would resist and be crushed or exterminated. On both sides there were many aggressive individuals who longed for war – unruly young Maoris who had grown up disciplined neither by their own nor European authority and who sought only excitement; frustrated settlers who believed that 'moral force is moral humbug when addressed to savages'. The Maori wars, perhaps like all others, began in men's minds before they were fought out in the fern and the bush.

The authorities were well aware of the increasing danger of war. In a dispatch in 1859 Gore Browne referred to the vast Maori lands in the North Island (only seven of twenty-six million acres had been purchased) and declared, 'The Europeans covet these lands and are determined to enter in and possess them –" *recte si possint, si non, quocunque modo*" [rightly, if possible, if not, then by any means at all].'

The imperial Government, he wrote, had declared unequivocally that even colonization must be regarded as a consideration subordinate to the duty of maintaining the substantial rights of the aborigines; but it was his opinion that unless some means were devised of reconciling the interests of the two races, 'collision attended with calamity to one Race, and annihilation to the other' was inevitable.

The only solution he could suggest was the one which had occurred to Sewell: more land purchases. The Maoris had more land than they needed; they must sell all they did not use. This was, of course, perfectly sound: after all, whenever there is a danger of war, if one side gives in, peace is easily maintained. But how could it be brought about? In 1858 and 1859 Gore Browne became increasingly hostile to the Kingites and the anti-land-sellers, to whose turbulent and wrong-headed opposition he attributed all the tension in New Zealand.

The most threatening situation was in Taranaki, where there had been continual trouble since the almost simultaneous arrival of the first settlers and of parties of Atiawa returning from slavery or exile. Taranaki presented, in a concentrated form, all the most difficult problems of racial relations in the country. There the land problem had always been most acute. In 1854 it had led to a Maori feud when a 'land seller' attempted to sell some land to which a prominent 'land holder' had claims. The settlers ignored the fact that a disputed purchase had caused the fighting. They blamed their difficulties on a seditious 'land league' which allegedly killed any Maoris who tried to sell land. There is, in fact, no reason to suppose that this inter-tribal land league ever existed in Taranaki. Rather the evidence suggests that the attempts to form such a league had failed dismally. Opinion in each tribe was deeply divided. But the settlers were faced with a phenomenon quite as formidable as a 'land league', if less dramatic: according to the local newspaper the anti-land-selling Maoris were in a majority of about five to one.

From 1854 to 1858, while the feud went on, murders, sieges and skirmishes, on or near the settlers' land, kept the Province in a perpetual uproar. Colonel Wynyard, who was the Administrator of the Colony in the interval between Grey's and Gore Browne's governorships, adopted a policy of non-interference, which Gore Browne continued. Since there were insufficient troops to enforce law and order, there was no real alternative to neutrality. But the settlers made no pretence of being impartial. They helped the 'land sellers' with supplies of ammunition and medicine, while calling on the Government to send troops to repress the 'land holders'. 'Are we, the sons of the greatest nation of the earth,' a correspondent in the local *Herald* asked, 'for ever to knuckle under to a parcel of savages?' There were many proposals, even one from a missionary, that the Government should confiscate the lands of Wiremu Kingi and other chiefs who opposed land sales. The Provincial Council, in 1858, petitioned the Government to abandon the system of requiring the assent of every claimant before making a purchase of land. Instead, it urged, the Government should divide disputed land and buy whatever proportion belonged to the 'friendlies' or 'the progress party', as the settlers called the 'land sellers'.

The Governor flatly refused to accede to this request, which meant buying land without the consent of all the owners, 'for the whole of the Maori Race maintain the right of the Minority to prevent the sale of land, held in common, with the utmost jealousy.' But the Government could see that the settlers were becoming desperate. They were short of capital as well as land. A depression in agricultural prices, in 1856, had hit them hard. To change over to pastoral farming seemed their only hope. Consequently they were more anxious than ever to acquire the open coastal land towards Waitara. There was imminent danger that, as they frequently threatened, they would intervene in the feuds to help the 'land sellers', particularly since, in 1858, these Maoris seemed likely to be exterminated. The chance that some settler, seeing the Maoris fighting on his land, would fire a round or two on behalf of the 'land sellers', was considerable.

In 1858 the Executive Council decided to announce that any Maoris fighting on European land would be treated as rebels. The authorities realized that such an order was risky, for, if the Maoris disobeyed, it would have to be enforced by the military. They decided, however, that the risk of insisting on this minimum of law and order was less than the likely consequences of continuing the policy of neutrality.

In March 1859 the Governor intervened in person. He went down to New Plymouth and at a meeting of Maoris announced the decision of the Executive Council. He added a few remarks on the subject of land purchase, advising the Maoris to sell their unoccupied land. He assured them that he would buy no land unless the owners agreed to sell, but that, on the other hand, he 'would not permit anyone to interfere in the sale of land unless he owned part of it'.

Immediately McLean had finished reading a translation of the Governor's speech, a Maori named Teira (Taylor) stood up and offered to sell land at the mouth of the Waitara. The Governor, after consulting with McLean and the Native

Minister, accepted the offer subject to confirmation of Teira's title. Teira then laid a *parawai*, a bordered mat, at the Governor's feet, as a symbol that he placed the land in his hands. Wiremu Kingi, the principal chief at the Waitara, objected to the sale, and, accompanied by most of his tribe, marched off in a huff.

A few days later Gore Browne explained to the settlers that, if Wiremu Kingi should have a 'joint interest' in the land, it would not be purchased without his consent, but that he would not allow him to 'exercise his right of chieftainship' to prevent the sale.

The Governor had come to the conclusion that the Taranaki feuds, the shortage of lands for settlement, and therefore the danger of war, were all due to the illegitimate interference of non-owners, whether Kingites, 'land leaguers', or chiefs, in land sales. He hoped that, by refusing to permit Kingi to bully Teira, he would be striking at the cause of the tension in the North Island. If he could resist unjust interference with Maori owners who wished to sell their land, while at the same time repudiating the demands of the settlers that he buy Maori land without waiting for the consent of all the owners, he might secure more land and establish a lasting peace.

This was how his policy in Taranaki appeared to Gore Browne. What he was actually doing was very different. To deny the rights of chiefs to a voice in land sales, on behalf of the tribe, was to abandon the established procedure of the Land Purchase Department. If the Government refused to hear the tribe speaking through the chiefs, there was no alternative but to buy land from any groups of Maori 'owners' who agreed to sell, which was not far from what the settlers had been demanding. The Governor was agreeably surprised by his sudden popularity in New Plymouth. It is abundantly clear, from his public utterances and private journals, that he had no idea that he was introducing a revolution in land purchase methods. Although the rights of chiefs in land sales had been pointed out to him by a Board of Inquiry into Native Affairs which he had set up in 1856, he did not understand this fundamental aspect of Maori land tenure. He realized that Maori land was owned in common; but he did not realize that it belonged to the tribe as a whole, not merely to the hereditary occupants.

His ignorance of the rights of the tribe and the chiefs was inexcusable; but he also imagined that the land-selling Maoris were in a majority, though too intimidated by the anti-land-sellers to speak out. This was an error which was extremely dangerous. The Waitara purchase was not, however, merely a tragedy of good intentions thwarted by ignorance. From first to last Gore Browne was badly advised – or not advised.

When the Governor went to New Plymouth he had no intention of buying land. It would have been very foolish of him to have thought of doing so at the very moment when he was trying to stop the feuds. When Teira offered him land he was taken aback, though he could scarcely refuse it, having just advised the Maoris to sell more land. Quite unintentionally, he found himself involved in the most difficult aspect of racial relations, a land purchase. McLean, and Robert Parris, the local government land purchase agent, were, however, well aware of Teira's impending offer – indeed they had been busily engaged for two years in promoting it. They did not warn the Governor that his remarks on land purchase might be followed by Teira's offer, might indeed be interpreted as encouraging him to make it. Nor did McLean correct the Governor's error about the land rights of chiefs, though none knew them better than he.

After the meeting in New Plymouth McLean continued, as in the past, to act quite independently. The Governor had emphasized that if Kingi were an 'owner', by which he meant if the chief had a joint claim based on a hereditary right of usufruct, the purchase would be given up. This was not, however, what McLean told Kingi. He informed him that if he owned any 'pieces' within the land owned by Teira, they would be excluded from the purchase. McLean proposed, in other words, to partition Maori land, as the local Provincial Council had recently demanded. This move cut off the Governor's retreat, for now it seemed to Kingi that he could not stop the sale either by speaking for the tribe or by laying claim to part of the land. He contented himself with a proud assertion of his right, on behalf of the tribe, to refuse the sale. He wrote to the Governor saying, 'I will not agree to our bedroom being sold (I mean Waitara here), for this bed belongs to the whole of us. . . . All I have to say to you, O Governor, is that none of this land will be given to you, never, never, not till I die.' This simply confirmed the Governor, who had been affronted by Kingi's behaviour in walking out of his meeting, in his impression that Kingi was an impudent bully who imagined that he could defy him.

The investigation of the title to the Waitara by McLean and Parris was a farce. Most of the authorities, from the Governor down (on McLean's advice), assumed that Kingi had no claims to make. Gore Browne felt himself 'pledged to effect the purchase', and on several occasions urged Parris to hasten his inquiries as much as was prudent. Parris eventually decided that the title of Teira, and his few supporters, was in order. In November they were paid an instalment of the purchase money. Parris wrote to McLean asking him to come and conclude the deal: 'Now is the time for turning the tables – a little show of determination with the present favourable change, will settle the whole question if some liberal provision of land is made for all.'

It is now known that Wiremu Kingi, and a considerable number of other Maoris who refused to sell, had hereditary claims to parts of the block of land offered to the Government by Teira. The latter had quarrelled with his chief over a woman, and sought revenge by selling the tribe's land to the European. '*He wahine, he whenua i mate ai te tangata,*' said the Maoris – 'Women and land are the reasons why men die.'

There is no reason for supposing that the authorities knew of Kingi's claims to the Waitara, though it is hard to believe that these were unknown to McLean. They all knew, however, that Kingi and some three hundred followers were actually living on the land in question, and had lived there since their return to Taranaki in 1848. Normally the mere fact of occupation would – rightly – have been regarded as *prima facie* evidence of a title. But Parris and McLean alleged that all these Maoris were living on the land with the permission of the owners, Teira and the other sellers. To defend the alleged rights of some twenty Maori property-owners to sell without interference from their chief, the Government was prepared to evict three hundred Maoris from tribal territory.

The Governor and his advisers were too emotionally involved in the purchase to see how it might appear – soon did appear – to more dispassionate observers. For different reasons, they all ardently desired to buy the Waitara. Parris had never made an important purchase. Both as a local settler and as a land purchase officer he wanted this success. McLean had, for twelve years, been thwarted by Kingi in his efforts to buy the Waitara. As soon as Grey heard, in Cape Town, of the events of 1859–60 in Taranaki (where he had in 1848 sent McLean to re-purchase the New Zealand Company claim between New Plymouth and the Waitara) he remarked that he fancied McLean had a grudge against Kingi. For McLean and Parris, Teira's offer was an opportunity to 'turn the tables' on Kingi. C. W. Richmond, who was both Native Minister and the elected representative of New Plymouth, would not stop the purchase. To him, Kingi was 'the bad genius of Taranaki'. On one occasion he made the extraordinary statement that 'Kingi's position at Waitara has been one of pure hostility to the interests of the settlement of which he has been occupying a part of the destined site.' The Governor, having, as he wrote privately, decided 'to put an end to many Maori difficulties by a vigorous and decisive act', was anxious to demonstrate his firmness. With the Government as enthusiastic as the settlers to acquire the Waitara, there was little chance of an impartial review of the facts.

By January 1860 Teira and his supporters, who had felt it wise to take refuge in New Plymouth, were growing impatient for the rest of the money, and wrote to the Governor complaining because the marriage of 'the beautiful woman, Waitara' – 'the land which we have given up to you' – was being deferred so long. 'This woman that we gave to you in the face of day is now lying cold. You had better turn her towards you and warm her that she may sleep comfortably in the middle of the bed.'

The authorities decided to survey the land, an action which had already led directly to the Wairau massacre and the feuds in Taranaki. They did not expect Kingi to show fight, being convinced that a demonstration of force would call his bluff. On the day of the survey Kingi sent some old women to pull out the surveyors' pegs. Martial law was declared. A few days later, at the cost of one dead private, the troops captured an empty *pa* which Kingi had just built on the disputed land at Waitara. It was to be twelve years before the old chief laid down his arms.

The history of New Zealand was distinguished from that of previous British settlements by the fact that the country was annexed when the evangelical movement was at the height of its influence on colonial policy. New Zealand was intended to set the world an example of humane colonization. The ideal was not attained. Racial relations soon came to resemble those on other frontiers. That the British Government failed, in particular, to achieve its professed desire 'to avoid, if possible, the disasters and the guilt of a sanguinary conflict with the Native Tribes', is no occasion for surprise: rather would it be a matter for astonishment if such wars, which seem everywhere to be part of the process of colonization, had not occurred.

Humanitarianism was a plant which flourished in the hothouse of English evangelicalism; it was to be many years before it was acclimatized to the harsh conditions of the frontier. Exeter Hall, the Church Missionary Society, the Aborigines Protection Society, and such bodies, set before Great Britain a noble aim. But what guidance did they offer to the governors of New Zealand when they were confronted by the bleak facts that the Maori nationalists and the settlers had incompatible ambitions, that the interests of the two races were not identical? It is difficult to see a solution to the problem in Taranaki. To stop settlement would have been an answer, but it was politically impossible: when FitzRoy offered to remove the settlers, they refused to go. Grey and Wynyard were obliged to ignore what they could not remedy. Then Gore Browne started a war by trying to stop it. Whether wiser men could have succeeded where he failed is a question which few people would care to answer.

VI: WHITE MAN'S ANGER

> For who can dwell with much delight
> On details bare of barbarous fight?
> War stripped of that superb disguise
> Of splendour which to youthful eyes
> Gives Terror more than Beauty's charms,
> And o'er Death's revel scatters rife
> Stern raptures of sublimest Life?
>
> ALFRED DOMETT, *Ranolf and Amohia*, 1883

'MOTHER,' Wiremu Kingi wrote to a famous chieftainess in November 1860, 'peace will not be made, I will continue to fight, and the Pakehas will be exterminated by me, by my younger brother Te Hapurona [his "general"] ... and by Waikato. ... It is well with your children and us, we die upon the land which you and your brothers left to us. I am now fulfilling the words of Rere and Mokau. This is why I am persisting. ... We are here eating the English bullets – My friends, my parents, this shall be my work forever. What though my people and I may die, we die for New Zealand.'

'Rere' was his father, whose dying word (among the Maoris traditionally the strongest of injunctions) had been to retain the ancestral lands at Waitara. 'Mokau' was another name of Te Rangihaeata, the famous chief who had been responsible, with his uncle, Te Rauparaha, for the Wairau massacre and other attacks on the settlers in the eighteen-forties, and who was noted for his opposition to the expansion of European settlement.

In the usual allusive Maori fashion of the day, Kingi's letter adumbrates what were, in practical terms, the chief issues in the 'Maori Wars', which the Maoris, more appropriately, called '*te riri pakeha*'–'white man's anger' or 'quarrel'. Could the Maoris keep their land, and in particular, the rich lands at Waitara and Waikato? Could they stop, or perhaps turn the tide of settlement? And there was another question. Could they ignore the authority of Queen and Parliament, and follow their King? Now that negotiation had failed and willing compromise seemed impossible, the answers were to be sought in battle.

Though, in the long run, the opponents were unevenly matched, for a time the Maoris had it all their own way. They had great courage, cunning, and skill; and as Kingi's letter indicates, an enviable morale. They were born to fighting and enjoyed it. But their chief resource was the land, which they knew and understood better than their foe. Wild, hostile to the stranger, unsurveyed, and indeed mostly unexplored by the white man, the land was the Maori's ally.

The Europeans quite underestimated the difficulty of their task. It was winter-time. New Plymouth was little more than a row of houses by the shore. Behind it lay mile after mile of 'broken country', rugged hills and gullies, swamp, fern, scrub, and the dense forest which the New Zealanders call 'bush'. The Maoris had almost complete freedom of movement. They were not encumbered by baggage, because their women travelled with them carrying potatoes or *kumara* (sweet potato), while at a pinch they could eat fern-root as well as birds. Within a short time the settlers were forced to leave their coastal farms, so near the bush from which the enemy might at any moment appear, and to congregate in New Plymouth. Many women and children were evacuated to Nelson. The rest were beleaguered while the Maoris plundered and destroyed where they liked. The Maori village at Waitara was burned by the troops, but the Maoris burned almost every farm-house in Taranaki and captured most of the stock. The soldiers could not be everywhere at once – at night they preferred to be within the walls of the town or their block-houses.

Wiremu Kingi was at first followed by about three hundred warriors, but the arrival of allies eventually raised the number of rebels to some fifteen hundred. He was soon joined by the tribes from southern Taranaki and by large war-parties who came from the Waikato against the will of the Maori King. Unable to control his more anti-European subjects, the King was forced to excuse their behaviour by proclaiming that Taranaki had been opened 'as a fighting ground for Maoris and Pakehas'. The south Taranaki tribes were already Kingites; now Wiremu Kingi also declared for King Potatau, although before the war he had steadfastly refused to do so. The conflict thus quickly assumed an aspect far more dangerous and general than that of a merely local quarrel, though fighting was temporarily confined to Taranaki.

The European troops (British soldiers, colonial militia and volunteers), increased from one thousand to about three, but it was some time before they formed an effective fighting force. The incapacity of the original commander, Colonel Gold, was rightly said to be a military phenomenon in itself. They were very disunited. From the first action of the war, the capture of Kingi's empty *pa*, the colonials conceived the greatest contempt for the imperial troops. They taunted the soldiers with such assertions as that 'there was more blood spilled in one field night in the Masonic Hotel than was spilled in the attack on [Kingi's] pa.' They were very scornful of the reluctance of the army to engage the Maoris in the bush, but showed little understanding of the difficulties which bush-fighting presented to regular troops. For their part, the British soldiers came to regard the colonial forces as ill-disciplined and unnecessarily harsh to the Maoris. This antagonism was to persist throughout the war.

To Frederic Rogers, the Under-Secretary of State for the Colonies, the first Taranaki war seemed 'the strangest war that ever was carried on'. In this campaign, as indeed throughout the wars, the Maoris adopted no comprehensive or co-ordinated strategy. Had they chosen to employ guerrilla tactics they would have been more dangerous, but they kept close to their traditional mode of war. They would build a *pa* at some inaccessible spot, preferably on a ridge or hill with swamp or bush in the rear to afford easy escape, and invite the Europeans to attack. When, on one occasion in June 1860, the troops accepted the challenge and launched a frontal attack, it proved as disastrous as during Hone Heke's rebellion.

Instead of allowing the Maoris to provoke him into making a costly assault on their defences, Gold's successor, General Pratt, adopted the tactics of driving saps (covered trenches), up to their fortifications, thus forcing them either to withdraw from the position or to risk making an attack themselves. These saps, one of which was almost a mile long, were ridiculed by the Maoris, who once offered to dig them in any direction for a shilling a day. Eventually, however, Pratt succeeded in inflicting two severe defeats on the rebels. The war-party from the

Waikato, who became bold and careless, suffered very heavy casualties.

In April 1861, after a year's inconclusive manœuvring and a few pitched battles, a truce was called. Some of the rebels made their peace, but Kingi retreated to the Waikato. No one believed the war was over. In Taranaki both Maori and European farming had almost ceased. Troops occupied the Waitara; rebels held European land south of New Plymouth. But the centre of attention had shifted to the Waikato. Potatau had died in 1860; his successor, King Tawhiao, was winning the allegiance of increasing numbers all over the island as the Maoris became convinced that the settlers meant to take their land by force. The more extremely nationalistic Kingites such as Rewi, the chief of the Ngatimaniapoto tribe, were advocating an attack on Auckland itself.

The crucial issue was whether the Kingites, as a body, would go on the war-path, and this largely depended on what attitude the Government took towards the Maori monarch, now that some of his subjects had interfered in Taranaki. To the Governor, the idea of giving any recognition to the Maori King was intolerable. He condemned the King movement as an 'unlawful combination', demanded submission to the Queen, and the return of plunder taken in Taranaki. When the Kingites refused to accept these terms, he decided, in mid-1861, to invade the Waikato and depose the King. Both the New Zealand General Assembly and the Colonial Office drew back before this prospect.

Though there had been a vocal minority of dissentients such as the Chief Justice, Sir William Martin, and Archdeacon Octavius Hadfield, as well as a few politicians, including William Fox the leader of the 'provincialist' Opposition, the majority of the settlers were in 1860 enthusiastic about the war. The Government was in a shaky position – it was defeated in most divisions on issues affecting the powers of the Provinces; but it was saved by the war. Several South Island 'Provincialists' supported its native and war policy and ensured a majority sufficient to keep it in office. These members, whose constituents were far from the battle and rarely saw a Maori, were among the most aggressive. Their ardent concern to defend

British honour against the traitorous rebels was too little tempered by any sense of the difficulties and dangers faced by the northern settlers. Most of the so-called 'peace party', on the other hand, were northerners.

In 1861, with the prospect of an extended war before them, the majority of Members of the House of Representatives were by no means convinced that the Governor's past policies or present intentions were wrong; but they were vividly conscious of the danger that, if the Kingites were attacked, they might fall on any of the northern settlements. The House decided that there were not enough troops to defend the settlements and opposed Gore Browne's plan to take the offensive.

At the same time the British authorities, who were beginning to think that the Governor had made a mistake at Waitara, were also becoming alarmed by his bellicose attitude towards the Maori King. The Secretary of State for the Colonies, the Duke of Newcastle, thought it absurd to go to war over a name. He could see no reason why the Maoris should not honour their King, 'whether his name be Potato or Brian Boru', provided they committed no breach of the peace. He decided to save the Governor from further error. Sir George Grey had written from Cape Town offering his services as a Commissioner to mediate in New Zealand. Perhaps Grey's great talents and prestige would enable him once again to establish a peaceful co-existence in New Zealand. He was sent back for a second term as Governor. Before he arrived McLean resigned the native secretaryship and the Stafford ministry lost office.

Though the political stage seemed set for a new drama, the action soon revealed not another play but merely a second act with a fresh cast. The chorus of grief stemming from the recent war sounded louder than Grey's tidings of peace; the Waitara purchase remained, an ominous backdrop.

Grey and the new Premier, William Fox, set about introducing in Maori districts a system of 'indirect rule' such as the Stafford ministry had advocated in 1858. Maori *runanga* (assemblies) in the various districts were to recommend to the Governor the laws they required. He could introduce them by Order-in-Council without seeking parliamentary assent. European doctors, magistrates and civil commissioners were to

reside among the Maoris in order to introduce them to some
of the virtues of western civilization. Perhaps it had been too
late in 1858; certainly it was too late now, amidst the resentments of an armed truce. Two years of sincere labour had little
effect. The Kingites were unalterably and understandably
suspicious of the Government's intentions.

One of the troubles was that Grey was absolutely obliged to
face two ways, a position which, in any case, from long practice,
he found congenial. He had to attempt to make peace, yet it
was essential that he should be ready for war. If the Kingites
attacked they could pass through bush and swamps and fall at
will upon any of the tiny settlements between the Waikato and
Auckland. Grey and his military advisers decided that the best
precaution against such tactics would be to extend as far as the
Waikato a road which ran south from Auckland and pointed
towards the heart of the Maori kingdom. The King tribes
would thus be threatened by instant invasion in the event of war.
The construction of the last few miles of the road was begun
soon after Grey's arrival. It was probably necessary – but it
convinced the Kingites that Grey meant to attack them. In the
prevailing atmosphere even his more innocent acts were regarded as hostile. For instance he tried to build a court-house
in the Waikato, but once they realized that it was going to look
remarkably like a block-house, the Maoris refused to allow it
to be completed. Grey's words did not help to allay their suspicion. When the Kingites asked him in January 1863 whether
he opposed the King he replied: 'I shall not fight against him
with the sword, but I shall dig around him till he falls of his
own accord.'

By the beginning of 1863 the country was tense and uneasy.
The settlers in Taranaki were demanding action against the
rebels who still held European land at Tataraimaka, south of
New Plymouth. There were many covetous eyes looking from
Auckland towards the rich valleys of the Waikato and its
tributary the Waipa. If Auckland was to share in the woollen
trade, which already promised to enrich the southern Provinces, these lands must come into European hands. Both races
felt that the truce was coming to an end. The Kingites proclaimed their policy: if the Governor's road were extended over

the Waikato river they would fight; if he tried to occupy Tataraimaka without returning Waitara, they would fight.

As soon as the completion of the military road as far as the banks of the Waikato afforded Auckland some protection, Grey turned his attention to Taranaki. He had become increasingly impatient with the Kingites, as he found both his prestige and his native policy of little avail. Now he arranged with General Cameron to reoccupy the European land at Tataraimaka, despite the repeated Maori warnings that they would regard this action as a *take*, a just cause for war. If the Waikato tribes interfered, the Governor decided that he would return to Auckland, force them to submit, and confiscate the land of rebels.

Grey was no more successful in solving Taranaki's problems in 1863 than in 1848. In April, troops took possession of the Tataraimaka block without opposition. The Governor then initiated a new investigation of the ownership of the Waitara. Though this inquiry was as incomplete and haphazard as the last, it led to the opposite conclusion. Grey decided that Gore Browne had been at fault, and decided to return the land to the Maori owners. Had he made this decision before taking Tataraimaka, it might have been possible to come to terms with the disaffected Maoris. But even now, instead of announcing his decision, he spent two weeks trying to make the new Domett ministry accept the responsibility for it. Ever since his return, Grey had been trying to reverse the situation, in which Gore Browne had placed himself, of having the responsibility for conducting native affairs but little effective power. Grey tried to take the decisions while making the ministers bear the responsibility, including that of paying for future wars. Both the imperial authorities and the colonial ministers wished to call the tune of Maori policy; but neither wanted to pay the piper.

While Grey and his ministers haggled, the Maoris acted. An assembly of Taranaki Maoris wrote to Rewi Maniapoto, the leader of the anti-European section of the King movement, asking his advice and saying that war seemed imminent: 'the work of the tribe is the gun; in a short time it will be firing constantly.' Rewi sent back word to attack. In May a small party of soldiers was ambushed near Tataraimaka. That evening the ministers at last agreed to abandon Waitara. They hoped that by so doing they would place themselves in a better light in England: the Waitara question would now be removed from discussion of the causes of the war.

After General Cameron had inflicted a severe defeat on the rebels in Taranaki, Grey brought most of the troops back to Auckland and invaded the Waikato. He claimed that he was making a punitive expedition against Rewi, because he had ordered the ambush in Taranaki. This was not an entirely adequate justification, for in the circumstances (thousands of Maoris being subjects of the King rather than of the Queen) Grey's provocative action at Tataraimaka had been the first act of aggression. Certainly this was how it seemed to the Kingites, who never had been effectively ruled by the British and who regarded the Governor and ministers more or less as a foreign government. Furthermore, if the invasion were intended to discipline Rewi, Grey was in fact punishing all the Waikato tribes for the act of a few. The consequence was that he drove Wiremu Tamihana and the moderates into the arms of the extremists.

Grey further alleged that he acted to forestall an imminent Maori advance against Auckland. Whether an attack was in preparation will never be known. There is no doubt that the extremists wanted to strike at the town, but it is very doubtful whether they would have done so in opposition to Wiremu Tamihana and the King, who had vetoed the proposal when most of the troops were in Taranaki and Auckland was defenceless. However, it is plain from Grey's actions, both in Taranaki and the Waikato, that the immediate reason for the renewed warfare was that he had decided to impose his will on the disaffected Maoris, since they would not voluntarily accept it. More fundamentally, the war arose from the same tensions which had led to war at Waitara, and which had been made worse by the first Taranaki campaign.

The Maoris, in control of the mountainous centre of the North Island, from Mount Egmont across to East Cape, from the Waikato Heads to Napier, were in an excellent position to seize the initiative by making sudden attacks wherever they chose. But the widespread Maori offensive which the settlers feared never occurred. The Maoris did, this time, accept the opportunity which the rough terrain presented for employing guerrilla tactics against the European lines of communication. A number of actions were fought along the road between the Waikato and Auckland. The settlers countered these tactics by forming a force of Forest Rangers, whose most famous commander was a flamboyant soldier of fortune, Gustavus Von Tempsky. Once a Prussian officer, he had seen action in Central America among the Mosquito Indians, and for all his swagger he was a dangerous opponent, skilled in guerrilla tactics and of rare courage. In the stealthy, swift, hand-to-hand actions in the bush, the Maoris probably took as much as they gave.

The decisive battles, once more, were on the site of Maori fortifications, built in the hope of fighting on advantageous terms. In the Waikato General Cameron had an advantage, for by employing small armoured gunboats he could outflank the *pa* along the river. On occasions he was able to by-pass *pa* altogether, but where he decided to carry prepared Maori positions by direct assault, it usually proved costly. At Rangiriri, on the banks of the Waikato, he forced nearly two hundred warriors to surrender, but only after his men had suffered well over a hundred casualties in unsuccessful attempts to storm the Maori parapets.

The assorted weapons of the Maoris, old flint-lock muskets, double-barrelled shot-guns, sporting rifles, native clubs, and spears were in the long run no match for gunboats, howitzers, Enfield rifles, and hand-grenades. Cameron captured the Maori King's capital at Ngaruawahia with little loss and advanced steadily up the river.

The King Maoris under Rewi Maniapoto made their last stand at a Maori village called Orakau. There, in an orchard of peaches, apples and nuts, amidst fields once ripe with wheat, maize or *kumara*, they built a *pa*. Not three miles from Cameron's advance post, it was a direct challenge to fight. The General accepted. For three days three hundred Maoris were shelled, shot at, and unsuccessfully assaulted by two thousand troops. At the last their water was gone, they had raw *kumara* to chew, and they had so little ammunition that they were firing wooden bullets. The General took pity on them and asked them to surrender. '*Ka whawhai tonu ake! Ake! Ake!*' Their reply will live as long as the wars are remembered. 'We will fight on forever, forever, forever!' To the entreaty that at least the women and children should be allowed to leave, the reply came that they would fight with the men.

This most famous battle of the wars ended, for the Maoris, in a defeat which has the ring of victory about it. On the afternoon of the third day, the Maoris charged out in a body towards some of the troops. Their audacity was their salvation. For a moment no one among the Europeans realized what was happening. Amidst the confusion, although a hundred and fifty died, half of the Maoris, including Rewi himself, vanished into the swamps.

The Waikato had fallen. The Bay of Plenty soon followed after a few desperate actions in which the friendly Arawa tribe –unlike the 'friendlies' in Taranaki–proved invaluable allies of the Europeans. In 1865 Wiremu Tamihana and his people made peace. Wiremu Kingi did not submit until 1872, the Maori King not until 1881; but they were living in exile, on the lands of other tribes in the interior. In 1864 it could be hoped that the war was almost over. Only Taranaki remained, and it was not likely that the rebels there could last long now that the main tribes of the King movement were defeated. But there was a new and intractable fact to be taken into account in Taranaki: *Pai marire* – the Good and Peaceful Religion. In 1862 the Angel Gabriel had appeared in a vision to Te Ua, a Maori who had fought the Europeans in Taranaki. This angelic visitation caused him to kill his child, as he wrote in a letter circulated among the tribes, as a redemption for his people, 'forgetful, desolate, and in doubt'. Te Ua founded a new faith, compounded of a little Old Testament morality and Christian doctrine and some primitive Maori religion. He invoked the Holy Trinity, but revived cannibalism. The services of the new Maori evangelism were held at a *niu*, a long pole, perhaps fifty feet high, with yard-arms from which hung ropes. The congregation revolved round this mast as round a maypole while the priests conducted a service of prayer. The 'angels of the wind' were said to visit the faithful during the service.

Te Ua taught his followers that this divine service and a strict adherence to his instruction would make them impervious to bullets if, when under fire, they raised their right hand and cried '*Pai marire, hau! Hau!*' The *Hau hau*, as these fanatics were called after this incantation, at first showed incredible boldness in battle; even the most practical demonstrations failed to convince the survivors that they had no magical protection against bullets.

Even before the war, Maori nationalists were beginning to reject some aspects of European life, economic as well as political. *Pai marire* was an attempt by some of the Maoris to turn their backs on Christianity and to establish a religion at least partly Maori. It was another 'adjustment movement', very reminiscent of the earlier *Papahurihia*. The *Hau hau* identified themselves to some extent with the Jews – calling their ministers *Teu* (Jews) and accepting the Jewish Sabbath. They believed that they were a second Chosen People, and that, with divine aid, they would return from the wilderness to their hereditary lands. *Pai marire* arose from the despair of defeat to bring a new hope to many rebels. The resistance to the settlers became more savage, more implacable.

The first *Hau hau* attacks were made in Taranaki a few days after the capture of the Orakau *pa*. But at first the Europeans did not appreciate the significance of the new religion or guess how formidable was the task ahead. They were busy quarrelling among themselves about the spoils of past battles.

In 1863 Grey had suggested that the Government should punish rebels by taking their lands. The Domett ministry seized upon the idea with a greedy enthusiasm, and produced a grandiose scheme whereby several million pounds were to be borrowed in England on the security of the profits expected from the sale of confiscated land to new immigrants. The rebels would thus pay not only for the war but to extend 'the legitimate progress of colonization'. It all sounded like the glowing prospectus of a new colonizing company: war was to be made to pay dividends.

Domett was a poet, a worthy representative of the gentry of the Wakefield settlements. He was not a very good poet; but he was a worse politician. As Premier, he was a mere figure of speech, a rhetorical flourish. Effective power in this ministry, as in the next (in which Fox found himself in an uneasy alliance) lay in the hands of two able, efficient, sharp Auckland lawyers, Frederick Whitaker and Thomas Russell. These men, like many other professional and business men in the capital, were deeply involved in land speculation. Earlier Premiers had at times lamented the lack of Aucklanders sufficiently presentable to be appointed as ministers; now Auckland was in power. Whitaker and Russell soon showed that, although they were no orators, they had a clear idea of the purposes of political authority. While the presence of Domett and Fox in the cabinet lent an air of respectability to their proceedings, they set about introducing measures likely to benefit themselves. In 1862 the Crown monopoly of the purchase of Maori land was abolished and, as the speculators had long demanded, 'free trade' allowed. Gossips in the House of Representatives whispered that this measure alone was worth £10,000 a year to Russell, whose extensive land speculations and whose flair for promoting companies were already the subject of wonder, envy, or disapproval, according to the beholder. No one could doubt that it was the Auckland speculators who would profit most from confiscations in the Waikato; or suppose that the two ministers would forgo the opportunity they now sought to create. Nor could anyone doubt that Maori welfare would be neglected: Whitaker had been the Attorney-General at the time of the Waitara purchase and again when the Waikato was invaded; Russell was noted for his 'strong views' on Maori questions; Domett, who was afire with the romantic vision of chivalric war which forms a somewhat tarnished theme in his verse, was as aggressive as his colleagues. But there was little open criticism in a House where so many members were directors or shareholders in the Bank of New Zealand or other companies which Russell had helped to found.

In 1864 a bitter quarrel arose between Grey and his ministers over the area of land which was to be confiscated. The British authorities joined in the fray with a salutary warning that confiscation might 'convert the Maoris into desperate banditti'. Other issues were involved. Late in 1863, on the insistence of the Duke of Newcastle, the Assembly and ministry had at last accepted the responsibility for administering native affairs, but in practice the unhappy division of authority continued. Grey was not the Governor to act solely on the advice of his ministers. Moreover, while there were large numbers of imperial troops in the country, the British Government expected him to have a say in Maori policy, lest the colonial ministers use the British soldier as an instrument of oppression. Consequently there was continual argument over the respective rights of Governor and responsible ministry.

The only solution was to withdraw the troops and let the colonists not only control Maori policy but fight any wars which might follow. This was precisely what the British Government wished to do. The House of Commons had in 1862 resolved that self-governing colonies ought to be responsible for their internal security. Since that time it had been the settled policy of the British Government to reduce its overseas military establishment. Some of the colonists were prepared to welcome the inevitable. When, in November 1864, the Fox – Whitaker Government resigned, Frederick Weld took office, pledged to inaugurate a 'self reliant' policy whereby the Ministry would dispense with imperial military aid.

The first fruit of colonial 'self reliance' was the confiscation of nearly three million acres of Maori land in the Waikato, on the East Coast, in Taranaki, and elsewhere. Though this was at least as much as the previous Government had wanted to take, Grey signed the proclamation without a word. It seems that his dispute with Fox and Whitaker had been a personal quarrel rather than a conflict of principle.

As an instrument of colonization, confiscation was a costly mistake: far from paying for the war, the confiscated lands proved a financial burden. As a measure of Maori policy it was a crime: it embittered relations with the Maoris for generations, while immediately bringing many recruits to the *Hau hau*. The Government seems to have aimed at securing good land rather than rebel land, so that confiscation, as a punishment, fell most unequally. The aggressive Ngatimaniapoto, for instance, escaped lightly; other tribes, who had played little part in the fighting, lost a great deal. Altogether it was the worst injustice ever perpetrated by a New Zealand government.

For all the Ministry's show of independence, it still had to rely, for a time, on General Cameron and his troops. Marching along the Taranaki coast in 1865, he showed a marked reluctance to risk the lives of his men. After being attacked in broad daylight while encamped in the coastal scrub, he kept to the beach, and moved so haltingly that the Maoris called him 'the lame seagull'. Like many of his men, he had had enough of action, and cared very little for motion. It seemed to him that the British army did most of the fighting and suffered most of the casualties in order to enable the settlers to take Maori land. Many of the soldiers had a great admiration for the Maoris, for their courage, for their chivalrous treatment of the wounded, for their 'sporting' attitude towards war. On more than one occasion the Maoris had asked for ammunition or water, or sent food to the soldiers, so that a fight could go on. The historian of the British army, J. W. Fortescue, has written that the British soldier found the Maoris 'on the whole the grandest native enemy that he had ever encountered'.

Another unpleasant verbal exchange occurred, this time between the Governor and the General. And Grey could fight with deed as well as word. Cameron was not eager to attack a *Hau hau* village called Weraroa. Believing he would need two thousand troops to subdue it, he by-passed it on his march into southern Taranaki. Grey then pretended that Cameron had refused to attack it and, having already received a *Hau hau* offer of surrender, took to the field himself. With a force of a few hundred colonial troops, he forced the Maoris to withdraw. The colonists acclaimed his feat as a famous victory, but it is not clear that anyone was beaten except the General. Certainly the *Hau hau* lived to fight another day.

In 1865 and 1866 all but one of the regiments sailed away. Thereafter the colonists and their Maori allies fought the war. Grey was summarily dismissed in 1868 for defying the Colonial Office once too often. In 1870 the last regiment was withdrawn, amidst howls of protest from the colonists, who felt that they were being sacrificed to the *Hau hau* in order to save a few pounds in Gladstone's budget.

It would be wearisome to relate all the sieges, the pursuits, the ambushes and skirmishes which, from time to time, disturbed Taranaki and the East Coast from 1865 to 1872. The fighting was more bitter, marred by the savagery which so often accompanies war between different races. Missionaries were murdered. Prisoners were killed by both sides, eaten by one. In 1868 the rebels found a talented guerrilla leader, bold, fierce and elusive. Te Kooti had been imprisoned in the Chatham Islands, almost certainly unjustly, on suspicion of being in league with the *Hau hau*. In 1868 he escaped and founded a new religion, *Ringatu*, which was a genuine Maori variant of Christianity, though retaining some elements of the *Hau hau* cult. He also proceeded to massacre the Poverty Bay settlers. It was fortunate for the settlers that there had been no Te Kooti in 1860 or 1863. Eventually, after a grim struggle, he was hounded into the 'King country', as the central part of the island is called to the present day. There he remained in peace for the rest of his life. So the wars drew to an end.

It is sometimes said that the wars were a set-back to the settlement of the North Island. Certainly many parts were devastated, or too dangerous for the farmer. But the obstacle to settlement had been the Maoris' refusal to sell land. At the cost of a long war, but of quite small casualties – about a thousand Europeans and friendly Maoris were killed – this resistance had now been overcome so that colonization could proceed. This was the chief result of the wars, as far as the settlers were concerned.

For the Maoris the consequences were more complicated. How many were killed is uncertain, though their losses have been estimated at about two thousand. The wars intensified their hatred of Europeans. Many concluded that even the missionaries had been insincere. They said that the missionary pointed towards heaven; while they looked up the settler stole their land. Thousands of Maoris abandoned the missionaries' churches in favour of none, or of one of the several new Maori religions, in varying degree Christian.

The effect of the wars which is easiest to appraise was the loss of Maori lands. The Maoris had sold about seven million acres in the North Island by 1860. Three million acres were confiscated, but in practice the Maoris were permitted to keep about half of this area. Between 1865 and 1892 they sold a further seven million acres. This left them eleven million acres, two and a half million of which were leased to settlers. Most of the rest was very rugged country for which the settlers had no pressing need.

The war having broken the Maoris' will to resist, the Land Courts then quietly separated them from their lands. The function of the courts was to ascertain Maori title and to issue a Crown freehold title to the owners who, now that Crown pre-emption was abolished, were free to sell either to settlers or to the Government. From 1865 to 1873 the court was bound by statute to name no more than ten owners to a piece of land, with the result that the rest were often dispossessed. After 1873 land was divided up among all the owners. This 'individualiz-ation' of land ownership had a disastrous effect. A Royal Commission reported in 1891 that 'The crowds of owners ... were like a flock of sheep without a shepherd, a watch-dog, or a leader. ... The right to occupy and cultivate possessed by their fathers became in their hands an estate which could be sold. The strength which lies in union was taken from them. The authority of their natural leaders was destroyed. They were surrounded by temptation. Eager for money wherewith to buy food, clothes and rum, they welcomed the paid agents, who plied them always with cash, and often with spirits.' Since nothing was done to help the Maoris to develop their land, the freehold tenure, which had long been advocated as a step to-wards civilization, was merely one more agent of destruction.

The land laws, which Parliament passed by the score, be-came a legal jungle within which the Maoris lost themselves and were preyed on by its natural denizens, the land specula-tors or their agents and shyster lawyers. Land agents would incite Maoris to apply to the courts for a title and would ad-vance the cost of surveying and legal fees. Only too often the Maoris would discover that they had mortgaged the land to pay for the Crown title. Storekeepers would give Maoris credit to the extent of thousands of pounds, and then force them, under threat of imprisonment, to hand over their land in payment. There was nothing illegal about most of these practices: they were good business.

Another evil effect of the white man's laws was that sittings of the land courts were held in towns. Very large parties of Maoris had to spend weeks or months there, waiting for their cases to be heard. Only too often they lived in squalid housing amidst scenes of drunkenness and debauchery, an easy prey to infective diseases.

Whenever the Maoris attempted to resist the advance of the settlers, by one means or another they were overthrown. For twenty years after their defeat in the Waikato, the Maori King and his followers lived in hostile isolation in the 'King country'. Few Europeans dared cross the *aukati* (boundary). Several who did were killed. The Kingites tried to keep Europeans and liquor out, but they also sought to incorporate elements of western culture into their own traditional life. They grew very large quantities of wheat and other food and traded across the border for European agricultural implements, clothes and other goods. They practised their own religion, *Tariao* (Morning Star), which was predominantly Christian. Visitors reported that they were living healthy and vigorous lives – and there is some evidence that their population was not declining as fast as in areas where Maoris had sold their land and let in settlers. The King tried to stop all land sales in their area, but in the eighties some Kingite tribes began to sell. The *aukati* shrank until, in 1883, John Bryce succeeded in detaching the Ngati-maniapoto tribe from the King. They let in the surveyors and the railway. Land selling and temptation followed.

At Parihaka, in southern Taranaki, a chief called Te Whiti, who was believed to have taken part in the fighting, founded another Maori religion based upon Scriptures and private revelations. He prophesied that a 'Day of Reckoning' would come when the *pakeha* would voluntarily depart and leave the Maoris to rule as in bygone days. His followers lived a virtuous and industrious life, but they were settled on land which had been confiscated. The Maoris believed, no doubt rightly, that McLean (who died in 1878) had promised them reserves; but the Government began to survey the land before these were granted. Te Whiti launched a passive resistance campaign. Parties of Maoris pulled out survey pegs, built fences across the disputed land, and began ploughing up neighbouring European farms as a form of protest. These tactics infuriated the settlers to the point of hysteria. Legislation was hurriedly passed making it possible to imprison Maoris indefinitely and without trial. Several hundred were gaoled while the Armed Constabulary occupied the district, but the campaign continued. In 1881 a military expedition, led by the Native Minister, John Bryce, and his predecessor, William Rolleston, who had resigned rather than use force, went to arrest Te Whiti. They were met by a couple of hundred children, singing and dancing. To immortalize this last, inglorious victory over the Maoris, the youthful poet Jessie Mackay wrote a neat parody:

> When can their glory fade?
> Oh! The wild charge they made!
>   New Zealand wondered
> Whether each doughty soul
> Paid for the pigs he stole,
>   Noble Twelve Hundred!

But it was of no use for Te Whiti or his sympathizers to meet guns with ridicule. The prophet was locked up and, after inadequate reserves had been made, his lands were unlocked. When he returned to Parihaka he built a model village with piped water and even electricity in a more practical endeavour to help his people to adjust to a European world, choosing which *pakeha* innovations they would adopt. But his influence and his village slowly decayed late in the century.

The white man's peace was as devastating as his wars. Land holding had meant keeping their self-respect; land selling usually meant demoralization. Many Maoris lived on liquor and credit. But the Europeans cannot be blamed entirely for this. Large sections of the Maoris seemed to have given up hope. They acted like the despairing remnants of a dying race, selling their lands at reckless speed as though they wished to dispose of their assets while they could still enjoy the proceeds. The population fell so rapidly that it was scarcely possible to dispute the view of Anthony Trollope, who spent a few months travelling in the country in 1872: 'There is scope for poetry in their past history. There is room for philanthropy as to their present condition. But in regard to their future – there is hardly a place for hope.'

PART TWO

COLONY INTO DOMINION
1870–1914

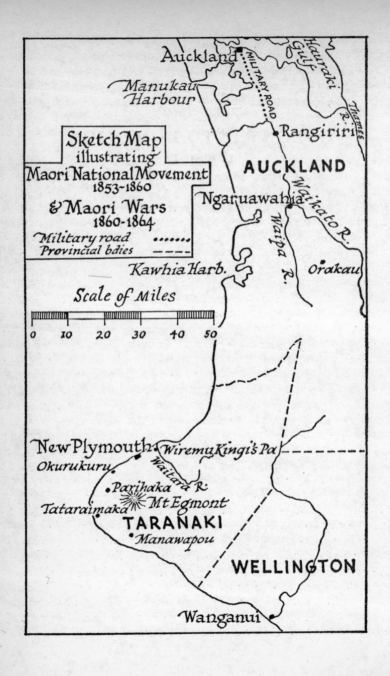

Sketch Map
illustrating
Maori National Movement
1853-1860
& Maori Wars
1860-1864

Military road ·······
Provincial bdies ------

Scale of Miles

0   10   20   30   40   50

Auckland

Manukau Harbour

Hauraki Gulf

Thames R.

MILITARY ROAD

Rangiriri

AUCKLAND

Waikato R.

Ngaruawahia

Waipa R.

Orakau

Kawhia Harb.

New Plymouth   Wiremu Kingi's Pa

Okurukuru   Waitara R.

Parihaka   Mt Egmont

Tataraimaka

TARANAKI

Manawapou

WELLINGTON

Wanganui

I: THE FRONTIER OF DEBT

The next point is, how to procure the money [for founding military settlements]? It is not necessary, and certainly it is not desirable, to raise any of this by additional taxation, whether the Colony could bear it or not. It is not right that the present generation should bear the whole expense of measures the benefit of which is to be reaped principally by their successors. To borrow on an Estate so rich in undeveloped resources, and so easily and rapidly improvable, as is a young Colony like New Zealand, and to borrow for the purpose of developing these resources and improving such an Estate, is not only prudent, but the simple duty of those who have the management of it. Ten or twenty years hence, the burdens now required to be taken up would scarcely be felt by the Colony. That is certain. Let, then, the power and prosperity, the material wealth that the Colony would necessarily grow into in the course of twenty or thirty years, be, as far as practicable, forestalled and realized at once. It would crush us to take the burden on ourselves alone; place it on the future . . .

The Premier, ALFRED DOMETT, 1863

THE American frontiersman is supposed to have gone into the forests, if Hollywood films are indicative of current mythology, with little but a gun and a handsome wife. In much the same way, the pioneering father-figure of contemporary New Zealand imagination was a man who went out to the 'back-blocks' (a term which originally referred to blocks of land purchased from the Maoris, but came to mean remote farming districts) with nothing but his courage and initiative in his creative hands. In fact he was more heavily burdened. The New Zealand pioneer bore a load of debt.

Although there were, especially near the towns, many small holdings on which poor men made a living eked out by labouring for wages, the successful farmers were generally sheep men, 'big men' who helped to establish not a subsistence but a capitalist economy. Most of them began their careers by borrowing. From the first the community as a whole also incurred considerable debts for, as in all 'under-developed' countries, progress waited on capital investment – a familiar observation which explains why a great deal of New Zealand's history has been concerned with credit, and why some of its most powerful leaders have been chiefly noted (or notorious) for their skill at making vast sums appear as though from nowhere and then, only too often, as unaccountably vanish.

As the Maori wars, 'the fire in the fern', died down, life in the colony was at a very low ebb. Gold production was falling. The prices of wool and wheat slumped in the late sixties. Business was almost at a standstill in the towns. On the London market the colony's credit was depressed as a result of the war and of the reckless management of finances in some of the Provinces; imports and public revenue were falling off, bankruptcies increasing; altogether there was good cause for the general pessimism. But it only needed one of the country's monetary magicians to give a hopeful wave of his wand for this whole scene to change into one of frenzied action and soaring ambition.

Julius Vogel, the first politician in New Zealand whose talents were at all remarkable, was a London Jew who, as a youth, abandoned his labours in the office of his grandfather, a merchant trading with South America, for the brighter prospects of the Victorian goldfields. From Australia he drifted on, with the tide of diggers, to Otago. There, after helping to start the first daily newspaper in New Zealand, he was soon drawn into provincial and then national, or more accurately, central politics. In 1870, as Treasurer in a new ministry led by William Fox, he propounded 'that grand go-ahead policy' with which his name is chiefly associated.

Vogel appreciated that the further advance of the colony was held up and settlement largely confined to coastal lands primarily because of inadequate transport. Roads were poor and few; there were under fifty miles of railway, in three different gauges, and only seven hundred miles of telegraph lines in the country. He proposed to borrow £10,000,000 in ten years to finance a rapid extension of transport facilities and a vigorous immigration scheme to provide the necessary labour. As security for this overseas loan he intended to set aside a public estate of 6,000,000 acres along the new railway lines and roads.

Before Lord Keynes was born, Vogel decided that what was needed to dispel a slump was not economy and caution but liberality and confidence; not retrenchment but increased government expenditure, which would create contracts and jobs, encourage the circulation of money and extend the community's purchasing power. With money, men and public works, the development of the country would proceed at an unprecedented pace. Still, this was flying very high, for there were fewer than a quarter of a million settlers in the country while, after thirty years of borrowing, the public debt was less than £8,000,000, of which £3,000,000 had been borrowed by the Provinces.

Vogel's biographer, R. M. Burdon, has suggested that one source of Vogel's policy is to be found in his experience of the expansion – and the expansive atmosphere – associated with the gold rushes. He hoped now to produce a similar situation artificially. But in any case Vogel was naturally drawn to such schemes. His public policies were extensions of that greedy and sanguine nature which was revealed in his inveterate gluttony and gambling. He suffered from gout as well as gold-fever. It is quite wrong to see him, as did some of his contemporaries, as a Machiavellian figure, for his plausibility and his success derived from a conviction born of temperament. As R. M. Burdon wrote: 'He was no cynical cozener of fools. The heroics of finance roused him to genuine emotional heights, and the call of a large loan on the London money market stirred his spirit as profoundly as the call to arms might rouse the soul of a warrior.'

The 'Provincialists' in Parliament wrecked Vogel's scheme from the start: in retaliation Vogel destroyed the Provinces. Some of the Provinces strongly objected to setting aside the lands which he intended should form the security for borrowing, and Vogel abandoned the proposal. Then the 'Provincialists' threw out a Forest Conservation Bill, a far-sighted measure to prevent the indiscriminate burning of the bush – a practice which had continued unchecked since the colony was established, and had, indeed, been common in pre-European times. Vogel hoped that the forests, carefully husbanded, might prove a national asset that would help pay for his public works. In 1876 he abolished the provincial governments. They were replaced by that confused multitude of road boards, rabbit boards, drainage, harbour, hospital and education boards, borough, county and city councils, which have ever since managed local affairs.

There was strong protest from Auckland, where Grey came out from his retirement on Kawau Island to lead the defence of his constitution of 1852; and from Otago, where there was much talk about the political separation of the two islands. In these Provinces the radicals feared a squatter-dominated central Government while the 'Provincialists' – the New Zealand equivalent of 'states-righters'– were unhappy about future financial arrangements. By the '1856 compact' the Provinces had gained the right to spend their land revenues. The Aucklanders, who had small land revenues but high customs revenues, suspected that this arrangement would somehow be maintained, so that the southern Provinces would keep their considerable income from land sales, while the central Government would continue to appropriate Auckland's customs duties. On the other hand in Otago the settlers feared that the 'compact' would be broken, so that the central Government and the poorer Provinces would enrich themselves at Otago's expense. In fact the central Government was eventually to take both revenues, the land fund being 'colonialized' by Grey himself when he became Premier in 1877.

The opposition of the far north and the far south was of no avail; the old question, whether New Zealand, politically speaking, should be one, two, six or nine, was at last answered in the singular. At first sight it may seem strange that the local governments fell so easily, for provincial rivalry and provincial – that is, parochial – thinking were deeply rooted and have persisted to the present day. But the provincial system was already in decline. Since the New Provinces Act of 1858 the central Government had been able to break up a Province, without consulting the wishes of its inhabitants as a whole, if a majority of settlers in any sizeable district wished to secede. The number of Provinces had risen to nine, while a tenth, Southland, after a brief independence had been re-absorbed by Otago. This Act ended any possibility that the provincial system might work, for none of the new Provinces had the resources to carry out their function of colonizing. By 1876 the Provinces had lost control of public works, railways and immigration. The central Government had taken over their debts and forbidden them to raise loans because their competition forced up interest rates. Despite relatively enlightened policies in Otago, Canterbury and Nelson they had failed in education. The second generation of New Zealand children was little better educated than the first. Only fifty-eight per cent of children aged five to fifteen years were on the school rolls, while the average daily attendance was a mere thirty-nine per cent of that age-group. New Zealand education lagged far behind that in Australia and the United States – in Massachusetts, for instance, the average daily attendance was seventy-three per cent. The Provinces could scarcely justify their existence, and they had many enemies. In Otago and Canterbury the squatters were so nervous of local radicals that they looked to the central Government to defend their lands; on the gold-fields of Westland, and elsewhere, recent immigrants had little interest in the inefficient Provinces. The 'Centralists', who had waited so long, saw their chance. Stafford prompted Vogel, until then an ultra-Provincialist, to abolish the provincial system of government. Since there was no provision for consulting the Provinces before amending the quasi-federal constitution, a simple majority in the central parliament was the only weapon that was required.

Vogel's scheme had lost its safeguards but not its attraction. Between 1870 and 1880 not ten but twenty millions were borrowed. The population doubled. 1,100 miles of rails, 4,000 miles of telegraph lines and many roads, public buildings and bridges were constructed. Also Vogel had arranged for a steamship service to San Francisco; two local steamship companies had been formed; a cable had been laid to Australia. All of this had not been achieved without waste and mismanagement. Some of the railways and roads were built merely to catch a few votes in the House or in the country, and served no purpose commensurate with their cost. Some of the contracts were ill-advised. The immigration scheme showed similar evidence of reckless haste. Conditions on some of the chartered ships were appalling; at the immigration depots the poorer families swarmed with lice; many of the newcomers, who poured in at the rate of 15,000 a year from 1875 to 1879, were described by older colonists as 'certificated scum'. Nevertheless the colony gained many essential public works together with thousands of useful settlers, Scandinavian (the founders of Dannevirke and Norsewood) and German as well as British. For a decade the economy, stimulated by Vogel's injections of capital, thrived as never before.

The pastoral industry made steady though unspectacular progress. The area of improved pasture was more than quadrupled during the seventies, while flocks grew rapidly until 1874. By crossing the Merino with the Lincoln and other strains, New Zealand sheep-breeders produced a new type of sheep, the Corriedale, which came to be prized both in America and Australia because it yielded both good wool and good quality lambs.

The introduction of American reapers and binders led, in the seventies, to 'bonanza' wheat farming, which reached its peak in the early eighties, when wheat accounted for nearly a fifth of the exports. It then declined as falling prices coincided with soil exhaustion, but for a short time parts of the South Island looked like eastern Australia or the American Middle West. As late as 1894, thirty-five reaping machines were to be seen at work on one farm. Thousands of casual labourers (the late nineteenth century was the great age of the 'swaggies') roamed the Canterbury plains in search of seasonal work. So profitable did this intensive farming of virgin soil prove that individuals were known to purchase land in Canterbury at the current fixed price of £2 an acre and make a net profit of £5 an acre on their first crop.

Improved transportation, paid for (or, rather, to be paid for) by the community, and the great profits of farming, pushed up land values. Private individuals pocketed the increment. Speculation in land reached a point feverish even for New Zealand. At the same time run-holders hastened the process of turning their leaseholds into freeholds. In Canterbury the Wakefield system of 'free selection' of land at a uniform price (now £2 per acre) placed little restraint on the aggregation of large holdings while prices were so high. Proprietors acquired the freehold of their estates within the area originally owned by the Canterbury Association, as they already had done outside those limits by virtue of Grey's cheap land regulations.

In the southern Provinces there was fierce competition between the pastoral tenants and the 'cockatoos', a name for small farmers which originated in Australia by analogy with the swarms of birds which descended on the land of the luckless farmer at harvest-time. It has persisted in New Zealand to the present day in the term 'cow cockies' for dairy farmers. The system of 'free selection' enabled a would-be 'cockatoo' to choose land in localities 'thrown open' to selectors (under certain conditions regarding residence, improvement, and area) and to buy the freehold. This was a direct threat to the holders of large leases. It led to a species of blackmail, for speculators could select choice pieces of a run and oblige the tenant to re-purchase at high prices; and offered great scope for malice. In 'The History of Mr and Mrs Miggs', some amusing doggerel written in the eighties, G. P. Williams recounted the sad fate of a 'station cowboy' who, dismissed for his frequent absences at race-meetings, decided that 'the proper course' was 'to start selecting land upon his boss's run'.

And some blocks upon his leasehold were thrown open. Michael heard,
On a certain purchase system which he thought he much preferred,
That convenient style of payment which is known as 'deferred'.

Now the laws throughout New Zealand with regard to buying land,
Which at divers times and places have been variously planned,
Form a code that's something fearful, something wonderful and grand.

And in that Provincial District where Waipapa county lay,
You can get a thousand acres and you haven't got to pay,
Ought but just a small deposit in a friendly sort of way.

But you mustn't own a freehold, and you mustn't have a run,
And you must be no relation to a party who has one ....

Miggs selects 1,000 acres on the run and, by marrying the cook, acquires a further adjoining 1,000 acres. They overcome the awkward requirement that they must sleep on their separate 'selections', by building a house across the boundary, but eventually they discover that

> ... throughout this blessed country, it is painful to
> relate,
> There's no fixity of tenure in regard to real estate,
> As its owner oft discovers from a hard and cruel fate
>
> For a river sometimes robs him of his title in a day;
> Though it serve to bound his section, it declines to
> make a stay,
> Or occasionally washes all his section clean away;
>
> Or the fierce Nor'-wester's fury will be sometimes so
> intense
> As to strip him of his holding, in a realistic sense,
> And deposit half his section up against his neighbour's
> fence.

In this case, after a 'landslip' moves their house, an inspector discovers that Mrs Miggs is not fulfilling the residential requirements. Like many other selectors, no doubt, they end up by answering an advertisement for a married couple with 'no encumbrance'.

The restrictions on selectors were not always as strict as those described in these verses. In self-defence against the cockatoos, squatters employed a series of ingenious stratagems known as 'spotting', 'grid-ironing' and 'dummying' which enabled them to keep their holdings while buying the freehold of only a small area. 'Spotting' was the purchase of strategic points, such as the mouth of a gorge, river-banks and other watering-places, so as to exclude rivals from large areas of adjacent land. Where land was auctioned the system known as 'grid-ironing' was useful: the leaseholder would buy a series of sections each of, say, twenty acres along a frontage, leaving perhaps eighteen acres between sections. Since no one but a poor man would want so small an area, the leaseholder could count on outbidding any rival. Where leaseholders were not permitted to 'select' land, or where conditions of residence were enforced, 'dummyism' was rife – that is, a leaseholder would pay some 'swaggie' to act as the ostensible selector and fulfil the requirements for him.

As in eastern Australia, where similar tactics were used, economic circumstances were not yet favourable to the small farmer with little capital. Free selection, deferred payment, and other enactments meant to encourage closer settlement gave more help to the great leaseholders. In 1883 forty-seven per cent of the 2,800,000 acres sold in Canterbury was controlled by 91 persons. In 1891, 584 persons owned 7,000,000 acres of the 12,500,000 acres in the possession of private owners in the whole country. Between 1868 and 1893 the number of land-owners perhaps quadrupled: the area they owned increased thirteenfold. In this circumstance lay the chief source of the greatest political struggle of the time.

Not everyone succumbed to the influence of Vogel's optimism, nor to the artificial glitter of prosperity on time payment. In 1872 Trollope thought the colony 'over-governed, over-legislated for, over-provided with officials, and over-burdened with national debt', an opinion which has had innumerable supporters ever since. He was sceptical of Vogel and remarked of his policy that 'what at first was taken for dash and good courage, seemed to many after a while to become recklessness and foolhardihood'. The projects of the colonists seemed far too ambitious. He was appalled by the fact that New Zealand Government expenditure was thirteen times as great, per head of population, as Canada's and higher absolutely than that in Victoria or New South Wales.

There were warning signs enough to justify such foreboding. For instance, although exports increased in value in the eighteen-seventies, a fall in their value per head of population showed that the progress in settlement and communications was not being matched in production and capacity to earn overseas funds. The colony's economic position was also being adversely affected by world-wide changes. The railway and the steamboat were making it possible to develop the vast lands of Russia, Australia and the United States and to transport their produce quickly to distant markets. In the latter country alone

4,000,000 acres of new land were brought into production between 1860 and 1900, while the yield of wheat rose from 173 to 522 million bushels. In 1873 wheat prices began to fall, a trend which continued, with little interruption, for twenty years. Wool prices began to fall in 1872, sharply in 1874, but in New Zealand such warnings were ignored in the general excitement. Economic depression was held off for a few more years while the colonists lived on borrowed wealth.

The banks in the seventies were carried away by Vogel's optimism and, parallel to the Government's scheme of borrowing, conducted their own borrowing – and lending – for development. Earlier in the century Australian and New Zealand banks had been handicapped by the absence of opportunity for short-term lending, by discounting bills, for instance, and had been slowly forced to conclude that English practices were not all suited to local conditions. In the eighteen-thirties the banks began to finance the pastoral movement in eastern Australia by assisting pastoralists to purchase stock. In 1843, despite the demur of the Colonial Office, a New South Wales Act made legal and regulated the practice, which was already a decade old, of lending on preferable liens on the next wool clip; it was not a great step to making advances on the security of land and then on all forms of property. By the early eighteen-sixties the New Zealand banks were lending directly and indirectly to squatters and other land-owners in circumstances in which the real security was in fact mortgages. In the eyes of English bankers such 'illiquid' securities were exceedingly dangerous but, in the colonial conditions, mortgage banking, when carefully controlled, made a valuable contribution to development. In the seventies, however, some of the banks, notably the 'local' Bank of New Zealand and the Colonial Bank, became quite reckless and permitted 'a frenzy of private borrowing'. Between 1872 and 1879 bank loans in New Zealand increased from £3·5 million to £13·8 million. The increase was associated with a shift in the emphasis of private investment away from the efficient 'export-oriented activities of mining, farming and grazing' towards housing and other 'domestic' enterprise, which was encouraged by the substantial rate of immigration. Much of the money was channelled into land speculation. The expansion was neither based on nor designed to stimulate the country's export earnings. It was financed largely with funds from the English or Australian branches of the banks, or with deposits collected in Great Britain at high rates of interest. Especially in Scotland, agents went literally to the customer's door to collect these fixed deposits. Then the banks were driven to take ever-increasing risks in their search for even higher rates on their New Zealand advances. The boom was bound to collapse as soon as these uncertain sources of overseas funds dried up.

In 1878 the failure of the City of Glasgow Bank, which had invested heavily in New Zealand land, added to growing misgivings in Britain about such securities. The difficulty of raising further deposits or other funds in Britain and the continuing fall in export prices at last brought New Zealand bankers to a cautious frame of mind. The Bank of New Zealand, in particular, was very hard pressed for money. In 1879 the banks – mainly the Bank of New Zealand – suddenly cut credit facilities by £1·5 million. The result was the ruin of many traders and shop-keepers and the collapse of the land boom. Even now, however, the Government tried to work the old magic before an increasingly less credulous audience. The Vogel Government, which, sometimes with a respectable figurehead as Premier, had been in power almost continuously since 1869, had fallen in 1877, but the new Premier, Sir George Grey, had an ardent borrower, James Macandrew, as Minister of Public Works and Immigration. In 1879 the Ministry sanctioned the largest loan of all. Even thereafter, though 'retrenchment' was the watchword of successive Governments, borrowing continued until the late eighties. In the years 1880–2, as public loan expenditures fell, bank advances substantially increased. They remained high until 1888, but not even the bankers could wish the depression away. They were again coerced by hard economic facts into caution. New Zealand's 'long depression' had begun. It was to last, with varying intensity at different times and places, from 1879 until 1896.

The South Island, which had probably done best out of the public works programme, and where the boom had been loudest, felt the effects of the slump most severely. Everyone was in some degree affected, but those who were hardest hit were small men, for the banks tried to protect their greatest debtors. The working men, who had not shared proportionately in the prosperity of recent years, were now struck down by falling wages and unemployment, while their ranks were swelled by ex-cockatoos and small business people. As early as 1877 there had been large meetings of unemployed; by 1879 they were in Christchurch revealing an angry temper and, when 'soup kitchens' were set up, demanding 'work not soup'. Not for the first time, recent immigrants found a sad contrast between the promise of the new land (or the promises of its agents) and the reality; once more most of them could not afford to return home. Unemployed workers unsuccessfully petitioned the President of the United States in 1880, and the House of Representatives in Victoria in 1885, for assistance to migrate. During the late eighties the departures exceeded the arrivals by many thousands. During 'the Exodus', as it was called, most of the emigrants went to Victoria, where in the eighties there was a borrowing boom like that earlier spree in New Zealand. As great a number, however, were to recross the Tasman when the Victorian bubble burst in the nineties.

The conditions of the urban workers steadily deteriorated through the eighties. Labour was so cheap that secondary industry was actually expanding and the country was able to export small quantities of its manufactures. In almost every trade employers were relying more and more on child and female labour. In 1888 respectable citizens – though not the trade unionists – were shocked to learn from a sermon on 'The Sin of Cheapness', delivered by a Presbyterian minister in Dunedin, that 'sweated labour' existed in the clothing industry. There was nothing novel about exploited labour, but a great many people found it intolerable that such an evil, which they believed had been left behind by the immigrant ships, should so soon be reproduced in 'this young fair land'. The indignation of the workers and their sympathizers was soon to lead to a political revolution.

Throughout the eighteen-seventies and -eighties the country was ruled by unstable alliances of cliques within the oligarchy of property owners which had dominated politics during the previous fifteen years. Despite the frequent reshuffling of the cabinet, it was so obvious that the changes of personnel involved no change that the governments came collectively to be called 'the continuous ministry'. It is generally regarded as having come into power with the Fox–Vogel combination of 1869 and gone out with Harry Atkinson in 1891. There was still nothing resembling modern political parties. Politics were mainly concerned with Maori land purchase, land sales, railways, roads and bridges – development-issues which provided no basis for a left-wing right-wing division of opinion. Instead, there was a competition among districts to attract the expenditure of public money.

After the abolition of the Provinces, with the help of Robert Stout and others, Sir George Grey tried to establish a Liberal Party. In 1879 he put forward a programme which included 'one man one vote', triennial assemblies, the compulsory government purchase of large estates and the 'free breakfast table', with a land tax to make up for the loss of customs revenues. For the first time in the colony a politician appealed directly to the masses in a democratic rhetoric. There was unusual excitement at the hustings and Grey polled well, but not well enough to win. There was too little of the radical sentiment to which he appealed for his oratory to be convincing. In the next decade poverty was to prove a greater agitator. All Grey had succeeded in doing was to add, to the existing assortment of cliques, new ones calling themselves 'Liberals', who were not strong enough to hold office alone.

From 1877–9 Grey had been Premier of a government of radicals like Ballance and Stout in alliance with far more conservative southern 'Provincialists'. In 1884–7 Stout entered an equally unhappy alliance with Julius Vogel. These two governments illustrate a further feature of the politics of the time. By twentieth-century standards there were quite unacceptably close links between business and politics.

In a basic sense, politics were about land values. To the general community, government borrowing for development held out the promise of rising production and export earnings. To the local settler it meant rising land values. And it offered the same hope to the businessmen and land speculators who had founded the Bank of New Zealand and other large companies. Where public and private advantages so coincided there were opportunities for legislators to benefit themselves which were not neglected.

A principal objective of the southern ministers in Grey's government, including Stout, was to float a land company, with the help of the Agent-General in London, Julius Vogel, so that it would appear to have official backing. Grey forced Vogel to resign from his office and his ministers to resign their provisional directorships. It has recently been shown that Vogel's objective in returning to New Zealand and politics in 1884 was to rescue the same company from liquidation by legislative action. One historian has called the Stout–Vogel ministry a 'speculators' government'. Nor was this company the only one with direct political involvements. A historian has demonstrated that one reason for the fall of Grey's government was the opposition – and defection from his supporters – of speculators in Maori land who wanted the Government to stop competing with them in buying land near and in the 'King country'.

It scarcely needs to be said that, in such political circumstances of weak alliances and divided aims, the radicals were unable to introduce many of the measures they advocated. An education Act, a trade union Act and the first land tax – which was promptly repealed by the next ministry – were passed by Grey and his colleagues, Robert Stout and John Ballance. Between 1884 and 1887 Stout and Ballance extended the use of leasehold and Ballance also tried to establish 'village settlements'. Some two thousand people were settled on plots of twenty to fifty acres, but the land was often as poor as the tenants and the scheme was not a success. In general the radicals lacked the support, either in the country or from their more conservative colleagues in these coalitions, necessary to push their schemes very far.

Many of the politicians who were calling themselves 'Liberals' were no more radical than their opponents, few of whom deserved the label of 'Conservative' that the 'Liberals' sought to fasten on them. Vogel was a financial adventurer. His faith in great private enterprises and in merchant princes, expressed in his novel, *Anno Domini 2000; or Women's Destiny*, would today mark him as conservative. But, like Sir John Hall, another leader of the colonial 'Establishment', he supported votes for women. So did Sir Harry Atkinson, who was Premier and held other offices several times in the seventies and eighties. He advocated proportional representation, and the leasehold tenure, which was a radical panacea. In 1882 he put forward a remarkable scheme of national insurance against old age, sickness, widowhood and orphanhood, to be financed partly by compulsory contributions and partly by the state. It was greeted with laughter.

William Rolleston was another early champion of the leasehold tenure. In 1882 he introduced legislation to stop the further sale of public lands and to establish a 'perpetual lease' at a low rental, though with periodic revaluations; but the Legislative Council, the local equivalent of the House of Lords and as full of decrepit conservatives as a contemporary squatters' club, frustrated his purpose by giving lessees a right of purchase at a cheap rate. The tenure became very popular, though whether because it was a form of lease, or because it offered an easy road to the freehold, it is hard to determine.

Above all the leaders of 'the continuous ministry' were at one with the local radicals in the alacrity with which they founded state enterprises and extended state control. In discussing his national insurance scheme Atkinson said he disagreed with writers like Herbert Spencer 'who would confine the functions of Government simply to police duties'. He thought that 'if we can really strike a fatal blow at pauperism, – then this matter is clearly within the proper functions of Government'. The lugubrious Rolleston might complain that every 'new Government function converts more and more the active and ambitious part of the public into hangers-on of the Government', but he supported the measure of a free, secular and compulsory state system of elementary education which was introduced in 1877 by another of the Canterbury gentry, C. C. Bowen. In the same period Rolleston also helped to found the University of New Zealand, which always relied on government money. Vogel established the Government Life

Insurance Office and that other great national institution, the
Public Trust Office. The fact that these leaders were no more
disinclined to extend the functions of the state than later more
radical politicians was a decisive influence on the country's
development.

Although there were no political parties in a modern sense,
there were certain foci for political disagreement, such as protection versus free trade, borrowing versus 'self-reliance', or
leasehold versus freehold, around which parties might coalesce.
But while politics ran on railway tracks, these were almost
peripheral. It took a prolonged economic depression, which
altered the order of political possibilities, to transform politics.

During the eighteen-eighties the old 'Establishment', dominated by squatters, speculators, merchants, British gentlemen
and their ladies, was falling apart in a wave of abscondences,
defalcations and bankruptcies, which ended in the collapse of
several of their financial agencies, including the Bank of New
Zealand; but a new order was growing in the womb of hard
times.

There had always been some radicals in the colony, but it
took the long depression, which seemed to prove that there was
little hope for individual improvement within the society created
by the pioneers, to produce a popular desire for sweeping
change. Within a few years of Grey's radical campaigns of
1877–9 a host of organizations had taken up his demands for
reform and added to the list. Among these reforming organizations were the trade unions, the Trades and Labour Councils,
the Knights of Labour (an American organization established
in New Zealand in 1889) and the Anti-Poverty League
(founded in Auckland in the same year to spread the 'single-tax'
theories of Henry George). Some wanted factory legislation,
protective tariffs, a state bank. The unions wanted the ex-
clusion of Asian immigrants and the cessation of government
assistance to British immigrants, since both Chinese and
British newcomers added to the pool of unemployed. Loudest
of all was the cry that land should be made available for small
farmers.

When the big estates had been built up the population had

been small, so that few were excluded from the land; there had been, in any case, only a limited scope for small farming. The colony had not long been able to compete with the grain-growing continents; there had been no large market for perishable produce. Consequently, since the economy had rested on wool, the squatter had been king, for wool-raising was a large-scale enterprise. Now, however, there was a much larger population, considerable unemployment, thousands of families waiting for a chance to leave the towns and begin farming. Moreover, the appetites of the land-hungry had been sharpened in 1882 by an achievement which was to transform New Zealand life: the *Dunedin* had carried the first cargo of frozen meat from New Zealand to England. At that time real wages and food consumption were rising in Britain, even during a depression, so that a large mass market was demanding food. At last the possibility was in sight of building up an export trade in meat, butter or cheese, all of which could be produced efficiently on relatively small holdings. But was it not also possible that the 'big men', who had promoted the initial experiment in refrigerated shipping, would grásp the opportunity of the future as they had that of the past? Would the country be carved into great cattle ranches as well as sheep-runs? This was improbable in the North Island, where most of the land was too rugged to be 'broken in' on a large scale with nineteenth-century equipment. Moreover, it was doubtful whether anyone had the capital necessary to try it. In the south, however, the outlook was less certain. There the land was locked up as much by financial stringency as by the greed of the monopolists. A large number of properties had fallen into the hands of banks, but the banks, in common with other mortgagees and with speculators who had bought land at the inflated values of the Vogel era, could not afford to sell at the prevailing low prices. A rise in land values, which waited on an improvement in commodity prices or easier credit, could break this economic deadlock; but it could not even then be taken for granted that the small farmer would come into his own. There were, however, other factors in the situation. It was unlikely that the British settler, accustomed in the colony to independence and, until recently, to high wages, would accept the status of peon. He possessed in his vote a weapon which might prevent the estate owners from offering him such a role. By 1890 the Liberals, who proposed to promote closer settlement by forcing estate owners to sub-divide their properties and by other methods, won the ardent support of thousands of potential farmers.

The spread of demands for radical reform and the fragility of the position of property owners, whose 'wealth' generally meant 'indebtedness', forced propertied persons into a defensive and conservative posture. Their chief fear was that the Colony's problem of paying the interest on overseas public debts would necessitate higher taxes. By 1888 six hundred thousand people had managed to borrow £38 million ($76 million). One government after another tried to find a way of paying for the past without raising an income tax, which was thought politically impossible. And one after another fell by threatening the security of the small politically powerful indebted class. Thus a class of conservatives, desperately trying to preserve its status, was created. Several conservative Political and Financial Reform Associations were formed in the towns. Their principal aim was so to 'retrench' government expenditure on education, the civil service and elsewhere that further taxation would be unnecessary. Many of the members were free traders who, in the New Zealand context, were extreme conservatives. Free trade meant cheap imports, and was calculated to bolster the position of farmers and estate owners. Tariff protection – economic nationalism – was a policy of radicals.

In 1887 a number of free traders, mainly rural, were elected to the House, the first coherent conservative group in New Zealand parliamentary history. They tried to ditch Atkinson, the leader of the Opposition, whom they thought dangerously radical, but failed. He became Premier again in that year after the defeat of the Stout–Vogel ministry. The conservatives after 1890 became the Opposition to the Liberals.

The depression produced two parties by creating two classes – classes which were nation-wide, for poverty ignored the Provinces. Provincialism lost much of its force for a further reason. For twenty years politicians had been squabbling round the 'pork barrel'. Now the barrel was empty. Borrowing on a large scale had become impossible. Thus the chief political issue, development, was eliminated. By 1889 the Liberals were growing united on a policy of radical land and labour legislation and of protective tariffs. In that year, after being divided and leaderless since the fall of the Stout–Vogel ministry, they elected John Ballance as their chief. Thereafter one may speak appropriately of the Liberal Party, though it was a very loose affair by modern standards. Thus the Colony now had groups of Conservatives and Liberals – in W. P. Reeves's phrase, 'parties of resistance and progress'.

The Liberals were immediately strengthened by an industrial crisis. The depression had strengthened the ideals of trade unionism while preventing their realization. There had been craft unions in the colony from the early days, but generally their career had been precarious and brief. In the seventies and eighties, however, active trade unionism was encouraged by industrial development; by the Vogel immigrants, many of whom were schooled in British unionism; and by Grey's Trade Union Act of 1878, which gave the unions legal recognition. Previously unorganized workers, including coal-miners, 'wharf lumpers' and seamen, formed unions, some of which embraced Australia as well as New Zealand. Trades and Labour Councils, representing regional groups of unions, were also established. None of these organizations, however, proved very robust amidst the prevailing unemployment; most of them, like the earlier unions, from time to time collapsed and had to be rebuilt. Nor did the slump provide ideal conditions for the aggressive unionism which was being imported from Australia. In 1890 the Australian maritime strike spread to New Zealand when a local ship was worked by non-union men in Sydney. The Maritime Council, which was affiliated with the Australian Council, called out its men; the wharf labourers followed; the shipowners employed unpaid 'volunteers' and 'black' labour. In both countries the strikes failed miserably. The New Zealand Maritime Council disintegrated. In both countries the failure of the industrial action caused the unionists to turn to politics; but instead of founding Labour Parties, like the Australians, the New Zealanders added their weight to the Liberals, many of whom had supported the strikers while Atkinson's Government stood aside in uneasy neutrality.

In December 1890, backed by the unions, the Trades and Labour Councils and the Knights of Labour, by the hungry and the land-hungry, by the recent immigrants, the Liberals were swept into office.

This was one of the really momentous elections in New Zealand history. As a turning-point in the country's development it has been compared with the 1832 Reform Bill in Great Britain. More exact, however, is the parallel with the 1828 election in the United States, when the Americans exchanged 'the Federalist decorum of Washington and John Adams, the courtly Virginia democracy of Jefferson', for the rule of Andrew Jackson and 'rough, rowdy back-country people in homespun'. Though there was a difference in philosophy between the democratic victors in the two countries, they shared their dislike of monopoly and distrust of banks.

The Conservatives fought a stiff rearguard action. At the instigation of the free traders, before resigning, Atkinson induced the Governor to appoint six extra Conservatives to the Legislative Council, in which the Liberals were scarcely represented. The Conservatives then used their control of the Council to the fullest extent for party purposes. For two years there was a struggle between the two Houses, one of them representing a declining, conservative, colonial aristocracy, the other a popular, Liberal majority, prophetic of the conflict between the English Houses of Parliament in the years 1906–11. In 1891 the Council passed the taxation bill and a bill, which both parties supported, to alter the tenure of future appointments to the Legislative Council from life to seven years. It rejected most other important Liberal measures, thus earning the name of 'the freezing chamber'. Early in 1892 Ballance, the new Premier, asked the Governor to appoint a number of additional Councillors. The Governor refused, and so did his successor, who arrived a few months later. The issues at stake were of major importance: not merely whether the Liberals could pass their legislation, but whether the Governor could decline to act on the advice of his ministers with regard to a domestic matter. Eventually the dispute was referred to the Colonial Office, which instructed the Governor to accept Ballance's advice. Twelve new Councillors were appointed; but not until 1899 did the Liberals quite dominate the Upper House.

With their defeat in the 1890 election, and after Ballance's victory over the question of appointments to the Legislative Council, the rule of the early colonial gentry, with their public school or university background, their Latin tags and cultivated English speech, their sheep-runs and their clubs, was done. Rarely, since that time, has any member of the former oligarchy held influential political office; rarely have Prime Ministers been either wealthy or well-educated, though a few have been well-read. The democracy was in power and the politician had to be, or at least to seem to be, if not a common man, then one of the common colonists. He should be big, preferably loud, certainly hearty; not, on any account, should he be suspected of feeling superior to the voters by reason of culture or fastidiousness. The country seems to have been none the worse for the change.

II: STATE EXPERIMENTS

New Zealand is the birth place of the Twentieth Century.

PROFESSOR FRANK PARSONS, PH.D., *The Story of New Zealand*,
Philadelphia, 1904

THE problem facing the Liberal ministry which took office in
January 1891 may be summed up in one word: misery. Canaan
had not fulfilled its promise. Thousands of people were living
in the towns in such circumstances as are painfully recorded in
John A. Lee's novel, *Children of the Poor*, while they were
denied access to the farm-lands outside. But though New
Zealand had failed to fulfil the high hopes of the pioneering
generation, these were not forgotten. It had, however, become
apparent that in order to achieve them it was not enough to
migrate to the new land; it was necessary by political action to
regulate the new economic and social order.

The New Zealand Liberal Party was a world apart from its
British namesake. In the colony, by the late eighteen-eighties,
only a few extreme Conservatives still followed Bentham or
Bright. Liberal leaders such as Robert Stout or John Ballance,
though they had been educated in the school of individualism
and *laissez-faire*, had come to believe that only state intervention could cure the country's ills. It was this belief in the
potential beneficence of the state that distinguished them from
the majority of British Liberals, but united them in one faith
with most of the radicals throughout the English-speaking
world. The political ideals of the New Zealand Liberals were
similar to those of the Fabians and other socialist groups in
England; the Nationalist Clubs, the Knights of Labour, and
the Populists in the United States; the Labour Parties in Australia. This was no accident, for they had all drunk from the
same intellectual springs. Scholarly radicals knew the works of
John Stuart Mill, and perhaps also those of A. R. Wallace, the
English land nationalizer. The ordinary man, who read few
books and read them well, was more likely to know *Progress and
Poverty* by the 'single taxer', Henry George, or *Looking Back-
ward*, a portrait of a socialist Utopia written by another
American, Edward Bellamy. These books were extraordinarily

popular. Through them, millions of people became acquainted, not only with the concepts of the classical economists and J. S. Mill, but with the heady socialist theories of Saint-Simon, Fourier, and Lassalle. Fabians, Populists and antipodean Labour and Liberal Parties alike received inspiration from their pages.

Mill's opinion was sought, more particularly by older Liberals, on all manner of questions – questions of franchise, tariffs, immigration, or liberty itself – but especially with regard to that quite fundamental colonial problem, land ownership. Mill, following Ricardo, held that the fortunate landowner received a gratuitous reward in the form of the excess value of his products over the return he would have gained had he farmed the poorest land which it was profitable to cultivate. For instance, supposing that the poorest land which would pay an ordinary profit yielded twenty bushels to the acre, then the farmer whose land yielded forty bushels for the same expenditure of labour and capital received a bonus of twenty bushels. This 'economic rent' was in effect both a result of the natural fertility of the soil and a social premium, for it was the growth of population which made it profitable to farm less and less fertile soil. Mill, who founded a Land Tenure Reform Association in England in 1870, held that this 'unearned increment', as he called it, should be taxed so that the community might share in the land values which it created.

The doctrine of 'economic rent' attracted a huge following in new countries where men were daily witnessing what seemed concrete examples of its relevance, land values rising – from nothing – as settlement advanced, and with the construction of public works paid for from public revenues. Henry George took Mill's theories to a logical conclusion by advocating that the state should confiscate 'rent' by placing a tax on land, but on no other form of property – an idea peculiarly attractive to the landless.

Like those of J. S. Mill, George's theories arose from a consideration of individual rights. In California, where huge areas were controlled by a few individuals and corporations, those rights, which included equal access to the land, were denied. He hoped to undermine 'the insidious forces that, producing inequality, destroy Liberty'. He hoped to preserve free capitalism by reforming it; but his views, spread in New Zealand and elsewhere by enthusiastic 'single tax' organizations, encouraged more radical ambitions. He popularized the idea of taxing the unimproved value of land: he also, unintentionally, popularized the idea of nationalization. If the land belonged to the community, why not confiscate the land instead of the rent?

In New Zealand almost all the land had recently come into private hands by purchase from the state. Moreover, many of the landless were recent immigrants who found themselves up against what seemed the same landlordism from which they had escaped in Ireland or Scotland. Needless to say, they felt no respect for their precursors. As an early New Zealand historian remarked, 'The class which cares least for the Pilgrim Fathers is that which immediately succeeds them.' To the Conservatives, who took the extremists' words too seriously, it seemed that Wakefield's prophecy of 1854 was fulfilled: he had warned the House of Representatives that, unless the land were opened to the people instead of to monopolists and speculators, 'a confiscating democracy' would arise.

Ballance, the new Premier, had written a pamphlet advocating land nationalization. In the trade unions and on the left wing of the Liberal Party there was a numerous minority prepared to go much further than land tenure reform and to attack, however cautiously, the capitalist system as a whole. Like Edward Bellamy, they emphasized equality rather than liberty – or rather, they believed that the liberties of the rich involved a form of slavery for the poor. 'Excessive individualism', Bellamy had written, is 'inconsistent with the public spirit.' Competition was the crime; co-operation would be the remedy. Bellamy longed for the time (which he imagined might be as far off as A.D. 2000!) when the nation would guarantee 'the nurture, education and comfortable maintenance of every citizen from the cradle to the grave.'

The leading exponent of this opinion was William Pember Reeves, the author of the first study of Socialism and Communism to be published in the colony, and the first Minister of Labour. He told the electors of Auckland in 1894 that he was a

Fabian socialist. On another occasion he spoke of the 'natural warfare between classes' and advocated the nationalization of the sources of production and the processes of industry. None of his colleagues in the cabinet would go with him there, even though he stressed that 'the ballot-box, not the barricade', must be the instrument of change, but several agreed with him that society, as then constituted, was 'clumsy, cruel and un-righteous'. Reeves's views were, in relation to public opinion in his time, more radical than those of any other person who has held cabinet office in New Zealand. He was, in Beatrice Webb's words, a 'radical collectivist', or, in a phrase he used himself, a 'state socialist'. Like Sidney Webb, when he spoke of the functions already performed by the state, he was wont to grow quite lyrical – or at least rhetorical. The state, he pro-claimed, was in New Zealand before 1890 already the greatest landlord, the public trustee, the builder of most roads and almost all railways, the educator of most of the people, the promoter of the largest life insurance business ... The list was formidable. Experience, the implication was clear, supported theory; for every interference by the state in 'the so-called "rights" of private employers and capitalists' was in his eyes 'a piece of socialism'. He ignored the warning given by Hubert Bland in the *Fabian Essays in Socialism*, that 'although Socialism involves State control, State control does not involve Socialism'.

Reeves presents the unusual spectacle of a radical becoming more radical in office. He was too extreme for his colleagues, and in 1896 he retreated to London as Agent-General. The Liberal Premier, Ballance (like his successor, Seddon), hoped not for the destruction of capitalism but for 'a reconciliation between capital and labour on a fair and equitable basis'. The whole outlook of the Liberals was, however, directed by an idealistic attitude towards the state. In varying degrees they believed in public ownership and enterprise, if not as ends in themselves, at least as useful means towards another end. For all of them, the final object was the fullest possible consumma-tion of the individual life. The state was to create a generalized sense of individual worth, in a word: equality. Writing in 1903 in the *Independent Review*, Reeves posed that question which the Liberals sought to answer in the affirmative: 'Is it possible to have a civilization which is no mere lacquer on the surface of society? Can a community be civilized throughout, and trained to consist of educated, vigorous men and women; efficient workers, yet not lacking in the essentials of refinement?'

Some Marxists have detected in New Zealand liberalism an idealization of the state akin to modern Fascism; but when Stout asked 'What were the State and the Government?' and replied 'The organized community', he was not repudiating the existence of classes so much as denying that the state was the executive committee of a ruling class. In a broad sense, the Liberals believed that the state was, in fact, the people. With the spread of education, they hoped that state action would increasingly become the co-operative action of an enlightened democracy. In a land without hereditary caste, they trusted to state action to minimize the significance of economic differences. The electorate has never been afraid of the state, and on the whole the state has served most of the people well. It must, however, be added in the same breath that New Zealand has not been quite without economic classes and that, on certain tense occasions, the government has acted as Marxists expect, intervening, for instance, in strikes to assist employers. There has, in other words, been a gap between the equalitarian ideal and the inequalities of reality. The desire to close it has been one of the chief stimuli of political change.

We have described the symptoms and sketched the treatments suggested. Something more should be said of the social doctors who had charge of the body politic. John Ballance was a man who has often been underestimated, largely because he died after two years in office. Retiring, modest, courteous, willing to compromise, he won the affection and loyalty of all his colleagues. This was no inconsiderable feat, for not only was his cabinet, in political, intellectual and administrative ability, probably the strongest ever formed in New Zealand, but also it contained masterful individuals quite incompatible without his presence. Reeves was the most articulate of the Liberals, the first New Zealand 'intellectual', the first local-born cabinet minister to exert any great influence in the country's affairs; but he was an isolated figure, abhorred by his class, the Canterbury gentry, yet remote from the trade unionists whom he led. Ballance and Reeves had the greatest share in working out the Liberal programme as a whole; but, in more ways than one, they seemed, in the short perspectives of contemporary vision, to be overshadowed by two mountainous men. One was a land reformer, John McKenzie, who had left a small farm in Scotland for another in Otago. By 1890 he was an experienced politician, shrewd yet straightforward and patently sincere. 'No art helped him to rise,' Reeves wrote of him, 'no tinsel was ever stitched onto his homespun; he would tell any set of men – even newspaper editors – what he thought of them, and had a gruff scorn of self-advertisement'. Though he was no orator (his angry, almost incoherent outbursts in the House of Representatives were notorious), yet 'when speaking for the reform for which he was literally giving his life, there were moments when this shepherd from the hills, passionately direct and lifted up by the greatness of his theme, could carry any audience away. Then you saw why he was a leader of men; then, watching him, you understood that in that gigantic body, and behind those grim and homely features, there was struggling for utterance a share of the unquenchable idealism, stormy sympathies, and vague poetry of the Gael.'

The other eminent member of the cabinet was Richard John Seddon, a hard-working politician who in 1890 was known chiefly for his clumsy verbosity. He had come out as a lad from Lancashire to Australia where he 'roughed it' for a couple of years and tried his luck on the 'diggings' before moving to the New Zealand gold-fields on the 'West Coast', the popular name for Westland. Ballance made him Minister of Public Works (an important portfolio), Mines, and Defence. In 1892, when the Premier became ill, he made Seddon, who had a considerable command of parliamentary procedure as well as the robust good health which Reeves and McKenzie lacked, the acting leader of the House. It was Ballance's intention, when the serious nature of his illness was made plain to him, to resign and to pass on the leadership to Robert Stout (who was not then a member of the House); but he died suddenly and the Governor automatically asked Seddon to form a ministry. McKenzie and Reeves, both close friends of Stout, at first refused to accept Seddon's leadership. Seddon consulted the aged Grey who advised him to go ahead. There was a symbolic fitness in this gesture – one of the country's greatest leaders passing the Liberal torch to a man who would prove to be another. McKenzie and Reeves capitulated. Stout was shortly afterwards re-elected to the Assembly, where he became a stubborn opponent of the new Premier; but he had few followers, the party was not seriously divided, and the New Zealand experiment could go on.

The first object of the new Government was to encourage closer settlement; it was their belief that in this way they could reduce unemployment and bring about a more effective utilization of the country's resources. They also believed small farming to be desirable in itself. To this end they meant to ensure that Crown lands should be alienated only to genuine settlers; to re-purchase estates for subdivision; and by means of taxation to force great landowners to subdivide their properties. They hoped to extend leasehold at the expense of freehold tenure because they believed land should be public property. In addition, they soon decided to make cheap loans available so that new settlers would not fail for want of initial capital.

The first measure affecting land was the repeal of the existing property tax, which penalized improvements and let salary and wage-earners escape free, and the introduction of graduated land and income taxes. To modern citizens these taxes seem delightfully low. Radical as it seemed at the time, the land tax, for all that it was an application of the theory of taxing the 'unearned increment', was so cautious that it was neither confiscatory nor even penal. A tax of a penny in the pound was levied on the unimproved value of all landed properties over £500 ($1,000) in value; holdings worth over £5,000 ($10,000) paid an additional graduated tax commencing at an eighth of a penny in the pound. Absentee owners paid a further twenty per cent. The Government hoped that 'the graduation screw', as the landowners called the tax, would 'burst up' the estates by making it costly to retain large, undeveloped properties. But it seems unlikely that this was a major cause of later subdivision. The taxes did not affect most of the largest holdings, which were Crown pastoral leases. Other factors were working more forcefully to encourage small-holding.

The Liberals passed several measures empowering the Government to re-purchase private lands for resettlement. By 1912, over 200 properties, comprising 1,300,000 acres, had been purchased and subdivided; 17,000 people were living on land which had been almost uninhabited. This was only a small proportion, about 3·2 per cent, of the 40,000,000 acres then in European occupation, but it looks more impressive when we recall that only 16,000,000 acres of that land was being cultivated (or that of the 32,000,000 acres which had been occupied in 1891, only 9,000,000 had been cultivated). Most of the land subdivided by the state was rapidly improved by the new tenants. Altogether the Liberals could congratulate themselves on an achievement which, though small by the canons of land nationalization, was great in its practical effect.

The Land and Income Tax Act was chiefly the work of Ballance; McKenzie framed the re-purchase laws and was also responsible, in 1892, for an Act consolidating the confused central and provincial land laws. For the first time there was one system of land regulations: an innovation which, like the creation of a public domain in the United States over a century earlier, must have contributed considerably to the growth of a sense of national unity. At the same time McKenzie introduced a reform affecting land tenure. The ideal tenure in the opinion of the Liberal leaders was a perpetual lease with periodic re-valuations, but they despaired of getting it through. On three occasions the House had approved the principle, but nothing had come of it. In 1891, the Legislative Council had slashed a bill incorporating this measure as they had Rolleston's in 1882. There were, moreover, a few freeholders on the Government side who were likely to revolt against so sweeping a repudiation of their beliefs. In 1892, more eager to get men on the land than to insist dogmatically on their favourite tenure, McKenzie and Ballance gave way and introduced a curious compromise. In the place of Rolleston's perpetual lease, which gave Crown tenants a right of purchase, they introduced a 'lease-in-perpetuity', a tenure which carried no right of purchase, but abandoned the periodical revaluations. For a low rental, state tenants were to receive a 999-year lease. The state could insist on genuine occupation and improvement and could regulate the size of holdings; but there was no provision to secure for the public purse a share in future increases in land values. The tenant had most of the advantages of the freehold without having to pay for it. The tenure proved popular; just over 2,000,000 acres were leased in this way in 1907 when it was amended; but naturally it was anathema to the land nationalizers. For the next twenty years 'the battle of the tenures' was fought as much within the Liberal ranks as between the two parties.

For much the same reasons of necessity – or expediency – the Liberal Government did not altogether forbid the sale of Crown lands. As Ballance said, though he thought this prohibition desirable, it would 'take a little time to educate the people up to that point'. Although discouraged by the Government, the sale of the freehold continued.

Theories of nationalization and the 'unearned increment' shaped the Liberals' land legislation and dictated their preference for leasehold and for taxing unimproved values (a principle which was also made optional as a basis for local body rates) but they were applied with moderation. The Government did not manage to retain the absolute ownership of the remaining public lands in state hands; the area of freehold land rose from 12.5 to 16.5 million acres between 1891 and 1911. They did, however, succeed in giving increased importance to the tenure they favoured. The area of Crown leasehold land increased from 14 to 19 million acres, from forty-four to forty-eight per cent of the occupied land.* Most of this land consisted of large pastoral leases – 12.5 million acres in 1891; 11 million acres in 1911. If this is subtracted from the total area of leasehold, it will be seen that the Liberals had a considerable success: excluding the pastoral leases, Crown leases rose from 1.5 to 8 million acres. But the significance of this change should not be exaggerated. Most of the good land, which had long been freehold, remained so. In the future a new 'freehold party' was to have as little success in changing the basic struc-

* See Table I.

ture of land tenure as the Liberals. Good land tended to be divided into small holdings and held in fee simple; millions of acres of poor land were suited to large holdings on pastoral leases. Although for thirty years the major political battles were fought over land tenure, economic and geographic facts had the last word.

Of all the Liberal measures of land policy the most influential was the Advances to Settlers Act of 1894 which was introduced by J. G. Ward, a previously unimportant minister who became Treasurer after Ballance's death. As we have seen, one of the gravest difficulties of the pioneers was shortage of capital. In the past interest rates as high as fifteen per cent had not been uncommon; even in the nineties eight per cent was quite usual. Like the followers of the Populist or the earlier Greenback and Free Silver movements in the United States, the New Zealand farmers, heavily in debt to banks or loan and mortgage companies, needed cheap and easily available loans. Would-be farmers were in the same position; a fact which led in the eighties to the unions' demand for a state bank. In 1894 the Government decided to resume overseas borrowing and to lend money, on first mortgage, to freeholders and holders of perpetual leases, at about five per cent interest. This measure was of immense value to working farmers. It is estimated that by 1908 it had saved settlers as much as £8,000,000 ($16,000,000) in interest.

It should be added, in parenthesis, that advances to settlers marked the beginning of a major change in Liberal policies. The Ballance Government had been elected on a programme which included the cessation of borrowing overseas. Now, though in a form somewhat disguised, the Seddon Government was resuming borrowing. The central feature of New Zealand politics before 1890 was already reasserting itself. It was increasingly to insist on its primacy over radical reforms in the years to come. And this was inevitable, for borrowing-for-development was essential to economic growth besides having an irresistible appeal to the dominant rural voters.

While the Liberals held office the number of land holdings rose from 43,000 to 74,000 though the area in European occupation increased by only 8,000,000 acres (from 32,000,000 to

40,000,000). There was, during the nineties, a marked trend towards smaller holdings. By 1911 the total land in private ownership which was in holdings of over 10,000 acres had been reduced from 7,000,000 to 3,000,000 acres. How far were these very substantial changes a result of the battery of Liberal Acts?

There is no doubt that the chief agents of change were the rising prices in Great Britain for food and the invention of refrigerated shipping. These benefited the small farmers. Prosperous farmers meant rising land prices which encouraged the owners of large holdings to sub-divide them.

Part of the basis for the new boom conditions after 1896 had been laid in the seventies with the Vogel communication network. During the depression valuable assets such as houses, urban buildings, fences, pastures, flocks and herds had been created. After 1888 there had been a reorientation of investment towards the efficient rural sector of the economy. Twenty-five years of effort had put the country in a position to take advantage of the new export opportunities. But here the Liberals' role was by no means negligible. They were in power for six of these depressed years, legislating (like Vogel) for the future.

A final point should be made. It seems that the main source of the increase in the number of small-holdings was not sub-division but the occupation of new land. The Liberals purchased 3,000,000 further acres of Maori land during 1891-1911. By this means, too, the Liberals gave would-be farmers what they wanted.

In general it seems fair to conclude that government policy was not the main agent of change in land holdings. But Liberal legislation did stimulate small-holdings and genuine settlement by encouraging those economic and technological changes which were making dairying and mixed farming prosperous industries.

The arguments about land tenure, which loomed so large in the politics of sixty years ago, are now almost forgotten. Other theories and measures, which then seemed less important, are now so familiar that there is less need for the historian, seeking to recapture something of the flavour of politics in the nineties, to describe them in detail. Labour legislation, for instance, though strenuously advocated by unions and warmly contested by extreme conservatives, aroused little general interest. Reeves records that only once was a debate on his Industrial Conciliation and Arbitration Bill attended by half the House – though it was twice mutilated by hostile amendment in the Legislative Council. In five years Reeves was responsible for fourteen measures regulating working hours, wages and factory conditions, and preventing 'sweating' or the exploitation of child labour. He introduced what was then the most progressive labour code in the world and the most comprehensive; one Act went so far as to prescribe the provision of chairs for shop-girls and the liberty to use them. No further labour reforms of importance were introduced in New Zealand until 1936.

Ballance set up a Labour Department under Reeves to administer the new laws, to inspect factories, shops, and shearing-sheds, and generally to scrutinize labour conditions. It did good work in relieving unemployment by transporting labourers to jobs. Reeves also conducted a short-lived experiment, inspired by the *Fabian Essays*, of forming co-operative 'labour farms' where unemployed were given the task of making new farms in the bush. Seddon was responsible for another example of what one newspaper regarded as 'Bellamyism': he began to let out minor public works such as road-making to small groups of men who contracted co-operatively to carry them out with government materials. This experiment, which also helped to relieve unemployment, proved most successful.

The most novel of the labour measures was Reeves's Industrial Conciliation and Arbitration Act. With the New Zealand Settlements Act of 1863, which confiscated Maori lands, and Ward's Advances to Settlers Act, it was one of the nineteenth-century legislative measures most decisive in moulding New Zealand society. It also influenced legislation in other countries, notably Australia, where, it seems, the idea had its origin. There had been machinery to arbitrate in industrial disputes in several places – in New York and Massachusetts, for instance, since 1886 – but it had rarely proved effective because its use was entirely voluntary. In Australia and New Zealand, after the strike of 1890, suggestions were made that arbitration be

made compulsory. In 1894 Reeves introduced the first compulsory system of state arbitration in the world.

The country was divided into districts in which Conciliation
Boards, elected by masters and workers, were set up. Reeves
believed that the majority of disputes would be settled by the
Boards, though he pointed out that they were not essential. If
the decision of a Board proved unsatisfactory, either party
could appeal to the Arbitration Court, which consisted of a
Supreme Court judge and two assessors elected by the employers' associations and the unions. An award of this court had
legal force. The system did not affect farm labour or unorganized labour.

The Industrial Conciliation and Arbitration Act was intended to stimulate and protect unionism, for Reeves considered,
with much justification, that the unions were too weak to safeguard the interests of workers against employers. The benefits
to be derived from registration led to a great increase in the
number of unions and an improvement in their efficacy. An
early award of the court giving 'preference to unions' over non-
union labour gave them further encouragement. Litigation
became a major industrial occupation. For some years the
Boards were a failure while the business of the Arbitration
Court multiplied. It had, in the words of a New South Wales
judge, 'a wider jurisdiction and greater powers than perhaps
any Court in the British dominions'. Over the next decade it
awarded many wage increases, thus ensuring that, in a period
of rising prices, prosperity was to some extent shared by the
industrial workers. It also helped to smooth class relations. The
economic conflict between employer and employee was to a
large extent transferred from the factory or political meeting to
the courts. There, as clause was pitted against clause, interpretation against interpretation, the economic became a legal
struggle, not muted, not blunted, but at a decent remove from
everyday life and suitably shrouded in legal abstraction. The
strange metamorphoses through which the arbitration system
passed – how an Act intended, as its sub-title indicated, 'to
encourage the formation of industrial unions', came to be used
to dragoon obstreperous unions – will be considered in later
chapters. It seems hardly too much to assert that the structure

of industrial relations in New Zealand, and to some extent the structure of society itself, has developed within the framework of the Act. Its influence is all the more remarkable when one considers that there was almost no demand for it: but for Reeves's persistence, it is improbable that it would have been introduced.

The Liberals completed the democratization of the state. The secret (or 'Australian') ballot had been adopted in 1869; manhood suffrage in 1879. In 1889 plural voting had been abolished, though property owners could still register in several electorates and choose where to vote. In 1893 this privilege was abolished too. In 1891 the tenure of members of the Legislative Council was altered from life to seven years.

A reform more radical than these was in 1893 forced on the Government. A small but determined number of women, led chiefly by the Women's Christian Temperance Union, had for several years been demanding the vote for women. Ballance had supported them and committed his party to adopting this measure, but after his death most of his colleagues were publicly tepid and in private warmly opposed to it. However, in 1893, when an electoral bill was before the House, Sir John Hall moved an amendment to enfranchise women. Seddon let it pass in the expectation that it would be rejected in the Legislative Council, and earn for that body the consequent opprobrium. To everyone's surprise, however, it passed by two votes and the women of New Zealand, preceded only by those in Wyoming, were enrolled with their menfolk.

Another important reform was pressed on an unwilling Government by its opponents. For some years the supporters of total abstinence, organized by the Women's Christian Temperance Union and the New Zealand Alliance, had been exceedingly active in New Zealand. Seddon was not sympathetic, and one reason for his doubts about female suffrage was the general opinion that it would strengthen the 'teetotallers', or 'wowsers', as the abstinence supporters were called. But the movement was very powerful; it found strong argument in the prevalence of drunkenness; it was led by a group of able agitators – in speech the 'wowsers' were, indeed, the least temperate people in the country. Moreover, in the House they were represented by Robert Stout. Since it was distinctly possible that Stout might split the Liberal Party over this issue, Seddon was in 1893 obliged to forestall him by introducing a 'local option'. This gave the voters the right to decide on the continuation or reduction of liquor licences in their electorates; a three-fifths majority could prohibit the sale of liquor altogether.

In the following year Seddon surmounted an even greater difficulty when the Bank of New Zealand announced that, failing state assistance, it would be forced to close its doors. Many businesses and estates, accepted as security on loans, had fallen into the hands of the banks, who now found themselves in possession of a mass of unsaleable properties while the interest was still to pay on their own borrowings abroad. Weighed down by its 'illiquid assets', the Bank of New Zealand was forced almost to liquidation by the withdrawal of English deposits and considerable losses during the Australian bank failures in 1893.

Seddon and Ward rushed the Bank of New Zealand Share Guarantee Act through the House and the Council in a night; the Governor signed it early in the morning; the bank and its shareholders and depositors, large and small, were saved. Henceforth the Government was to appoint the chief officers of the bank and a majority of the directors, though it should be added that for many years to come it made little use of its power to dictate banking policy.

In 1896 Seddon had to face yet another crisis when it was discovered that Ward's personal finances were in a hopeless state. He had been speculating recklessly in grain and frozen meat and had an enormous overdraft with the Colonial Bank, whose affairs were in as bad a condition as his own. Worse, while he was at the mercy of that bank, he was responsible, as the Colonial Treasurer, for negotiating a most discreditable arrangement by which it was to be taken over by the state-guaranteed Bank of New Zealand. It seems clear that Ward hoped his own debts would be placed under the same sheltering wing; but this proved impossible. Despite Seddon's efforts to protect him, he was forced to resign and to go bankrupt. He was, however, triumphantly re-elected and soon rejoined the cabinet, though not as Treasurer.

During these affairs Seddon's remarkable political judgement was slowly revealed. He was shrewd, resilient, devious in
method, straightforward in speech, conciliatory to his foes. He
grew in political stature as well as authority. One after another
he surmounted crises which would probably have led to the
defeat of any previous Premier. Most of the Liberal legislation
might never have reached the statute book but for his astute
leadership. He was a shelter belt which protected the delicate
experimental plantations of Reeves and McKenzie. Furthermore, he was responsible for one important innovation himself.
For some years the left-wing Liberals had half-heartedly been
demanding an old age pension. In 1898, after a famous parliamentary battle in which 1,400 speeches were made, Seddon wore
out the opposition in an uninterrupted ninety-hour sitting.
The aged poor received their small pension – providing that
they were of good repute, sober, and had not deserted their
family or been recently in gaol.

There is no need to describe further the amalgam of democratic and humanitarian legislation which made New Zealand
for a time the most radical state in the world. French political
scientists, American radicals, English statesmen and political
philosophers made pilgrimages to the distant colony. At the
Eighty Club in London, Asquith described it as 'a laboratory
in which political and social experiments are every day made
for the information and instruction of the older countries of the
world'. He paid tribute to the 'series of measures of social and
industrial reform to which, in an equal period of time, I believe
it would be impossible for any other community to form a
parallel'.

European visitors were often at a loss to explain the New
Zealand legislation of the nineties. What were they to make of
the 'colonial governmentalism' of these so-called Liberals; of a
radical country where socialists were rarities? European visitors
such as André Siegfried and Albert Métin were astonished by
the relative absence of political theorizing, as the latter neatly
indicated in the title of his book on the Australasian colonies –
Le Socialisme sans doctrines (1901). The colonist might well
have quoted in reply the earlier observation of Alexis de
Tocqueville that the French interest in general ideas arose from

the fact that for centuries, because of their system of government, they could only speculate on the best methods of conducting public affairs, having no opportunity to correct their ideas by experience. Métin himself wryly confessed that, if Europe was more rich in the doctrines of socialism, these antipodean colonies were richer in socialist realities.

Some writers have gone so far as to suggest that the radical measures of the Liberals were the response of practical men to practical problems and owed nothing to theory. This is absurd; it is impossible to understand their legislation except in relation to contemporary theories. The Liberals had a doctrine, but they were not doctrinaires. As Reeves told Siegfried, his socialism was experimental, not theoretical. Although he believed capitalism would not permanently work, he appreciated that there was negligible support for a frontal attack on it. He endeavoured to secure as much as was practicable for the unionists within the framework of free enterprise. Ballance and McKenzie, too, acted as do all successful politicians – they adjusted their aspirations to fit the facts. But it is easy to exaggerate their moderation. They effected an enormous extension of the powers of the state; in many respects their measures were regarded, in their own day, as socialistic.

We should not apply that term today. Their 'state socialism' may be viewed in a longer perspective. In 1911 no Marxist Party had held power, and, except for short periods in Australia, no Labour Party. Since then we have seen many Labour Parties in office, sparing of socialist measures and seeking to generalize the benefits of capitalism. The New Zealand Liberals were among the first to step on a political road along which millions have since walked towards the Welfare State. Whether it will prove a dead end remains to be seen. That democratic and egalitarian aspiration, that yearning for what was later termed 'social justice', which the Liberals inherited from the pioneering generation and to which they gave a measure of tangible expression decisive enough to mould the future history of the country, is the main element in the New Zealand tradition.

III: COW COCKIES AND RED FEDS

Harmony is impossible between two conflicting forces. Hence the expression 'harmony between capitalism and Labor' is all bunkum.

The Maoriland Worker, 24 November 1911

The farmers of the country should present a united front to the socialistic demands of the proletariat, and to the semi-socialistic legislation of the Government.

Auckland Provincial Executive of the Farmers' Union, 1908

FROM the mid-nineties until 1906 New Zealand was ruled by a benevolent despot known as 'King Dick'. Successive elections became little more than plebiscites which registered the over-whelming public approval of the leader. Richard John Seddon, this colonial king, rid himself of Reeves in 1896; by 1899 McKenzie was too ill to take part in politics; Stout was pro-moted to the political silence of the Supreme Court. Neither in the cabinet, where he surrounded himself with men who, with the exception of Ward, were nonentities, nor in the House was there anyone to rival Seddon's pre-eminence. He had a remarkable presence. Whether at public meetings, on the race-track, or in a bar, he drew ordinary men to him – and won their votes. The 1890 election has been likened to that of 1828 in the United States. Seddon became New Zealand's Andrew Jackson, and the picture drawn of the American leader in a recent history may aptly be applied to the New Zealander.

The contemporary campaign picture of him as an illiterate, irascible, rabble-rousing radical was far from the truth. He was not learned, but he was by no means ignorant and his mind was sharp. He was a pragmatic man . . . who recognized and seized opportunities with an almost incredibly accurate sense of timing. He possessed, as one contemporary remarked, a scent for the trail of political opinion as delicate as a bird dog's; he was peculiarly adept at following when he seemed to lead.

The impression of Beatrice Webb, a cultivated woman ac-customed to the society of English politicians, is not without interest. When she met Seddon in London in 1897 she thought him 'incurably rough in manner', 'a gross, illiterate but forceful man, more like a Trade Union official in such an industry as steel-smelting than an M.P.'. A year later, when she and her husband visited Seddon in his own kingdom, she recognized his great courage and ability. Though he still seemed 'intensely vulgar', he was also 'shrewd, quick, genial'.

While Seddon ruled, the Conservative Opposition was at successive elections reduced to a disorganized, apathetic and by 1900 leaderless handful of whom the *Sydney Bulletin* remarked in 1902, 'They have hardly [in a dozen years] carried even a snatch division on a question about a culvert on a back-country road. They could hardly remember how to draft a Bill now, and they have forgotten what success looks like.' Noisier, but scarcely more formidable, was a group of independent Liberals whose chief ambition was to fill their countrymen's tankards with cold water or hot tea. Seddon's despotism forced these men, including their able leader, T. E. Taylor, into a carping and factious opposition which led them ultimately to silly and discreditable lengths such as making accusations of corruption which they could not substantiate.

Seddon's generous nature was not restricted by too nice a conscience, and he habitually went beyond the stricter dictates of political morality in helping his friends, filling the Civil Service with 'temporary clerks' of the right political colour and handing out other favours where expedient. His critics screamed corruption, but to the Webbs, 'fresh from the Augean stables of America', 'the customary Government favouritism and genial tolerance of fallen human nature' seemed 'peccadillos'. In all probability there had been more serious political corruption in the days of the oligarchy than during the Liberal period. The worst feature of the Seddon régime was an intolerable pettiness. Seddon was known to have hauled a minister over the coals for ordering a new scuttle. As a senior Civil Servant wrote privately: 'Fancy being Premier and having to decide whether you would give a billet as charwoman to Mrs Jones or Mrs Brown, and what effect it would have from a party point of view.'

At first Seddon was little more than an ordinary politician preoccupied with the acquisition and exercise of power. He seemed to his intimates rather to despise the worshipping voters and to regard them as pawns in his game. In a cabinet meeting in 1901 he gave Ward the following advice on his political tactics: 'You should always keep something up your sleeve for next year. Keep the b—s on a string and then they'll keep you in office.' But with advancing years, finding his authority so easy to maintain, he yearned for higher things and sought not merely to rule but to serve his people. His proudest boast became, 'I am a humanist.' In innumerable ways he sought to improve education, labour conditions, or the welfare of widows or children, and to consolidate administratively the earlier legislative advance. Nor was that momentum quite lost. In 1903 he pushed through a measure of immense importance, the introduction of free places in secondary schools. There was, however, no more radical legislation like that of 1894. As rising prices and easier access to the land satisfied the small farmer; as better working conditions and the wage increases provided by industrial arbitration comforted the city worker; the radical impetus of 1890 died down in the community and in the party. Seddon became a political Santa Claus who, if he could not give each child his desire, at least provided something for everybody. When, in 1899, he tried to join the two wings of his party in a national organization, the Liberal-Labour federation, one veteran Liberal wrote protesting that the Labour interest was a class, not a national interest.

The claim of the Liberals to be a National Party rests on its unreserved adoption of the great principle of equality before the Constitution of their country for all New Zealanders without distinction of person, class or calling. From this follows the obligation that its public policy shall be marked by a broad, human spirit, and that amid the inevitable conflict of interests, the progress and welfare of all shall receive equally careful consideration.

For some years the Liberal attempt to provide adequate satisfaction for all sections of the community was a conspicuous success. By the beginning of the twentieth century the colonists were among the most prosperous people in the world and they were rapidly increasing. Between 1881 and 1921 the New Zealand rate of population growth of 23 per 1,000 per annum was higher than that of any country for which statistics were available. To many travellers New Zealand seemed too good to be true. One of its most enthusiastic admirers, a man who did a great deal to publicize its achievements, was Henry Demarest Lloyd, a noted American progressive who in 1900 published a book about New Zealand entitled *A Country Without Strikes*. To him the absence of strikes – there were none between 1894 and 1906 – and the material conditions of the workers meant that the industrial millennium had arrived. To a New Zealand friend he wrote, 'My greatest trouble is going to be to avoid getting the reputation of being a Munchausen by simply telling the truth about you.' William Cuff, an English Baptist pastor who described his trip to the antipodes in *Sunny Memories of Australasia* 1904), thought that New Zealand was best described in Deuteronomy:

A land of wheat, and barley and vines, and fig leaves,
    and pomegranates;
a land of olive oil, and honey;
A land wherein thou shalt eat bread without scarceness,
thou shalt not lack anything in it.

The settlers were the first to agree; nor was their satisfaction unjustified. Something of the pioneering ideal had been achieved. If the colony was not yet 'God's Own Country', as Seddon alleged, it had secured the reasonable comfort which most of mankind seek. In one respect it touched greatness; in its care for the poor and the laggard. The mood of the Seddonian age was the most expansive that the country had experienced, less flashy than that of the time of Vogel, but more assured because more soundly based: based, the economist would say, on rising prices; on hard work and a just society, the moralist would add; on humanism in politics, the Premier declared.

Everywhere there were signs of confidence. Even the Maoris – though few of them can have known it – had grounds for hope. It was commonly assumed, even after 1900, that they were dying out, but the census told a different story. In 1896 their population reached its nadir, 42,000. By 1901 there was a slight increase. By 1921 there were 56,000 Maoris, as many as at the time of the first census, just before the Anglo-Maori wars.

The reasons for this change are not well understood, but it is likely that a growing resistance to European diseases was more important than better medical care.

The rise in numbers, which indicated that the race had a future, was accompanied by the appearance of a new Maori leadership which began to exert a significant influence after 1900.

During the nineties the principal Maori political responses to European rule, though satisfying to the participants, were not well judged or likely to succeed. In several parts of the North Island, for instance, Maoris refused to pay dog taxes aimed at controlling the numbers of Maori dogs, which worried European sheep. Some Maoris were gaoled.

More important were two movements which aimed at achieving some form of Home Rule for Maoris. In the eighteen-eighties the Maori Kingites twice sent delegations to London to ask the British to grant them Maori self-government. Their requests were politely declined. Then, in the early nineties the King party set up a Great Council, *Kauhanganui*, modelled on the Parliament in Wellington. There was a premier and cabinet, including a Minister for Pakeha Affairs. It passed many Acts of no efficacy. The King, Tawhiao, issued a proclamation banishing all *pakeha* from New Zealand except blacksmiths, carpenters and storekeepers.

Another very numerous group of Maoris, with leaders from North Auckland, the East Coast and Hawkes Bay (districts where many Maoris had been 'loyal' during the wars), set up a Maori Parliament which held sessions from 1892 to 1902. This movement was known as *kotahitanga*, union, a name which went back to the unity movement of the eighteen-fifties. It aimed at the full implementation of the Treaty of Waitangi and interpreted that to mean a form of limited self-government for the Maoris. It wanted the European Parliament to give the Maori Parliament control of Maori land, property and personal rights. But bills to this end introduced by Hone Heke, Member for Northern Maori and grand-nephew of the warrior of the forties, were regularly ignored in the Parliament in Wellington.

Both these movements aimed at improving the lot of the Maoris without accepting complete assimilation by the *pakeha*, but the Europeans were no more willing to tolerate Maori separatism in 1893 than in 1863.

More effective leadership, which involved the selection of more appropriate methods, was ultimately provided by 'old boys' of an Anglican school for Maoris, Te Aute College, who in the late nineties formed an association which came to be called the Young Maori Party. Its leaders were better educated than most Europeans and equally at home in Maori or European society. Its secretary, Apirana Ngata, was a graduate in law and arts. Maui Pomare and Peter Buck (Te Rangi Hiroa) were graduates in medicine. At first the 'evangelistic fervour' of these and other young men to reconstruct and purify Maori society ran into the stone wall of traditionalism, but they learnt the arts of politics. Ngata managed to secure the support of the Maori Parliament, which was itself coming to concentrate on practical questions of land settlement and management.

Though they benefited from old-age pensions and government efforts to improve Maori schooling, before 1900 the Maoris owed little enough to the Liberals. In 1894, convinced by a Royal Commission of the evils of free trade in Maori land, the Government had resumed the chief responsibility for land purchase, but still permitted many private sales. The Liberals' vigorous prosecution of land purchase hastened the approach of landlessness. In 1892 the Maoris still owned about a third of the North Island. They sold a further 3,000,000 acres by 1911. It was a sense that they were selling their future as well as their past that produced a consolidation of Maori opinion at meetings all over the country in favour of ending land sales and of placing the control of their remaining lands in the hands of Maori boards, councils or *komiti*.

The Liberals were not unresponsive to Maori wishes: there was in the cabinet an able half-caste Maori, James Carroll. In 1900 the Government passed two Acts influenced by bills drafted by Ngata and supported by the Maori Parliament. Maori Land Councils were set up to provide for local management of Maori land and to encourage leasing instead of sales. This Act was not a success and was amended by the Government in 1905 partly in response to the growing European demand for freehold. The second Act set up Maori Councils, a form of local self-government to promote Maori welfare. Ngata became the organizing secretary; Pomare and Buck became medical officers. The excitement and value of their work is clear in some remarks made by Sir Peter Buck many years later:

In preaching health propaganda, a good many prejudices had to be overcome as diplomatically as possible. Sometimes an objection could be met by reference to ancient customs or institutions. At a large gathering of the Ngati Ruanui tribe in South Taranaki, the old men raised a violent objection to the action of Maori Councils in urging the building of latrines of the type used by Europeans in country districts. The project was criticized as a *pakeha* innovation absolutely foreign to Maori institutions. It so happened that the story of the first latrine built by Rupe in the tenth heaven had been given to Sir George Grey by a learned man of this same Ngati Ruanui tribe. I was, therefore, able to quote in detail from the Maori text of their own authority and, furthermore, to point out that when their ancestor Turi settled on the south bank of the Patea River, in addition to building his house, Matangirei; his village, Rangitawhi; and other items; he also built his latrine which he named Paepaehakehake. Thus, the latrine was an integral part of every fortified village, but our ancestors had abandoned this ancient institution when they left the hilltops for the flat lands after European contact. Therefore, I argued, the Government was merely attempting to restore an ancient health measure which had been forgotten and was advising a form of structure to suit the change in village sites. I was young and nervous but I mustered sufficient courage to turn to an old tattooed man sitting in a corner of the crowded meeting house and say, 'O Sir! You have the symbols of authority and learning on your face. Tell me, have I lied?' The old man smiled approvingly and replied, 'Speak on, O descendant of Te Rangipuahoaho.' Te Rangipuahoaho was a gifted elder of my own tribe and I have always regarded the old man's commendation as the greatest compliment I have ever received.

Carroll was displeased with the demands of the Maori Councils for more power – full Maori self-government had not been intended – and by 1906 they were allowed to wither away. Their failure encouraged Ngata, Buck and Pomare to enter politics and the European Parliament to seek a more direct influence on Maori welfare. Still, an important start had been made. An American historian, John A. Williams, has written that the Maoris and their problems had assumed 'a new place in national life'.

In 1889, in offering to the public some ballads that had 'a flavour of the colonial soil', the young Jessie Mackay had spoken of the cultural ambitions of 'young New Zealand' and had trusted that 'the dawning of a national spirit' would 'brighten into the noonday of a nation's prosperity'. In vain. The 'march of progress and intellect' of which she spoke soon came almost to a halt, or at best proceeded haltingly. Twenty years later high noon seemed as far off as ever. Nevertheless, though it was not to lead directly to any national literary fulfilment, her verse and that of W. P. Reeves marked a new direction in New Zealand writing.

In 1889 Jessie Mackay published *The Spirit of the Rangatira*. In the same year Reeves and G. P. Williams jointly published *Colonial Couplets*. Two years later there appeared in Christchurch two more volumes from the three poets. Williams was avowedly an 'old chum' writing about his 'adopted country'; but in the verses of Reeves and Mackay, and especially in those written later in the nineties or soon after 1900, may be found the first signs of an indigenous as opposed to an immigrant literature.

The change must have been due primarily to the fact that by 1890 the local-born Europeans at last outnumbered their expatriate parents. In a later chapter we shall see that this circumstance was associated with other evidences of emerging nationalism. Another stimulus to local writing was the depression of the eighties, which challenged the colonists not merely to reconsider the organization of their society and its purpose but to express in prose or verse their sense of injustice or their vision of a better life. In the complacent years after 1900 they were happy to relax in the comfort of not having to think too hard.

The poets of the nineties made a firm distinction between 'poetry' and 'verse'. On the whole it is their 'verse' which has lasted well. Many of their occasional or political verses are expressed in firm rhetoric and witty phrase. When they wrote 'poetry', however, they walked unerringly into all the traps of a poor tradition and produced pale echoes of Tennyson – or

Longfellow. 'Poetry' was pretty. Too often it dealt with sickly, romantic themes from the history and legend of the Celt or Cretan. Their attempts to write on New Zealand themes have served rather as warnings than as guides to their successors. To most modern writers it has not seemed possible to communicate their experience of the bush by describing the flora in the manner of Reeves, or imaginatively to enter into the Maori universe by recounting its legends, as Jessie Mackay attempted to do.

The same may be said of another variety of verse. In the latter years of the century, when the sheep-run, though smaller, was still as typical of the New Zealand as of the Australian scene, many local versifiers wrote of the 'swagger' boiling his billy, of the shearer and his mate, in the approved Australian style. Such writers – David McKee Wright was one – escaped the pretension of their more high-brow rivals, but fell as frequently into sentimentality; they had, however, less far to fall. Their ballads were often entertaining, but the tradition was a stream which ran into the sand.

Occasionally the pioneer poets succeeded in matching manner to mood, in expressing some just perception without overreaching their technical ability, as in Pember Reeves's poem, *A Colonist in His Garden.* Its theme has been an obsession in New Zealand writing, the conflicting claims on the settler of his homeland and his country by adoption. Reeves pictures a Colonist reading a letter from a friend who calls him back to 'England, life and art'.

> Write not that you content can be,
> Pent by that drear and shipless sea
>   Round lonely islands rolled,
> Isles nigh as empty as their deep,
> Where men but talk of gold and sheep
>   And think of sheep and gold.
>
> A land without a past; a race
> Set in the rut of commonplace;
>   Where Demos overfed
> Allows no gulf, respects no height;
> And grace and colour, music, light,
>   From sturdy scorn are fled.

As he reads the Colonist mentally replies that he has turned a desert into his new England, where 'Skies without music, mute through time, Now hear the skylark's rippling climb'; that in his garden he has surrounded himself with

> . . . smells, sweet English, every one,
> And English turf to tread upon,
>   And English blackbird's song.

Then he turns to this fine statement in justification of the pioneering life:

> 'No art?' Who serve an art more great
> Than we, rough architects of State
>   With the old Earth at strife?
> 'No colour?' On the silent waste
> In pigments not to be effaced,
>   We paint the hues of life.

This is plainly a South Island poem; the 'silent waste' was the great plains of Canterbury, almost uninhabited by man or beast when the settlers arrived. The first contributions towards a native literature came from Canterbury where, from the first, there had been a lively tradition of writing gentlemanly occasional verse. Reeves grew up among the cultivated families of Christchurch. Jessie Mackay inherited, in addition, the Scottish tradition of balladry which retained some of its vigour in Otago. Such facts must console the ghosts of Edward Gibbon Wakefield and John Robert Godley for their failures, justify their efforts, and perhaps signify the realization of their larger dream.

Edith Searle Grossman, one of a brilliant group of early women graduates of Canterbury University College, was one of the first colonial-born novelists whose writings deserve mention if they defy reading. As with Jessie Mackay and Reeves, the reformer in her took precedence over the artist. Her early novels were feminist tracts as the former's verses were frequently prohibitionist propaganda.

In art, as in literature, the late eighties and the nineties were a time of great activity. In the chief towns the art societies, art galleries, and schools of art were founded. There was much speculation about the possibility of producing a national art or literature. The first editorial of the *New Zealand Illustrated Magazine* in 1899 heralded the end of 'the era of "colonialism"' and announced: 'We stand in the parting of the ways. The young scion of New Zealand national life has began [*sic*] to awake to a knowledge of itself.' The new magazine would 'be truly New Zealand in matter and in manner'. But once again the cultural ambitions of precocious nationalism were not to be achieved. Of all those who wrote for the *Illustrated Magazine*, the historians and anthropologists such as Guy H. Scholefield, James Cowan and Elsdon Best were to make the greatest contribution to local intellectual life. It is noteworthy, too, that the most successful writings of W. P. Reeves were his histories, *The Long White Cloud* and *State Experiments in Australia and New Zealand*.

New Zealand was not yet able to make her artists or poets feel at home. In this coarse colonial society (where Beatrice Webb thought 'the educated or quasi-educated classes' the most provincial people on the face of the earth) it was still true, as its first historian, Dr Thomson, had remarked forty years earlier, that ditchers were more esteemed than poets. New Zealand was still, as one poet, B. E. Baughan wrote in 1908, 'a country to come'. When Pember Reeves's Colonist, standing in his garden, refused the invitation to return to England and art, his creator had already settled in London. In the early nineteen-hundreds both Katherine Mansfield and Frances Hodgkins (who had been one of the illustrators of the *Illustrated Magazine*), after visiting the Old World and returning, hesitantly, to the colony, departed for ever from its shores. So too did the physicist, Lord Rutherford, another Canterbury graduate. The most eminent New Zealanders of their day in the world of art, literature, or intellect, had to leave in order to achieve their maturity. They were accompanied by a steady stream of their most intelligent countrymen. The 'export of brains' became one of New Zealand's chief contributions to the world. And not brains alone; talent of all kinds joined in the exodus. New Zealand could rarely find a place for its most able children; nor did it, in general, feel competent to estimate their worth. It was possible for a few politicians and footballers, and for Sir Truby King, the founder of the Plunket system of caring for babies, to win a permanent place in local esteem by local achievement. In rugby, domestic politics and child welfare, the New Zealanders trusted their judgement; not so in most respects. 'Young New Zealanders when abroad,' the *New Zealand Times* asserted in 1891, 'can generally manage to hold their own in whatever society they are cast.' The remark revealed not so much smugness as the usual colonial sense of inferiority. To 'hold his own' abroad, to win fame abroad, was the hall-mark of the New Zealand Hero.

There were other more numerous sections of the community who, early in the present century, were becoming discontented with the Liberal heaven. Before Seddon died in 1906 he was under attack from left and right in his own party. There had always been freeholders as well as leaseholders within the Liberal ranks. Each group, increasingly importunate, urged him to adopt its panacea. There had always been employers as well as representatives of labour within the latitudinarian fold. After 1896 some of the latter began to feel that their interests were being neglected. The labour and business sections of the party began to quarrel bitterly over labour policy. The agitation over these two issues led to a double revolt which split the Liberals and led ultimately to the formation of the two chief parties of this century – the Reform Party which, in combination with the remnants of the Liberals, eventually became the modern National Party, and the Labour Party. The Liberals, as in many other countries, were caught in a political no-man's-land between the opposing armies of sectional and class warfare, and either captured or destroyed.

During the Liberal era there was a considerable industrial expansion, notably in the clothing and processing industries, but also in the metal trades, in printing and in saw-milling, and in new industries such as wire-making, fibrous-plaster works and electrical supply. The number of industrial employees rose by two-thirds, while the arbitration system, which offered its benefits only to registered unions, encouraged the multiplication of trade unions. In 1893 there had been only thirty-seven, but by 1906 there were two hundred and seventy-four. The workers once again began to feel their strength and some of them to overestimate it. The fact that the average membership of unions was in 1906 only about a hundred and twenty-four suggests the extent to which unionism was an artificial creation of the state and lacking in natural vigour. The unionists were by no means the most powerful section of the community. They carried less weight with the Government than the farmers, and no more than small shopkeepers and business men. As early as 1895 Seddon had declared that the country had had as much labour legislation as it could swallow. Some of the urban wage-earners began to speculate whether they might do better by following the example of their Australian brethren and establishing their own party instead of supporting the Liberals. In 1898 a Trades and Labour Conference resolved that a Labour Party should be set up. Seddon tried to forestall them by founding the Liberal-Labour Federation, but he was unable to satisfy Labour's demands for more radical legislation without offending his middle-class and farmer supporters. As Edward Tregear, the brawny, ardent, Utopian socialist and poet who was Secretary of the Labour Department, wrote a few years later: 'There had been a feeling (perhaps unconscious) that they [the Government] had to settle every Session how few bones could be thrown to the growling Labour Dog to keep him from actually biting.'

Soon after 1900 the workers had an additional grievance – that they were not sharing proportionately in the country's increasing prosperity. The Arbitration Court judges, now somewhat less sympathetic than formerly to the unions, refused to adopt suggestions that they should introduce profit-sharing and contented themselves with fixing minimum wages. From 1902 to 1906 wages were nearly stationary while the cost of living grew dearer; 'effective' wages, measured in terms of food and housing, began to decline, and despite some recovery about 1910, remained markedly lower than in 1903. In 1906 there was a strike for the first time in a decade. Meanwhile the employers, who had been hostile to arbitration, were coming to regard it as a leash for the now quite unruly Labour Dog.

In 1904 the Trades and Labour Councils at last set up a Political Labour League which supported several candidates in the elections of 1905 and 1908; in 1910 it was succeeded by the first Labour Party which was two years later reorganized as the United Labour Party. It comprised a group of Trades and Labour Council officials and ex-'Lib-Labs' (Liberal-Labour supporters). Its programme reflected the moderate radicalism of its founders, not least that of its chief architect, 'Professor' W. T. Mills, a visiting labour evangelist from Milwaukee. It opposed monopolies, in the American progressive tradition, but was not socialist in the sense of aiming at the abolition of private property. There were, however, political groups further to the left.

About 1901 a Socialist Party was founded in several towns by followers of the English socialist, Robert Blatchford, and other cliques. Edward Tregear described this party, one of the leaders of which was an American called La Monte, 'a firebrand agitator', in a letter to H. D. Lloyd in Wisconsin:

> We are suffering from the presence of a small body of mutineers. . . . They call themselves Socialists; they are really the drunken, shirking, fringe of trade-unionism, who deliriously think that because they are failures, and the Street-Arabs of Individualism, they would become the shining lights of a better social order. How little they know! Oh that I had them by the neck in the Socialist's world of two centuries ahead!

In 1908 various socialist groups established the New Zealand Socialist Party, a weak organization that lasted for a few years. Its programme was notable for the influence of the syndicalist doctrines of the newly founded I.W.W. (Industrial Workers of the World) which had been brought to New Zealand by a miner returning from the United States. This man, Pat Hickey, and W. T. Armstrong were the only New Zealanders prominent in the radical movement of the time.

Hickey helped Paddy Webb and Bob Semple, two Australian socialists and future New Zealand cabinet ministers, to form branches of the Socialist Party on the West Coast. Then they led a more formidable 'mutiny' against the 'Lib-Labs'. In 1908 there was a local strike which aroused the miners against the industrial conciliation and arbitration system. They formed a Federation of Miners which soon expanded to become the Federation of Labour, to which, within a few years, were affiliated a number of other unions including most of the miners and waterside workers.

The 1912 constitution of the 'Red Federation' began with the preamble of the I.W.W. constitution which, in turn, parroted the phraseology of Marx and Engels:

The working class and the employing class have nothing in common.   .

Between these two classes a struggle must go on until the workers of the world organize as a class, take possession of the earth and the machinery of production, and abolish the wage system. . . .

It is the historic mission of the working class to do away with capitalism.

In contrast to the United Labour Party, the 'Red Feds' eschewed political action. Like the I.W.W., they hoped that the growth of trade unionism would form 'the structure of the new society within the shell of the old'. They would fight in the factories, not on the floor of the House; not the vote but the strike would be their weapon. Consequently they were bitterly antagonistic to the arbitration system which sought to minimize class antagonism, to do away with the need for the strike by improving labour conditions peacefully, and thus to keep capitalism functioning smoothly.

From 1908 onwards a number of unions cancelled their registration under the Arbitration Act in the hope of gaining better pay by direct negotiation with their employers or by striking; others went on strike in defiance of the awards of the Arbitration Court; but the total number of strikes was quite small. The 'Red Feds'' rejection of the principle of industrial arbitration was not generally accepted by working men even within the Federation of Labour, which included only perhaps a fifth of unionists. In a country with no large-scale industry there were few strong unions except on the wharves and in the mines and railways; unions with small or scattered membership found the arbitration system a blessing. Moreover there was too little of that 'hunger and want' to which the I.W.W. preamble referred to produce more than a handful of revolutionaries. Only a few workers were convinced by Marxian dogma that the state could never promote their welfare. The majority still seemed to regard their 'historic mission' as the achievement of bourgeois living standards, of bourgeois respectability, rather than the abolition of the bourgeoisie. The 'Lib-Labs' and the Trades and Labour Councils spoke for the majority of workers when they demanded higher wages and criticized the administration of arbitration rather than the system itself. The 'Red Fed' leaders were so far in the vanguard of the proletariat that they were out of sight of the main body of unionists.

The growth of industry was paralleled by the much more rapid rise of dairying; between 1896 and 1914 butter production went up nearly 500 per cent and the output of cheese by over 1,000 per cent. Dairy produce became a major export. The 'cow cockies' became an important, numerous section of the community; and one long resentful of the influence of organized labour. An opportunity to make themselves heard more clearly came in 1899 when some well-to-do farmers formed a Farmers' Union. By reason of their numbers, the 'cockies' quickly became the dominant influence in the new organization.

The appearance of 'unionism' among farmers led to an accentuation of a feature of political life which, though not new, had not previously been very important: the rivalry of town and country. According to a popular cliché, the farmers were 'the backbone of the country'. Since the export of primary produce was the basis of New Zealand wealth, it followed that the welfare of the farmers should be the first concern of the Government. The general aim of the Farmers' Union was to see that the Government appreciated the force of this argument.

One of the specific objectives of the Union was the abolition of the very moderate protective tariff. In the eyes of many a farmer the 'townies' were mostly parasites who, sheltering behind the tariffs, lived by selling him dear and inferior goods. Moreover, the farmers considered that the tariff, by creating jobs in unnecessary industries, was responsible for the shortage of rural labour.

Soon after 1900 the Union adopted a second major objective: to secure for those farmers who occupied land on lease-in-perpetuity, the right to acquire the freehold. There were several reasons why many of the class of small farmers brought into being by John McKenzie now wanted the freehold. They feared that, if for any reason they gave up their lease, they might lose the value of the improvements they had made. More powerful was the feeling that not even a 999-year lease provided a tenure as secure as private ownership, which enabled the farmer to enjoy his acres at his ease and to pass them on without question to his heirs. Love of the land was not, however, as ubiquitous as the zest for gambling. From the earliest times until the present day the New Zealand farmers, as might be expected in a country where local tradition and ancestral piety are newly rooted, have been speculators in land values. This is revealed by the very high rate of land transfer. From 1900 until 1937, for instance, while the value of farm production was quadrupled, it has been calculated that mortgage indebtedness rose sevenfold and the land transferred from one owner to another was greater than the area of the country! One of the aims of the holders of leases-in-perpetuity was to cash in on rising land values. The Farmers' Union demanded for them the right to purchase their land at roughly its original value, which would enable them to sell for a handsome dividend – the 'unearned increment'.

Only 10,400 farmers, a minority of the state tenants and far fewer than the number of freeholders, occupied land on the lease-in-perpetuity in 1907. Not all of them, by any means, wanted the fee simple, as events were to show. Yet the demand for it was an explosive ingredient in politics. 'Freehold' became the focus of a system of socio-political attitudes. It was a potent symbol, evocative of a whole political creed; a catch-cry irresistible to rural conservatives and individualists. The freehold, it was proclaimed, would build up a nation 'independent, free, thrifty, sturdy, and clean, both physically and morally'. As in the earlier Grange movement or the farmers' Alliances in the United States, there was in farmers' unionism a strong puritanical streak. Rural life was regarded as essentially wholesome; the morality of townsmen was (and is) suspect. Like the Yeoman of England, the small farmer stood (in his own eyes, at least) for strong and simple virtues. The cry of 'Freehold' aroused the farmers to great fervour; it was given point by the existence of the 'Red Feds' and the land nationalizers. To farmers the future seemed to lie between socialistic, loafing 'townies' and hard-working, individualistic, freeholding countrymen. Once a party was able to present itself as the standard-bearer for the rural way of life, the support of a majority of farmers was assured.

The issues were not, of course, so clear-cut. The farmers were not as individualistic as they imagined. For instance they combined to form their own butter and cheese factories, over half of which, by 1903, were 'co-ops'. They looked to the state for cheap loans and assistance of all kinds, so that J. G. Findlay, one member of the Liberal cabinet, felt justified in declaring 'it's all Socialism – but it's farmers' socialism'. Nevertheless, though the country, like the town, continued to have faith in the state, there was a definite split in the Liberal movement; one which had been inherent in the Liberal creed and policy since 1890. The radicalism of Reeves had led to even more radical doctrines and to the establishment of political parties appealing specifically to unionists. The enthusiasm of McKenzie for the welfare of small farmers had encouraged the rise of a new group of individualistic capitalists.

In the programme and sentiments of the Farmers' Union there was clearly a basis for a new political party. In 1902 a group of Opposition members of the House of Representatives, led by an Auckland farmer, William Massey, were discussing the formation of a Country Party. Again in 1910–11 the Farmers' Union was debating the same possibility. But this move was forestalled when the existing political Opposition adopted part of the programme of the Farmers' Union and absorbed its potential rival. When a Country Party was established in the twenties, at the same time as similar parties in Canada and Australia, it had little success.

For some years after its formation the Farmers' Union operated as a non-political organization (its motto was 'Principles – not Party') in the sense of refusing to back either the Government or the Opposition. Neither party had promised to grant the freehold on the Union's terms; both accepted the tariffs, the maintenance of which was urged by both the unions and the Employers' Federation. Moreover, the Farmers' Union was precluded from taking sides because its membership included Liberals as well as Conservatives. Instead it endeavoured to influence both parties. Candidates in rural electorates were urged to approve its programme, tactics which led to the return of increasing numbers of freeholders as Liberal members.

The difficulties which the rise of vociferous sectional opinion on the left and right of the Liberals created for the Government were immense. It was being pulled apart by opposing political magnets. J. G. Ward, who succeeded Seddon as Premier in 1906, found that he had little room for manœuvre. In 1906 the Minister of Lands and Agriculture, Robert McNab, introduced a bill strengthening the leasehold. The opposition was so strong that it was dropped. Next year Ward tried to meet the wishes of the freeholders, whether Liberals or not, by abolishing the lease-in-perpetuity. In its place he introduced short renewable leases with periodic revaluations. The tenants were given the right to buy their land outright at its current value. Had the farmers' agitation arisen solely from a desire for the freehold, this should have satisfied them; but the agitation continued unabated. Ward could not give away the 'unearned increment', by selling the land at its original value, without alienating the leaseholders. He did try in 1909 to go further towards meeting the Farmers' Union's terms, but the outcry from the radicals in his party pulled him up short.

Perhaps the Government's difficulties were insoluble. Certainly Ward seemed less able than Seddon to cope with them. Everything seemed to be going against the Liberals. In 1907-9 there was a brief recession coinciding with the 1908 election. The Government's programme of 'a rest in legislation' had little appeal. Twenty-one per cent of the qualified voters rested at home on polling day. The Liberals lost a number of seats, mainly rural, to the Opposition. Established farmers in long-settled areas had rarely voted Liberal. But pioneers on new, rough land had needed government assistance and voted Liberal. Now, with state aid and hard work, they, too, were becoming prosperous, were beginning to think like successful farmers, and to vote for the Opposition.

While Ward tried to stand as still as possible between business and labour, freeholders and leaseholders, the Opposition was advancing with increasing confidence towards power. In the eighteen-nineties, while the parliamentary Opposition became increasingly ineffectual, a group of National Associations, which had been established by business men and some farmers, like William Massey, had been quietly promoting conservative views and conservative candidates. These organizations looked back to, or derived from, the Reform Associations of 1887. In 1903 Massey had become Leader of the Opposition, which had been leaderless for four years. He was supported, from 1905 onwards, by the Political Reform League, which succeeded the National Associations. This was potentially an enormous improvement in the prospects of the Opposition, because of the superior organizing and campaign technique of the Reform League. Massey was prepared to adopt Seddonian electioneering tactics; was ready, so it seemed to the older generation of conservatives, to stoop to conquer. Moreover, though not one of the unpopular and discredited estate-owners, he was a farmer who could be identified with the rural virtues.* Yet the Opposition remained weak. In the 1905 election it was reduced to fifteen members. Estate-owners and business men did not provide a sufficiently large nucleus for a rich man's conservative party.

In 1908, with the help of the League, Massey's Opposition made some ground. Next year it adopted the name 'Reform Party' and by 1911 it had accepted the freehold policy of the Farmers' Union which, now partially reconciled to accepting the continuance of tariffs, was converted for the time being into an organ of the political Opposition. But the Opposition was itself transformed into a poor man's conservative party that derived its chief support from the dairy farmers. It did not propose to overturn the immensely popular Liberal legislation except with regard to the grant of freehold. It promised a reform of the Civil Service and honest administration. As an

---

* According to tradition, Massey was building a haystack on his farm in the Mangere district when a telegram arrived asking him to stand for Parliament. The message had to be handed up to him on a pitchfork. Had Massey been a radical, some farmer would have remarked, instead, on the symbolic fact that *mangere* is the Maori word for 'lazy'.

agrarian and business party, it promised a firmer resistance to the militant unions and a halt to 'socialist' legislation.

At the election of 1911 the Reform and Labour vote rose considerably while the Liberal support, diminished at the extremes, fell from sixty per cent to forty-one per cent of the European votes cast. Reform won most of the North Island rural seats, whose importance was out of proportion to the number of rural voters. Since the eighteen-eighties the electoral system had included a 'country quota' which, by adding a fictitious twenty-eight per cent to the rural population when electoral boundaries were determined, gave the countryside that much extra political representation.

In the following year the Liberals fell after twenty years of power. Their fall meant more than a change of government: it represented a shift in the social and geographic location of power. Since the gold-rushes and the Maori wars, the South Island had been the wealthier and politically the more influential. The growth of dairying meant the growing importance of the North Island, with its mild winters, generous rainfall, and good pastures throughout the year. In the twentieth century it increasingly became more populous and richer than the South Island. With the election of a small farmers' Government, the southern predominance in politics was also at an end.

Massey gave the freehold to the holders of the old lease-in-perpetuity. The years 1912 and 1913 witnessed the most violent scenes since the Anglo-Maori wars as the Government, the employers, and the 'cow cockies' smashed the 'Red Feds'.

As early as 1901 Edward Tregear had foreseen how a recalcitrant union which withdrew from the arbitration system might be forced back under the Act. If no registered union existed in a trade in any district, it was possible for any fifteen persons to form one and obtain from the Arbitration Court an award which would then apply to all the workers in the industry. Members of the previous union would be obliged to join the new one. This device, which, unionists complained, gave them the choice of 'starvation or arbitration', was first employed against a labourers' union in Auckland in 1911. In the next year it led to violence in the gold-mining town of

Waihi when the Miners' Union, which had cancelled its registration and joined the Federation of Labour, went on strike. An 'arbitrationist' miners' union (the strikers used the older and blunter term of 'scab' union) was formed. The owners brought in strike-breakers, including a good number of 'toughs'. The Government moved in large detachments of police who protected them. There was a series of clashes between the strikers and the strike-breakers or the police. One of the strikers was killed, most of their leaders were imprisoned and many more were driven out of town by the strike-breakers while the police looked on.

The forcible action of the Government and employers at Waihi served to some extent to consolidate unionist opinion. Almost every union in the country was represented at a 'Unity Conference' in 1913 when the 'Red Feds' and most of the United Labour Party joined forces to form two new organizations, the United Federation of Labour and a Social Democratic Party. The president of their political party was Edward Tregear, once the head of the Labour Department, but now disgusted with the arbitration system he had helped to found. In the new constitution the I.W.W. preamble was dropped, but despite superficial signs of compromise, the new organizations were dominated by 'Red Feds'. Labour unity was still some way off; an I.W.W. group refused to join, while the 'single taxers' and some of the 'Lib-Labs' kept the more conservative United Labour Party in existence. The majority of unions did not affiliate with the new Federation, having no inclination to risk their status under the Arbitration Act by striking.

The 'Red Feds' had not so far tried to call a general strike. During a waterside strike in Timaru the conservatives had tried on a small scale the experiment of enrolling farmers as strike-breakers. In 1913 both sides had an opportunity thoroughly to test their main armaments; and the 'Red Feds'' biggest gun misfired.

On the Wellington wharves a 'lock-out' led to a strike. One strike led to another through the ports and mining towns. The Government formed a force of 'special constables'. The Farmers' Union organized its effort on military lines and enrolled mounted farmers as 'specials' and others to form 'arbitration-ist' unions to work the wharves and even to man ships. Naval and military forces protected them. In Wellington there was some fighting between the strikers and 'Massey's Cossacks'. The 'Red Feds' called a general strike, but, except in Auckland, where for a short time there was a general stoppage of work, the unionists ignored them.

The challenge of the 'Red Feds' to the arbitration system was decisively defeated. Some of them were imprisoned for sedition. In the Waikato the Prime Minister handed out medals to the dairy farmers who had acted as strike-breakers. Next year aggressive instincts were given a larger outlet and, during the First World War, a wave of patriotic fervour completed the rout of 'foreign socialism'. The Federation of Labour was disrupted and the Social Democratic Party dwindled to insignificance. For the 'khaki election' of 1914 there was no national Labour organization. Candidates were nominated by the Social Democrats, Trades and Labour Councils and Labour Representation Committees formed by local Labour groups. In addition there were some Independent Labour candidates.

Massey was bitterly disappointed by the result. The Reform vote rose considerably, but despite his appeals for loyalty to the Empire, despite his stand against the 'Red Feds', despite freehold, he won a majority of only two seats. Labour retained its representation of six seats. In 1915, when Ward joined Massey in a wartime coalition, the Labour members became the official Parliamentary Opposition.

The greatest barrier to the advance of Labour had been the fraternal warfare between militants and moderates. This was, if not ended, at least contained when, in 1916, the various Labour and Socialist groups formed the present Labour Party. Socialism was still the objective, but the new party accepted the arbitration system and the necessity of constitutional processes of change instead of industrial revolution. In 1913 the militants had learned something of the power of Parliament. But another reason for their new willingness to co-operate with the moderates was that they entertained the contemporary delusion of international socialists that the war heralded the collapse of the capitalist system. Hence it was essential that the workers should be united and ready to take over, even if the class-conscious vanguard had to make concessions of principle to secure that unity. They also wanted Labour solidarity to oppose conscription, which they feared might disrupt the radical movement.

So the dream faded. The Liberal dream of a national unity overriding sectional differences, of effective equality, of 'a fair go' for all, had not fitted the facts of a capitalistic life. When would it take shape again?

IV: NEW ZEALANDERS AND BRITONS

It may be well to notice here that as Auckland considers herself to be the cream of New Zealand, so does New Zealand consider herself to be the cream of the British empire. The pretension is made in, I think, every British colony that I visited. I remember that it was insisted upon with absolute confidence in Barbados . . . that it was hinted at in Jamaica with as much energy as was left for any opinion in that unhappy island; and that in Bermuda a confidence in potatoes, onions and oleanders had produced the same effect. In Canada the conviction is so rife that a visitor hardly cares to dispute it. In New South Wales it crops out even in those soft murmurings with which men there regret their mother country. . . . But in New Zealand the assurance is altogether of a different nature. The New Zealander among John Bulls is the most John Bullish. He admits the supremacy of England to every place in the world, only he is more English than any Englishman at home. He tells you that he has the same climate, – only somewhat improved; that he grows the same produce, – only with somewhat heavier crops; that he has the same beautiful scenery at his doors, – only somewhat grander in its nature and more diversified in its details; that he follows the same pursuits, and after the same fashion, – but with less of misery, less of want, and a more general participation in the gifts which God has given to the country. . . . All good things have been given to this happy land, and, when the Maori has melted, here will be the navel of the earth. I know nothing to allege against the assurance. It is a land happy in its climate; – very happy in its promises. . . . I must specially observe one point as to which the New Zealand colonist imitates his brethren and ancestors at home, – and far surpasses his Australian rival. He is very fond of getting drunk. And I would observe to the New Zealander generally, as I have to other colonists, that if he would blow his own trumpet somewhat less loudly, the music would gain in its effect upon the world at large.

ANTHONY TROLLOPE, *Australia and New Zealand*, 1873

EVER since the late nineteenth century New Zealand has commonly been considered the most dutiful of Britain's daughters. It is a reputation which many New Zealanders, especially Prime Ministers, intent on making an impression in London, or on securing commercial concessions, have fostered at every oratorical opportunity. Few Canadians, Australians or South Africans have cared to contest the claim – though George Reid, the Premier of New South Wales, debated it hotly with Seddon at the Colonial Conference of 1897.

In New Zealand anti-British prejudice has been less vocal or widespread; local national sentiment less aggressive and later in developing than in the older colonies. It is indisputable that the people have, in general, remained attached – attached, a modern Prime Minister has said, by bonds of sentiment, trade and debt – to the United Kingdom. But their reputation for a somewhat excessive devotion has not always been justified and it obscures the ever-changing quality of their feelings for their ancestral homeland. In New Zealand the Union Jack has been hoisted over some unlikely projects and for many motives.

More than to any other single cause, New Zealand originally owed her name for clinging to the motherland to the policy of her Government, from the eighteen-eighties until the First World War, in supporting the campaign for imperial federation. Although most of the other colonial Governments at times pursued the same ideal, New Zealand alone was persistent. Her attempts, by means of federation, to strengthen the imperial ties which Little Englanders and colonial nationalists sought to loosen, was often interpreted as implying a distaste for local autonomy, a desire to follow safely behind maternal skirts. Nothing could have been further from the truth. To appreciate the reasons why many New Zealand politicians were federationists, it is necessary to glance back to a time when the colony's reputation was very different.

For much of the nineteenth century New Zealand was a most troublesome dependent, unwanted in the first place and often regretted. Apart from providing the usual run of native wars and financial difficulties, the colony's affairs seemed to breed contentious advocates: first Wakefield, then Grey, obstinate and casuistical, then a series of politicians independent and pertinacious. The disputes began before the first New Zealand Company ships hoisted sail at Gravesend and continued with little intermission until the end of the Maori wars. Then came Vogel, who seemed to one of the harassed Colonial

Office staff 'the most audacious adventurer that perhaps ...
ever held power in a British Colony'.

The colonists received their self-governing constitution, in
1852, after relatively little opposition; and responsible government, in 1856, with remarkably few restrictions. Their Parliament even had the power, subject to the British right of
disallowing colonial legislation, to control waste lands and, after
1857, to alter their constitution, two of the matters which Lord
Durham had thought should be subject to direct imperial control. Like most other colonists, however, they were dissatisfied,
and devoted themselves to whittling away what powers remained in the hands of the Governor and the British authorities.
Before the Maori wars they tried to dictate native policy, despite
the fact that Governor Gore Browne had reserved it from ministerial control. After the Maori wars, when they had won the
right to govern the Maoris, there were plenty of other causes of
friction.

At times their demands were too extreme for other colonies.
In the years 1868–73, for instance, when the Australian and
New Zealand colonies were agitating for the right to make
reciprocal tariff agreements, Vogel went further and, in the
name of 'fiscal freedom', demanded the right to negotiate trade
agreements with a foreign power, the United States. In addition he urged the abrogation of British most-favoured-nation
treaties which forbade colonial tariff preferences to Britain
unless they extended to Germany and Belgium. On the first
point he was not supported by the Australian Governments,
and his demands were ignored, but the British Government
gave way over the issue of inter-colonial preferences.

At the first Colonial Conference, which was held in London
in 1887 on the occasion of Queen Victoria's Golden Jubilee,
the New Zealand representative again pressed for an independent right of negotiating commercial treaties and once more
received no sympathy from the British or other colonial representatives. At this conference, and during Ballance's ministry, the colony was also active in pressing for a diminution of
the powers of governors.

On the only occasion in the nineteenth century when the
colonists were not eager to extend their autonomy, relations

with Great Britain were at their worst. The exception is instructive. It was the period, during the sixties, when the colonists endeavoured to escape the responsibility for governing the Maoris – which the British Government now thrust on them – because they could not face up to paying for the Maori wars. In the eyes of a good many people in London, including the Duke of Newcastle, the Colonial Secretary, it was a war in defence of the colonists' property; but to the settlers it seemed that they were fighting Britain's war, a war in the cause of Britain's civilizing and colonizing mission.

When the last imperial troops were withdrawn in 1870 the colonists were hurt and indignant at being left unprotected, though at the same time, as Anthony Trollope observed during his visit shortly afterwards, they were convinced that the wars had been won by colonial troops. A few hotheads were heard to mutter seditious suggestions of annexation by the United States. Vogel himself urged that, unless the British Government could guarantee adequate support, it should 'sanction an arrangement with foreign powers that in the event of war the colony should be treated as neutral'. On the whole, however, open disaffection was short-lived. The resentments engendered during the Maori wars merely strengthened the colonists' resolve to secure as much influence as possible over their own affairs and sharpened the tone in which they voiced their demands.

The colonial leaders of the sixties were antagonistic to the British authorities because they were already out of touch with British opinion. They left England in the hey-day of the Colonial Reformers and the Church Missionary Society; and they would not readily abandon the intellectual and emotional baggage they brought with them. But now, in England, the Manchester School of free trade was in session. Colonies were out of favour. The colonists could not really understand why the British troops were withdrawn, because they could not comprehend the economic pacifism of men like John Bright, or Professor Goldwin Smith (one of their chief aversions), who had said that colonies were an 'expensive and perilous connexion'. The *Southern Cross* sneered that 'peace is advocated because peace is cheap'. It seemed to the colonists that, under Gladstone, England was losing touch with her finest tradition, of which they were the chief standard-bearers: the tradition of empire. Empire, Alfred Domett wrote in *Ranolf and Amohia*, was never won

> By slow hack-hearts that never knew
> A spur beyond material greed!
> The mere 'utilitarian' crew
> Whose huckstering God is only Gold;
> That 'cheaply bought' is 'dearly sold',
> Their sordid creed and single heed.

The colonists never reflected how much they owed to the free traders. There were no American revolutions in the nineteenth century because Great Britain was disinclined to resist the colonists' demands for increasing freedom. More than to any other factor, this compliance was due to the influence of free trade doctrine, which denied the economic value of colonies, while affirming that their political destiny was independence. What impressed the settlers was a parallel effect of free trade thought – the disinclination of Great Britain to extend her imperial commitments by further annexations; for they had never ceased to believe the conclusion which a New Zealand pamphleteer had reached in 1851:

'Be fruitful, and multiply, and replenish the earth, and subdue it.' This blessing, first pronounced on man, would seem indeed to have been peculiarly inherited by the British people

Some of the colonists adopted this attitude in another question, as productive of disputes with London as the Maori wars, that of imperial expansion in the Pacific. Even in the eighteen-forties Grey had visions of a British Empire in the Pacific centring on New Zealand. In the same period Bishop Selwyn launched the Melanesian mission, thus creating spiritual claims to responsibility among the islands. Later Vogel repeatedly urged that New Zealand should be allowed to 'earn for reluctant Great Britain ... a grand island dominion', and wanted to annex Samoa, Fiji, indeed most of the islands in the South Pacific. Robert Stout took up the mission in the next decade. Simultaneously the Australians followed a similar policy. But Great Britain turned a deaf ear alike to these requests and to the colonists' gloomy warnings with regard to German or French ambitions in the Pacific. There was something ludicrous in the grandiose pretensions of the settlers. At the spectacle of —

> Vogel and Seddon howling empire from an empty coast
> A vast ocean laughter
> Echoed unheard. . . .

In general the British Government regarded annexation as a last unwelcome expedient to be resorted to only when naval visits, consular representation, 'spheres of influence', protectorates, and so on, had proved inadequate. Queensland's annexation of New Guinea in 1883 was repudiated just as Stout's offer to annex Samoa in the following year was snubbed. The Colonial Office was too shrewd not to see that the colonists were calling on Great Britain, in the name of the British Empire, to pursue imperial interests of their own.

The programme of 'Oceania for the Anglo-Saxons' was largely inspired by traders in Sydney and Auckland, the main centres for South Pacific commerce. Vogel's scheme in 1874 to form a company to colonize and civilize the South Pacific islands, for instance, was suggested by Frederick Whitaker and other Auckland business men. Nevertheless, it remains true that the settlers saw themselves as carrying on the British imperial mission. With Kipling, they asked,

And what should they know of England who only England know?

Some of the colonists set out to recall Great Britain to her task. The Royal Colonial Institute in 1868, the Imperial Federation League in 1884, the British Empire League a decade later, all numbered among their most energetic founders colonials, Canadians and Australians as well as New Zealanders, living in England. The reaction against the anti-imperialist views of the extreme free traders has been traced to the protests of these 'Anglo-colonials' against the withdrawal of imperial troops from New Zealand in 1868. In the last two decades of the century, the New Zealand colonists welcomed 'the revival of imperialism' and the adoption of a more truculent policy by the British Government. They took up the imperial chorus with practised voices. Great Britain had at last seen the light.

The great epidemic of chauvinism, of exaggerated and aggressive nationalist or racialist doctrine, which infected many

European peoples at this time, which carried the United States to war with Spain, Germany to *Weltpolitik* and disaster, in British countries took the form of jingoism. The fall of Khartoum and the death of Gordon produced a flood of sentimental and obstreperous verse in New Zealand, while New South Wales sent troops to the Sudan. In the same year, 1885, there was an exaggerated fear of a war between Britain and Russia. J. A. Froude, who was in New Zealand at the time, found that 'the patriotism of the colonists was inflammable as gunpowder'. 'Auckland wearied me with its valiant talk.' This feeling reached its height during the South African War when the Canadians, Australians, and New Zealanders vied with one another in helping Great Britain to repress the Boers. In Christchurch the meetings of a few courageous pro-Boers, an epithet applied to independent men, like T. E. Taylor, who tried to regard events with some detachment, were broken up by youthful zealots singing 'We're the Soldiers of the Queen', and the speakers were pursued home by the mob. This sort of hysterical 'imperialism', compounded of a crude and intolerant racial prejudice and militarism, as much as of love of the motherland, was to persist in New Zealand for a long time.

The articles of faith of the first generation of colonists were these: that it was the mission of the British to expand and rule the uncivilized world; that unfettered self-government was the birthright of those chosen spirits, the colonists, who carried out this noble task. Both ideas were inherited and accepted by the New Zealand Governments of the late nineteenth century, but it was becoming increasingly obvious that something was lacking in this simple creed. How was it possible to reconcile the affirmation of the value of empire with the fact of the steady extension of colonial autonomy? It was difficult to conceive of an empire consisting of fully autonomous units. Was the fate of the empire envisaged as a constant state of expansion and disintegration? Where, in short, was the empire going? In New Zealand some politicians, including Sir George Grey, foresaw, in the dim, rosy future, a supra-imperial polity, English-speaking union, as the answer to the problem. Somewhat more popular, however, was the idea of imperial federation. In 1885 the House of Representatives, though not in a very serious mood, simultaneously adopted resolutions favouring both these ideals.

As long ago as 1852, John Robert Godley, the founder of Canterbury and one of the foremost advocates of colonial autonomy, had foreseen the need for an 'Imperial Congress' to administer the common business of England and her realms. In the eighteen-sixties Vogel had advocated the same ideal. Between 1884 and 1893 the Imperial Federation League came and went, rent by internal dispute, and dispirited because of the lack of public interest. Federation, it was clear, was not politically feasible in the foreseeable future. A number of organizations launched a campaign for the lesser objective of an 'imperial council' which, without legislative or executive power, might perform a useful advisory function in matters of common interest and would perhaps prove a step in the direction of federation. This project was advocated by some of the New Zealand Liberals. At the Colonial Conference of 1897 Seddon supported Chamberlain in arguing for a council, against the protests of most of the Australian Premiers, who believed that it would amount to creating 'fresh political bonds'. In 1905 W. P. Reeves took a leading part in inducing the Secretary of State for the Colonies, Alfred Lyttelton, to suggest to the colonies that the Colonial Conference should be transformed into an Imperial Council with a permanent secretariat. At the 1907 Conference the chief advocates of a council were New Zealand's J. G. Ward and Alfred Deakin of Australia. The former, in 1911, put forward an ill-considered and confused case for an imperial 'council' or even a 'parliament'. The Liberals' aim, throughout these years, was not merely to reconcile colonial autonomy with imperial unity or co-operation, but at the same time to extend New Zealand's power of influencing her own destiny.

In urging the House of Representatives to send troops to the South African War, Seddon had argued that, by helping to bear the burden of empire, they would build up a case for having a voice in its government. In this remark lies the clue to the hope which lay behind New Zealand support of imperial federation or an imperial council: the hope of acquiring a voice in the formulation of British foreign policy. This was the chief remaining restriction on the powers of the colonial government. War, peace, and the general direction of foreign relations were still determined by the British Government without consulting the self-governing colonies. The New Zealand leaders hoped, however, for more than a right to be consulted in an imperial council. They wanted, Ward informed the Imperial Conference of 1907, 'a distinct line of demarcation between the responsibility we accept of our own free will and the responsibility which may be imposed on us without prior discussion'. Above all, he said, they wanted to keep clear of England's 'continental troubles'. The Liberals were not content to follow Britain's lead; they dreamed, indeed, of changing British policy. As Robert Stout explained in 1887 to English readers of the *Nineteenth Century*, Great Britain 'should be as independent of European politics as the United States is now'. Instead of being a European power, she should become 'the centre of a world-wide dominion', the focus of an imperial federation. Part of their plan was to press Great Britain to pursue New Zealand's ambitions of expansion in the Pacific.

The motives of the New Zealand imperial federationists changed with the times. Ward's attitude, which reflected a growing uneasiness about the possibility of German aggression in the Pacific, was markedly defensive in comparison with Seddon's. The arguments they put forward, administrative, constitutional or racialist, varied too. But invariably their policy revealed a great dissatisfaction with existing imperial relations. The Canadians were, on the whole, content with their lot; some of them, like a few British leaders, were beginning to see the way from Empire to Commonwealth. The New Zealand leaders, like the English imperial federationists, were too logical. They simply disbelieved in the possibility that so anomalous an organization as the modern Commonwealth could ever be. Moreover, they were, more than the Canadians, conscious of the remnants of British authority. Asquith's characterization of the autonomy of the Dominions as 'absolute, unfettered and complete' seemed to them mere rhetoric. Great Britain had the right to veto Dominion legislation and the power – soon to be exercised – to commit them to war without prior consultation. The New Zealand Liberals wished to bring the constitution of the empire into 'some kind of harmony' with the conceptions of Asquith, or of Laurier, who had already termed its self-governing peoples 'a galaxy of free nations'. They hoped, however, that the Dominions, once free, would form with Great Britain a federation which would leave their domestic powers of self-government unimpaired, while extending their influence in external affairs. In the nineteen-twenties these roles were to be reversed: the Canadians – and South Africans – were to feel the need to remove all anachronistic vestiges of Britain's old power; the New Zealanders – and Australians – were by then satisfied with their position.

The New Zealand Liberals were less nationalistic in their outlook than many politicians in other Dominions. The Australians and Canadians, for instance, wanted their own navies; the Canadians already looked forward to pursuing an independent foreign policy; but to Ward or Seddon, conscious of the weakness of their own and other Dominions in a world increasingly militaristic, such an independence must be wholly illusory. They thought New Zealand could achieve a more effective independence by influencing the formulation of imperial policy. But enough has been said to show that they had no intention of returning, as some of their critics feared, to an outmoded colonial status. Like the Canadians and Australians, they cherished their independence. Though the talk was now in terms of 'imperialism' rather than of 'autonomy', the fundamental aims of New Zealand policy had neither changed nor become more dependent since the days of Vogel. There were, indeed, signs of a growing maturity of outlook.

In 1885 J. A. Froude had met a gentleman whose views typified the colonial mentality of the first generation:

He expressed the greatest loyalty to England, which he declared to be the universal feeling of the whole Colony; but it was a loyalty which implied that we were to continue to do everything for them – protect their coasts, lend them money as long as they wanted it, and allow them to elect a governor who should be entirely independent of us. He repudiated all forms of confederation, would not hear of a political association with the rest of the empire, rejected with scorn Mr Dalley's notion that the colonies should contribute to the expenses of the navy. . . . Let us do all this cheerfully and then we should see how attached they would be to us.

From 1885 onwards the New Zealand Government showed itself willing to accept some of the responsibilities of autonomy.

Many specific policies of the Liberals were inspired by an emergent colonial nationalism: their protective tariff policy; their adoption of a 'white New Zealand' immigration policy in response to the trade unions' demands; their hostility towards the residual powers of the Colonial Office; their constant endeavour – as Ward said after the colony became a Dominion in 1907 – to 'raise the status of New Zealand'. Ward and Reeves entered Parliament in 1887 as leaders of a so-called 'Young New Zealand' party. Like Findlay and other colonial-born leaders, but unlike most earlier politicians, they thought of themselves always as 'New Zealanders', not as Britons overseas. And Seddon, though a Lancashire lad, had more claims to the title of a national leader than any Prime Minister for thirty years to come.

New Zealand imperialism may best be seen in action in the policies of Seddon who was, needless to say, its loudest spokesman. At every opportunity he embellished his speeches with the heartiest of imperial sentiments, and showed a brash readiness to advise Great Britain and the other colonies on all manner of questions: on the correct (relentless) treatment of captured Boer generals; on the best management of native peoples; or on the necessity of adopting imperial preference. A favourite pastime was abusing the English free traders, 'the sloths and urchins of our public and political life' and ranting about 'the foreign trade cancer' which, for want of preferential tariffs, was 'insidiously at work' destroying the empire. In one speech in London in 1902, blind to 'invisible exports', he announced that England had an unfavourable balance of trade of £161,000,000 and had 'to send out as many golden sovereigns to foreign countries to meet the difference'. On his arrival in London on this occasion, his demands for attention and his determination 'to get a good start' on the other Premiers seemed most inconsiderate to the public servants in the Colonial Office, but they could think of no way (to quote an official minute) to 'avoid giving him a *private* carriage and servants from the first'. Though superior persons found his 'push' very trying, he was the darling of the crowds and the popular press. At the coronation of Edward VII, King Dick earned the place in public esteem which, three coronations later, was to be won by Queen Salote of Tonga.

Sensitive New Zealanders, also, deplored Seddon's 'oratorical indiscretions' and 'clamorous patriotism' which, they feared, were giving 'a sort of Gilbertian complexion to our political life'. More than once he was denounced in the House of Representatives. for squandering the country's liberty by working for an imperial council or an imperial trade policy. That there was no substance to the charge is, however, obvious from the contrast between the noble unselfishness expressed in his speeches and the shrewd regard for local interest to be detected in his policies. After advocating imperial preferences at the 1902 Colonial Conference, he raised the local tariffs against non-British goods, a procedure which involved no sacrifice and conferred little benefit on British manufacturers. Thereafter he threatened that, unless the United Kingdom granted reciprocal concessions, the result must be 'inevitable dismemberment'. Similarly he gave warning that, unless a further penny per pound for mutton was forthcoming, he must negotiate reciprocal trade agreements with foreign countries.

Seddon's love for 'the dear Old Country' did not prevent him from asserting that the fact that Fiji was still a Crown Colony was 'a dark blot' and urging that it should be 'federated' with New Zealand. He wanted part of Samoa and also Tonga, which was a British protectorate. During a visit to the United States he bluntly informed President McKinley of New Zealand's interest in Hawaii. His agitations caused no small stir in the South Seas. From time to time his agents inspired surprising but opportune petitions from chiefs in Fiji who were anxious to come under the sway of his sceptre. On one occasion the Governor of Fiji warned the Fijians that the New Zealanders were after their lands. Presidents and Prime Ministers, too, were less suggestible than island chiefs. The United States annexed Hawaii. Great Britain kept

Fiji and abandoned Samoa to the Germans and Americans. New Zealand was allowed, in 1901, to annex the Cook Islands – a small reward for half a century of pleading.

Though one cannot question the sincerity of Seddon's emotional brand of imperialism, it was equivocal as well as confused, and it served many purposes. Like many kings before him, Seddon discovered the efficacy of foreign adventures as a means of distracting the electorate from humdrum domestic policies. The enthusiasm aroused by the South African War helped him to massacre the Conservatives in two successive elections. Not the least important aspect of its value was the immense personal satisfaction he felt, after graduating from a West Coast Road Board to the House of Representatives in Wellington, in stepping on to the imperial platform in London, where there was elbow-room for his vast energies and a world-wide auditorium for his tremendous voice. From 'Digger's Hut to Privy Council': of course it went to his head. He was not the last New Zealand Premier who, after patting a prince's head, became a chronic sufferer from royal fever.

In New Zealand the colonists welcomed the unprecedented experience of having a Premier who cut a figure in London. They loved the spectacle. Yet for the Liberal Government's campaign for annexing islands or for an imperial council there was neither a public demand nor popular support. In New Zealand, alone of the self-governing colonies, there was no local Imperial Federation League. The Royal Colonial Institute had a tiny membership of the respectable rich. Neither the public nor the Press took more than a languid interest in the Imperial Conferences. Even in Parliament the debates on imperial relations were poorly attended. Of those few members who took the subject seriously as many opposed as supported the idea of federation. The Liberal Premiers made no attempt to interest the public in the proposed imperial council. Indeed they took no interest in it themselves between the Colonial Conferences. Federation or imperial council were Liberal products not for local consumption.

There is no reason for supposing that the electorate would have opposed the creation of fresh imperial ties, though there were strong protests when, in 1911, Ward went so far as to suggest an elected imperial parliament, in which the Dominions' representatives would be outnumbered by the British. In general it is plain that the voters were utterly indifferent. Foreign relations were a matter quite remote from their interests. If they could be said to have had any opinion at all, it was one of satisfaction with the existing situation. They would enjoy self-government within the empire. In Ballance's words, they would be 'New Zealanders and Britons'. Their twin loyalties were neatly revealed in some remarks made by one politician in 1890 in a debate on the question of federation with the Australian colonies.

New Zealand should be a country for New-Zealanders. With the wings of Great Britain over us we need look to no other country or colony for protection ... we are here the pioneers of a great nation, and shall, no doubt, have a glorious future. . . . I think we shall become in every respect a country quite as great as Australia, and with a nationality of our own.

'New Zealand for the New Zealanders.' Such nationalist slogans (it might well, thirty years before, have been the motto of the Maori King party) came into use at the same time as those of super-imperialism. Often the two varieties were used by different people, but they are as frequently found, especially in political speeches, in combination. A nation of imperialists? There was no paradox. The New Zealander never did consider his two loyalties incompatible. Very frequently, however, the shouts of imperialism have deafened historians to the portentous piping of infant nationalism. In literature, in politics, and in trade unionism alike, the first evidences of nationalism are to be detected in this period.

To some extent New Zealand nationalism was imitative of that in Australia, as may be seen, for example, in the formation of New Zealand Natives Associations in Auckland, Hokitika, and Christchurch in the late eighties and nineties, on the model of the similarly-named Australian bodies. But the evidence of national feeling is too widespread for it to be dismissed as entirely artificial.

The growth of the New Zealand nation was very different from that of many new nations. It had few prophets and even fewer of the demagogues, xenophobes or ignoramuses who so often appear as nationalist leaders. It did not arise at the will of a Mazzini or a Cavour, who created a nation by proclaiming its existence or by force of arms; it grew up in defiance of the tradition among the better-educated section of the population that New Zealand was 'the Britain of the South'. The educated and wealthy were conscious of British intellectual and social leadership. A sense of nationality arose first among the in-articulate majority. Its parents were Place and Time.

By about 1890 the local-born European New Zealanders outnumbered the immigrants. They still heard of their ances-tral 'Home' from parent or grandparent, but it was far off, unreal to them. Free from the recollection of another land, which might lead them to assess New Zealand as a visitor would, they grew up with unqualified feelings for their native country. No longer a 'settler', the new New Zealander came to form for his home town or district the same attachment that the Maori had felt long before. He grew up in Christchurch, which looks across the patchwork of the Canterbury plains to the Southern Alps, where

> Rock, air and water meet
> Where crags debate
> The dividing cloud.

He was from Wellington, a town which has somehow elbowed a space between a superb harbour and encircling ranges of aggressive hills. He belonged to Auckland, with its mangroves and mudflats, its reefs, volcanic cones, and dark islands, remin-iscent rather of Fiji than of a temperate land, with its tidal inlets knitting together the sprawling suburbs. He came, perhaps, from some country district: 'Komata ... a dark green creek hung over with yellowing willows and the clay bank scarred with gorse and the water running cold and fast ... Komata with the hills going up behind the crumbling Maori cowshed, gorse bright in the paddocks, a scatter of cows moving in to milking.' Wherever he came from there were, not far away, beaches or hills, with the sombre 'bush', its foliage as much brown or ochre as green, coming down to fence-line, or river-bank, or dunes of black iron-sand. Such familiar scenes inspired a new image of New Zealand in the mind of the new New Zealander.

It is impossible in a paragraph to communicate to the stranger the appearance of the country. It cannot be done by analogy. The New Zealand traveller is often reminded of his country. A gully in California, carpeted with scrub ... a glimpse of the sea over a ridge crested with pines in Provence ... the view across an English moor.... But in its general aspect it is unique. Within a small area there is a remarkable variety of scenery: mountains to challenge the Swiss; 'sounds' to rival the Norwegian fiords; plains so large that, crossing them, a man feels himself in the centre of a continent; beaches to compare with the Australian; beech forest and dense rain forest; a thermal region and glow-worm caves of unworldly beauty. As it was fifty years ago, so it is today, rough, untamed. The farms look newly occupied. The towns, mostly wooden bungalows, each with its eighth- or quarter-acre 'section', appear unfinished, temporary. Man has not been here long, and there is little of his handiwork to admire. What is beautiful belongs to nature – nature which men have despoiled and burned. Only in a few localities is there landscape which resembles the polished, man-made beauty of the English countryside. The light, too, is not veiled as in England; it stares with a Mediterranean boldness. But the historian must surrender the task of description or comparison to poet or painter. If, in this passage, the American or British reader finds nothing to call up in his mind an image of these islands, he may, at least, imagine readily the feelings of the New Zealanders for their home.

Patriotism was confirmed by another sort of local pride. The New Zealanders were proud of their political and economic achievements; and of their success in establishing themselves in a new land. Above all, they were justly proud of their feats of arms – though the justice of their wars is not now equally plain – against Maori, Boer, and soon, Turk and German. In this, at least, they were confident that they were as good as the best. Almost as important was their joy in the feats of their rugby teams one of which, in a tour of Great Britain in 1905, lost only one and that an ever-to-be-debated game with Wales.

Travel, in war or peace, and contact with new immigrants, brought a consciousness of owning to values in some respects different from those of other English-speaking peoples, of possessing, in subtle ways, a manner of life which, though not unlike that in Australia, England or California, had a flavour of its own. One focus of this sense of being different, and therefore of nationalism, was the local use of the English language.

Writing in 1898, W. P. Reeves remarked that he had 'listened in vain for any national twang, drawl or peculiar intonation'. Perhaps he had a poor ear, but in any case what is now generally called 'the New Zealand accent'– though 'intonation' would be a more precise term – must have been the speech of a minority. By the time of the First World War it was probably characteristic of a majority of New Zealanders. It became the subject of heated controversy in which considerations of beauty or effectiveness of speech were usually lost amidst feelings of snobbery or inferiority, an inheritance from class-conscious Britain; for whatever else this local speech may be, it is plainly not that approved by educated persons in the south of England. Only in the last twenty years has there been much disposition among educated people to accept the fact that there is a New Zealand form of spoken English.

The historian must be excused from discussing the fundamentals of New Zealand speech (though he might confess a personal opinion that it is, in quality of sound, far inferior to the English of Virginia or Eire) but he may venture a few remarks on its obscure origins. Climate, so often adduced as an explanation of national differences, seems scarcely relevant. The most important influence was social heredity. New Zealand was settled from every part of Great Britain, and all of the regional and class dialects were mixed up as they never had been in their homeland. A major ingredient seems to have been the speech of ordinary folk in the counties near London from which many of the early settlers came. It is still possible today, especially in Essex, to hear speech strikingly similar to that heard in New Zealand. Strangely enough, some of the same sounds – for instance, the long, flat 'a' in such phrases as 'park the car'– may also be heard among educated Bostonians: it is said that, in the foundation of New England, Essex exerted more influence than the rest of the counties combined. A second important influence was Australian speech,* which New Zealand speech resembles in a great many ways. In England it is a common experience for New Zealanders to be taken for Australians – and in Australia, or North America, for Englishmen.

New Zealand speech developed among children, out of the babel of voices they heard at school – or at home. It cannot, however, be explained simply as a dialectal omelet. The contiguity of so many forms of English, for instance, made people very speech-conscious, a fact which might help to account for one of the characteristics of New Zealand speech at its worst – a peculiar inhibition, a seeking, as it were, to avoid all distinction. A lad who in his native village spoke Lancashire with a warm freedom, on moving to New Zealand, could not but be continually aware that to others his voice sounded unusual, uncouth. A common reaction must have been to develop an inconspicuous mumble.

Another social attitude which led to the same result was the reaction of the mass of the settlers against the British class system and their antagonism towards the ruling classes. In New Zealand if a person used the intonation natural to an English gentlemen he was likely to be considered to be 'giving himself airs'; to be 'affected', even effeminate. The local-born generally took care not to speak what is now called 'standard English'; it was, in any case, the native dialect of only a small minority of immigrants. Lazy speech, poorly produced and badly enunciated, was a frequent result.

All New Zealanders do not, even today, speak with the local intonation. A minority speak 'standard English', while many more attempt to do so, with varying results. It would seem, however, that the pronunciations described in Daniel Jones's dictionary, despite the labours of elocutionists, can never be heard generally in a land where they have always been rare.

* Australian speech was also, no doubt, greatly influenced by London usage, but it is not, as is often asserted, very like Cockney. No one who has compared the Australian drawl with the Cockney chatter (with its glottal stops), or who has heard an Australian and a Cockney say 'How now brown cow', could confuse the two. The diphthong [aɪ] replacing standard English [eɪ] in the first syllable of 'basin' or the second of 'Australian' is, however, a common feature of the two dialects.

When does a nation become a nation? In the sense that a nation is a group of people who, for historical or other reasons, consider themselves to be a nation, its rise is a process never completed. In the case of New Zealand no one could pretend that it has, even today, in all respects outgrown its colonial past and achieved cultural or political maturity; no one could ignore the presence of non-national attitudes among some sections of the community. But these observations imply criteria which would require a nation to be entirely self-contained, and which are, therefore, meaningless. The only useful requirement is that there should be a fairly general sense of nationality in a community.

The beginnings of this consciousness of nationality are in New Zealand to be detected in the eighteen-eighties and -nineties. Thereafter two events were decisive. One was the decision not to join the Australian federation. Grey and other New Zealand delegates took part in the conventions which prepared for federation, and several politicians favoured joining, though probably a majority agreed with Sir John Hall and John Ballance in thinking that the 1,200 miles of Tasman Sea were so many arguments against becoming an Australian state. Yet even in 1900, it was not quite certain that New Zealand would not join. It was believed that a significant section of the population wished the colony to link itself with Australian destiny. Seddon tried to induce Chamberlain so to amend the Commonwealth Act that, for a few years, it would be open for New Zealand to join on the same terms as the original states. But there was no more general a demand for federation with Australia than for imperial federation. Indeed, it is probably accurate to go further and say that the majority of New Zealanders did not wish to become Australians. It had been a basis of New Zealand Company propaganda that New Zealand would be unlike the neighbouring colonies. Sixty years of living in a new country had made the prophecy seem justified to many New Zealanders. Their feeling that they were not Australian was a major influence on the growth of national sentiment. Australians tended to define themselves as non-British. By seeing themselves as 'non-Aus', New Zealanders could continue to feel both New Zealanders and Britons. New

Zealand was to continue as a trading rival of the neighbouring continent and a rival for the hegemony of the South Pacific. In the same period trade with Australia, which had once been New Zealand's biggest market, was becoming of minor importance in comparison with the rising trade with Great Britain.

The close contacts which had existed for a century between the two countries became loose and infrequent. What remained was a feeling of comradeship and a friendly rivalry in which the Australians regarded the 'Kiwis' as genteel country cousins while the latter professed to see the 'Aussies' as coarse fellows whose ancestry, in the interests of courtesy, should be ignored. Significantly enough, the term 'Australasia', once commonly used to refer collectively to both countries, fell into disfavour; the word 'Anzac' (Australian and New Zealand Army Corps), which was coined at Gallipoli, remains to express the close friendship of two increasingly distinct peoples.

The decision not to federate with the Australian colonies committed the New Zealand Europeans, as it were, to continue the process of becoming New Zealanders. They were more alone than before in the Pacific. The other decisive event was the First World War. For the first time the New Zealanders were involved in international responsibilities. Over 100,000 served in the forces overseas and a few thousand more at home: altogether over ten per cent of the population. They fought bravely at Gallipoli and in France. They could brag that they were the first to occupy enemy territory – New Zealand at last secured part of Samoa. W. P. Morrell, who in 1935 first interpreted the history of New Zealand as the growth of a nation, concluded that New Zealand announced its manhood to the world on the bloody slopes of Gallipoli in 1915.

The men who fought, fought for the Empire, but also for New Zealand. The Empire belonged to the realm of imagination : New Zealand belonged to the realm of experience. They thought of it as their country. They might not be reasoners, thinking of nationality in terms of status or of history, but they were nationalists for all that. . . . By the very fact of coming to the Old World and coming in a body, they could not but realize that they had as New Zealanders their own individuality, that they were not, as Seeley had once thought, merely Englishmen living overseas.

After the war there was a very general agreement among the New Zealanders that they were a new nation. But who could celebrate? The cost of fighting for the Empire and becoming a nation was appalling for a people of only a million. Nearly 17,000 men – one in sixty-five of the population – did not return from battle. This death-roll was greater than that of Belgium, which had six times the population and was a battle-field. The total New Zealand casualties, 58,000, represented one in seventeen of the population. Then came the influenza pandemic, which carried off another 5,500 citizens. But it is impossible to count the cost. In many respects the country's growth seemed to falter in the years of mourning after the war. The Government hesitated to grasp the opportunity for independence held out by events. Not until the nineteen-thirties was the national consciousness at last to find its voice in politics and literature.

PART THREE

NEW ZEALAND
1914–1968

TASMAN SEA

Waipu
Puhoi
Auckland
Coromandel Penin.
Mercury Bay
Thames
Waihi (1876)
Bay of Plenty
East C.
NORTH ISLAND
Rotorua
Gisborne
NewPlymouth
TARANAKI
L.Taupo
Napier
Poverty Bay
Wanganui
Golden Bay
Otaki
Norsewood
Dannevirke
WELLINGTON
HAWKES BAY
Nelson
Wairau
Wellington
Greymouth
NELSON
Strait
Hokitika
MARLBOROUGH
WESTLAND
Southern Alps
CANTERBURY
Christchurch
Banks Penin.
Akaroa
SOUTH ISLAND
OTAGO
Dunedin
Dusky Sd.
Southland
Foveaux Str.
STEWART IS.

Scale of Miles

0   50   100   150   200

NEW ZEALAND
1876
Provincial Boundaries _ _ _

I: INSECURITY

And if these things be so oh men then what
of these beleaguered victims this our race
betrayed alike by Fate's gigantic plot
here in this far-pitched perilous hostile place
this solitary hard-assaulted spot
fixed at the friendless outer edge of space.

R. A. K. MASON, 'Sonnet of Brotherhood', 1924

SOME of the great questions which perturbed the New Zealanders in the years preceding the war were answered during
the nineteen-twenties. The dispute between the leaseholders
and freeholders, for instance, faded to a murmur which could
scarcely be heard amidst the din of politics. The Labour Party
tried to carry on the radical Liberal ideal with regard to land by
advocating a tenure known as 'usehold' (their opponents called
it 'loosehold') but soon discovered that it was a liability. No
one could hope to woo the rural voters without acknowledging
their true god whose name was Private Property. Before long
Labour was to find that the way to the farmers' hearts was not
to doubt the god but to nationalize his church – the bank – and
to check the rapacity of the priests.

It must not be supposed, however, because the leaseholders
were almost silenced, that every farmer now had the freehold.
Despite the opportunities which the Reform Government in
1912 and thereafter gave to leaseholders to convert their tenure, by 1928 there was no significant change in the total area
leased by the state.* The area of freehold land had risen steadily
since the eighteen-nineties, as new land was brought into
production, but the area of leasehold had remained relatively
constant. Some fifteen million acres are held on Crown
leases to the present day; much of the best land, as we
have seen, has been freehold since before 1890. The only significant effect of the Reform legislation was on the old leases-in-
perpetuity, but even in this case only 3,000 of the original
11,000 properties had been converted to freehold by 1928, less
than a quarter of the two million acres concerned. Many of the

* See Table I.

farmers who occupied the public domain, having discovered –
despite the freehold dogma – that some types of lease were
eminently satisfactory, made no move to exchange a lease and a
rent for the fee simple and a mortgage. Thus, though the land-
taxers and nationalizers made few converts and lost their
evangelical fervour, a good many farmers continued quietly to
enjoy the favours of their old deity, Public Ownership.

Another crusade fizzled out after the war. The teetotallers
almost succeeded, in 1919, in winning their campaign. Only
the votes of the Servicemen overseas, ninety per cent of whom
voted 'wet', saved the New Zealanders from that unlawful
thirst which tantalized the Americans in the twenties. Thereafter the enthusiasm and numbers of the prohibitionists declined. One minor victory was won by the 'blue ribbon' brigade; in 1917 all bars closed nightly at six o'clock, and they
continued to do so until 1967.

There were other questions which time had answered; but
though in many respects the country entered a new phase of
its development after the war, it would be misleading to exaggerate the differences between one decade and the next. Many
difficulties, still unresolved, have remained to perplex successive governments and generations. Such a problem has been
the industrial arbitration system which has been hit alternately
by the employer's right hand and the trade unionist's left.
Twice, since the First World War, the labour movement has
been split between those favouring strikes and those who looked
to Parliament and arbitration to improve the workers' condition. The greatest problem of all has not changed: the country's
dependence on economic trends abroad.

Because of persisting issues such as these, New Zealand's
development reveals a considerable degree of continuity. Indeed, in a very general sense, its history between the world
wars recapitulates that from the Maori wars to the South
African War. In each case peace brought depression; in each
case the Government resorted to borrowing to stimulate the
economy. The eighteen-seventies were the years of uneasy
prosperity under Vogel's leadership. Though in the mid-
nineteen-twenties there was a marked improvement in economic conditions, these years seemed prosperous only in

comparison with those that preceded and followed them; at the time, people were conscious of the uneasiness rather than the prosperity. In each case there followed severe depressions, beginning in 1879 and in 1929. Twice the electors, dissatisfied with conservative government, looked to financial adventurers – in 1884 Vogel; Ward in 1928 – to rescue them. Both failed, and the voters, still shy of growing radical movements, re-elected their traditional leaders, who introduced economies and hoped the storm would pass. On each occasion ministers, Atkinson after 1887 and Coates after 1931, were forced towards unorthodox policies which alarmed the extreme conservatives without satisfying the radicals. Then, in 1890 and 1935, parties of 'state socialists' were at last granted office by great and enthusiastic majorities. The South African War and the Second World War soon came to temper radicalism with an imperial patriotism.

To watch the riders, to enjoy the spectacle, is often a more enchanting pastime than contemplating the merry-go-round itself, or speculating about the nature of the machinery. William Massey was Premier from 1912 until his death in 1925. Inevitably comparing him with Richard Seddon, who also ruled for thirteen years, historians have emphasized Massey's probity, thus by implication echoing a popular view that the term 'honest politician' is paradoxical. Massey was Seddon's equal as a parliamentary tactician; he was as verbose; he bore quite as excessive a load of portfolios; he was similarly peripatetic in pursuit of voters; he was as hearty and as genial in manner; but he cuts rather less of a figure in New Zealand history. Unlike Seddon he never overcame the limitations of his education and upbringing. 'King Dick' was as unlettered as 'Farmer Bill' but in some respects his boundless ambition carried him to a wider vision. Massey lacked his predecessor's air of greatness or his appeal to the public imagination; he walked on narrower ways and less securely. Seddon, the West Coast publican, was sufficiently flexible to accept the existence of conflicting interests and capable of comprehending something of the problems of farmers, labourers, and shopkeepers alike. Only the bankers and estate-owners were the objects of his permanent suspicion. Massey, the Auckland farmer, however, remained the worthy representative of his class. The premise of Massey's political philosophy, a cliché of the nineteen-twenties, was that New Zealand was 'the Empire's outlying farm'. Many people, apart from the farmers, agreed with his deduction that nothing must harm the primary producers, upon whose output the community's prosperity rested; but it did not necessarily follow, as the Prime Minister seemed to assume, that industrial problems were the invention of agitators. The only consolation he could offer to unionists was to suggest that they raise their wages by working longer hours.

One virtue which Massey possessed and which in Seddon was quite lacking was modesty. He could appreciate ability and welcome in his company men more enlightened than himself or equally able. His first cabinet contained five graduates, three from Cambridge, one from Oxford, and one, Maui Pomare, with an American doctorate of medicine. To one of them, F. H. D. Bell, a member of one of the old oligarchic families, the Premier frequently deferred. It should be added that the policy of the Government reflected the views of its supporters rather than the learning and enlightenment which was gathered in the cabinet room.

Seddon's histrionics encourage colourful description, but most writers have found Massey, though in some ways a more admirable person, a more difficult subject for a verbal portrait. In a private letter, one of the most prominent South Island members of his party wrote of his leader, shortly before Reform came to power: 'Hopelessly stereotyped in everything, lacking one original idea, unimaginative as a clam, unsympathetic as a grindstone, too conscientious to be tactful, he goes on his way guided by a hard, cold, obstinate bigotry which is proof against argument, entreaty, ridicule, or the lessons of the past.' Though it might be phrased in less impatient and resentful terms, this description does give some idea of Massey's qualities. He was an earnest student of the Bible, a Presbyterian from Ulster, inflexible and of narrow outlook. His obstinacy and honesty were inseparable from his religion. He was, everyone agreed, a man of great strength of character, rightly admired for his courage and persistence in the face of adversity.

He encountered little else. The Reform Party was in power from 1912 until 1928 without once winning half the votes; during Massey's premiership, only in 1919 did it win a clear majority of the parliamentary seats. He was, in consequence, usually obliged to manœuvre for the votes of the two parties in opposition. His political career was one long struggle: after nineteen years in opposition, he had to face the strikes, then the war, then the post-war depression. That he endured it all and for so long speaks of uncommon qualities in a man who at first seemed no more than a solid 'country member'.

Although, as W. P. Morrell wrote, it required 'a continuous exercise of imagination to realize that New Zealand was at war on the other side of the world', the country's war effort was out of all proportion even to filial duty. Eventually, however, the endless stream of casualties, the strain of keeping nearly half the eligible male population in arms, began to tell. By 1917 even Ward, whose party had joined with Reform in a wartime coalition, felt that the Dominion could send no more men to feed the guns. In the previous year the more militant labour leaders opposed the introduction of conscription for military service. Some of them, including several future cabinet ministers, were gaoled for sedition. Class feeling continued to be as bitter as it had been just prior to the war. While the labour movement as a whole demanded 'the conscription of wealth' as well as of men, the farmers added a chorus of imprecation against the profiteering of middlemen.

War naturally encouraged centralized authority. The British Government purchased New Zealand's chief exports under a 'war commandeer', thus eliminating competitive marketing. The New Zealand Government in 1915 set up a Board of Trade with power to control prices and later to prevent profiteering and virtually to regulate the internal economy. Where it thought necessary, the Government did not hesitate to supplement the Board's powers with other forms of state intervention. In 1917, for instance, when it considered meat prices were too high in Auckland, the Government opened state shops which sold meat cheaply and forced the master butchers to reduce their prices. Except with regard to price control, however, the administration of the Board of Trade was apathetic; it failed to become, as it might have, the twin luminary of the Arbitration Court in the economic firmament. Nevertheless, business men and farmers found the various restrictions very irksome.

Labour was restless because the economic controls did not go far enough. Although the Board of Trade prevented prices from rising as rapidly as in many countries, they did rise considerably. The unionists, still tied to Arbitration Court awards, found their standard of living falling. There was a new wave of industrial trouble. In 1918 the court was empowered to follow Australian example by fixing a minimum wage for all industries, a practice which was followed until the mid-twenties.

Although the population was in general prosperous, the last two years of war were a time of many stresses. Hatred of Germans welled over on to supposed enemies within the ranks. Wartime frustrations produced neuroses which, like others, found outlets in channels far from their source. Sectarianism, which has often been the New Zealand substitute for religion, produced a second war on the home front.

There had always been much Protestant hostility to the Catholic minority. It centred in the Orange Lodges and found expression especially in disputes over education. Protestants campaigned for non-sectarian bible lessons in state schools; Catholics for state aid for private schools. This rivalry became very heated before the war when Catholic attacks on a Bible-in-Schools League aroused great resentment. In 1913 a Catholic Federation was established to press for 'state aid'. In retaliation the Protestant Political Association was formed in 1917. Its founder was a malignant, bigoted, Australian Baptist minister, Howard Elliott, who believed that Rome was responsible for causing the war.

The *Ne Temere* decree ruling on mixed marriages provided one issue. Wartime provided others, such as a dispute over the conscription of Catholic theological students and teachers. But above all the Irish rebellion, and the sympathy for the rebels expressed by leading Catholics, aroused suspicion of sedition and hostility towards supposed traitors. The air was thick with talk of Catholic plots in the public service. Near-pornographic anti-Catholic propaganda circulated widely. Allegations of immorality in convents and the public horsewhipping of Elliott by the brother of a traduced nun provided a public spectacle. But soon his hysterical excesses alienated all but the most virulent of his supporters.

The P.P.A. was violently anti-Labour, for it regarded that party as dominated by Rome. Nor could it accept the Liberals – Ward was a Catholic. It supported Reform, but Massey, an ex-Orangeman himself, came to find it an embarrassment. Its vigorous campaigning may have played some part in a by-election and in the post-war election, when sectarian tensions were unusually savage. But the sectarian plague died away.

Ward left the wartime coalition in 1919 and announced a programme, calculated to challenge Labour, which included a state bank, nationalized coal-mines, government control of freezing works and a large loan. But to no avail. He lost his seat and the Liberal share of the votes dropped to twenty-nine per cent.

Labour came out with a red-hot blue print for a socialist society. It offered the forty-hour week, a nationalized and free medical service, state banks, state shipping, state factories, and even state farms which, it hoped, would lead to state control of food supplies. Labour's opponents, as for many years to come, concentrated their attack on its opposition to conscription and its alleged sympathy for Soviet Russia. Worse, the Labour Party was even suspected of being pro-German. One newspaper regarded Labour protests against the peace treaty as unpatriotic, as evidence of 'disloyalty to the Empire and of sympathy for the most criminal nation on earth'. The Labour vote rose, however, to almost a quarter of the total.

Reform won thirty-six per cent of the European votes and forty-three of the seventy-six European seats on a programme of shreds and patches: it promised to care for ex-Servicemen and maternity patients; to make a small increase in old age pensions; to grant state assistance in the marketing of primary produce; and to continue imperial preference – a shred of socialism, a patch of patriotism, a humanitarian thread, and an imperialist ribbon on the ragged conservative cloak.

For a little time New Zealanders believed the war had been won. They enjoyed two years of post-war intoxication, and the people who enjoyed it most were the land agents. While the high wartime prices for primary produce continued, enabling the country to share in the British credit boom, the Government spent large sums of money to provide farms for ex-Servicemen. In buying land to cut up into soldier settlements it sometimes paid excessive prices, knowing that this must encourage speculation, in response to what it felt to be an irresistible public demand. In addition it made loans to ex-Servicemen for private purchases. The effect of turning loose 22,000 new purchasers, waving £22,600,000 of borrowed money, on an already inflated real-estate market, may readily be imagined. Veterans swarmed over the countryside, knocking on farmers' doors, and asking them to sell. It has been estimated that nearly half the occupied land changed hands between 1915 and 1924 during an orgy of gambling on land values. Returned soldiers took on a burden of mortgage-debt far beyond their means in the expectation that prices would continue to rise, though there was little reason for their optimism. Already the pastoral industry was thriving because of high prices, not because of increased efficiency – though the quantity and value of exports was rising, there had been a lessening of productivity per person. Now experienced farmers were, only too often, being replaced by inexperienced ex-Servicemen.

The boom lasted only two years. The farmers were eager to return to pre-war competitive marketing; but no sooner was the wartime requisition of the main exports terminated in 1920–1 than overseas prices for primary produce began to fall rapidly. Many farmers found themselves in a desperate position, burdened with mortgages and interest based on the previous high and rising prices. A good many ex-Servicemen gave up their holdings while, over the next few years, the Government had to write several million pounds off the value of soldiers' properties.

Though prices rallied somewhat in 1923–5, they fell again, and continued to fluctuate through the twenties: uncertain prices were the chief source of the pervasive sense of insecurity in the community during the next few years. New Zealand had no 'lost generation'; its flappers were too few to attract much attention; it did, however, have its 'aspirin age'. The cause of the New Zealanders' headaches was more likely to be worry than wine.

The nineteen-twenties saw many changes in New Zealand life. The use of superphosphate manures, tractors, electric milking machines and herd-testing to improve the yield of butterfat per cow led to a great expansion of dairying. (By 1913 New Zealand had already claimed to be the largest exporter of dairy produce.) The rapid adoption of motor vehicles, improvement in road surfaces, hydro-electricity and electric light brought improvement in the lives of many people. Yet wherever one looks at life in New Zealand during the nineteen-twenties there is evidence of a loss of confidence, hesitancy, disillusionment. Life seemed more circumscribed than at any time since the eighties. These were years of loud talk and little faith. And they were followed, in the early thirties, by a period of hysteria. New Zealand became the paradise of the fake magician. The farmers flocked to the many currency cranks and were prepared to believe that 'funny money' might save them from their creditors. In the cities folk crowded into the town halls to be hypnotized in batches by modern medicine men; they carried away 'blessed' handkerchiefs to cure all their complaints. Some of the odder and American religions made a great many converts. In 1933 the New Zealand Legion, a semi-fascist organization (its task, like that of Mazzini's Nation, 'a living flame') sprang up ('unswerving, undaunted and unafraid') to abolish party government and bring dynamic leadership to the nation. Fortunately it was a weed which, flourishing in sour ground, was soon crowded out by healthier growths when rising prices fertilized the land.

Nowhere did the confident affirmations sound more hollow, nowhere was the loss of heart more obvious, than in the country's foreign relations. The Government adopted an attitude of passive regret towards the creation of the modern Commonwealth. Just as Massey had in 1907 opposed the adoption of the title 'Dominion' on the grounds that so pretentious a name would make New Zealand ridiculous, now, in office, he declined to participate in the formulation of the concept of 'dominion status'. Although New Zealand signed the peace treaty separately, entered the League of Nations as an independent member, and was later on her own initiative to negotiate commercial treaties with a number of foreign states, Massey consistently denied that the Dominions were, for international purposes, sovereign states. The Dominions had, he and his colleagues urged, merely entered into a 'partnership' with Great Britain for the management of 'the British Empire as a single, undivided unity'. Massey thought the League utterly useless and a waste of money; international co-operation was not to be compared with the Royal Navy as an instrument for defending New Zealand. Consequently for many years the Government took merely a perfunctory interest in the League; in ten years only three delegations were sent to the annual conferences of the International Labour Organization; the Dominion ratified none of its conventions until 1938.

The Liberals had sought a voice in British foreign policy in the hope of changing it, of deflecting Britain's course from the path of European diplomacy to that of world politics, but all the Reform ministers' talk of 'imperial partnership' amounted to little more than a docile acquiescence in British leadership. They were consulted; they expressed their opinion; they accepted the decisions made in London. Though they believed they were pursuing the same policy as the Liberals, and though their arguments were often similar to those of such Liberals as Sir John Findlay, the spirit of New Zealand policy had changed. So too had the circumstances. It was hardly possible now to mistake the direction in which the British Commonwealth was moving. The New Zealand Government was trying to resist the inevitable. It deplored the Balfour Report, which defined Great Britain and the Dominions as 'autonomous communities ... equal in status' and united only by 'a common allegiance to the Crown'. It sniffed at the Statute of Westminster, which brought the legal position of the Dominions into conformity with their practical status.

To Massey and his ministers the British Commonwealth was a mystical, indeed, they could not doubt, a sanctified institution; a political family: to try to give it legal definition seemed almost blasphemy. Even discussion on the subject was to be deprecated, as one minister, William Downie Stewart, testified: 'To me it appears that there is a certain degree of danger in searching minutely into the advantages and disadvantages of the existing commonwealth association. For such a process is apt to concentrate on the material aspect of the problem and to draw up a balance sheet of gain and losses in which little count is taken of the intangible idealistic and spiritual factors.' Only a minority of parliamentarians, as one Labour member put it, were 'sorry that in this country we should take pride in our insufficiency'. One economist concluded, with much justification, that the New Zealanders suffered from a 'mother complex'– so far had the Government fallen from Seddon's rough assertiveness. Strangely enough, Australia too, rudely nationalistic in the nineties, also declined to adopt the Statute and unqualified independence within the British Commonwealth of Nations.

The failure of political imagination revealed by New Zealand's foreign and imperial policy has been attributed to the influence of Massey, who was not only an Ulsterman, reared, as it were, in England's protective arms, but a British Israelite. It would be difficult to imagine a combination more likely to produce an exalted British patriotism. More generally, the failure must be attributed to an acute sense of dependence brought about by the war and the post-war depression and, most important of all, to the utter dependence of the dairy farmers – and, therefore, of the country – on the British market.

These were the days of 'compulsory loyalism'. 'Patriotism', if one believed the schoolmasters, was a synonym of 'imperialism'. The men had become more self-consciously New Zealanders rather than Britons during the war, but they seemed not to appreciate that, within the British Commonwealth, loyalty to the Crown was not incompatible with an independent outlook in world affairs. In their foreign relations – in which, as in the past, they took little interest – they were still willing to follow the British Government. In 1922 Lloyd George tried to panic the Dominions into sending military aid during the

'Chanak' crisis. The cabinet agreed, after a few minutes' deliberation, without consulting Parliament. Next morning 12,000 volunteered for service without being asked, though whether from imperial fervour, a desire for revenge on the Turk, or from the universal desire of New Zealanders to see the world, no one inquired. There were, however, some signs of a changing outlook. The Labour Party was steadfastly internationalist in its ideas on foreign policy. The existence of the League of Nations Union showed that there was, in the late twenties, a growing minority which took an intelligent interest in world affairs; during the early thirties, as the European fascists and Japanese militarists revealed their aims, there was a more general interest in the international situation than at any previous time. Some of the younger generation grew bored with the incessant talk of British virtue and, an historian observed in 1930, rather resented even the closeness of the country's cultural ties with Great Britain, because they savoured of 'intellectual tutelage'.

One international responsibility the Reform ministry accepted willingly: the result did not encourage further assertions of independence. After the war New Zealand was granted a League of Nations mandate to govern Western Samoa. The Government began to promote economic development, health and educational measures, and a greater measure of local self-government than had existed under German rule. Unfortunately this zeal was not matched by official experience or knowledge and the administration succeeded in alienating the great majority of the population. Local traders were soon up in arms because the authorities began to experiment in marketing copra (the state also took a hand in the marketing of New Zealand primary produce at this time). In 1925 the Government endeavoured to incorporate in its administrative machinery the indigenous governmental institutions of the villages, thus combining democracy and native custom. Official understanding of Samoan custom had not gone far enough. The Samoans regarded the new system of administration as a quite revolutionary interference with their customs. Samoan traditionalism was aroused against the endeavour of the Administrator, General G. S. Richardson, to hasten the inevitable process of change. During the past century Samoan leaders had suffered enough change, including the appalling loss of something like twenty per cent of the population in a few weeks, in one of the most disastrous epidemics of this century, from the post-war influenza. This was brought by passengers in a ship from Auckland, a fact which the Samoans did not forgive. The well-meaning Richardson they regarded as a martinet. The *Faipule* who sat in the advisory council, the *Fono*, they regarded not as district representatives but as government officials. And, as a recent historian has written, even 'the holder of government office was still, in a time of crisis, the slave of the world of custom'.

A Samoan national movement, the *Mau*, which in many ways resembled the Maori King movement, sprang up to resist further Europeanization. Its slogan, which, ironically enough, had been formulated by the Government as the aim of its re-forms, was *Samoa mo Samoa*, 'Samoa for the Samoans'. The next few years were a dismal record of passive resistance (even to a campaign to destroy the rhinoceros beetle), ineffective repression and, in 1929, bloodshed. The lesson learned by the British Government in New Zealand, was now, sadly and slowly, learned by the New Zealand authorities in Samoa: benevolence is not enough.

Party politics in the post-war years exemplify the prevailing state of insecurity. In general, New Zealand political history has been unusually stable. From about 1870, by which time the departure of Governor Grey and the imperial garrison had left the ministry fully 'responsible' for domestic government, New Zealand was, until 1891, ruled by an oligarchy chiefly representative of the pastoralists and speculators. For a further twenty-one years, until 1912, the Liberal Party, chiefly backed by the small farmers and unionists, though with much business support, was supreme. For fourteen years, from 1935 to 1949, the Labour Party held power. Since then the National Party has been in office for all but three years. By contrast, during the intervening twenty-three years from 1912 to 1935 there was an unstable three-party system. The Reform Party, with its small farming and business allegiance, was for most of the time predominant, but its authority was precarious. It was not at any time assured of sufficiently strong support from the voters' to enable it to absorb one of its rivals, or to destroy the other as Labour managed to do in the nineteen-thirties.

It is not self-evident that two parties are better than more, but such has been the general opinion in New Zealand. Throughout the twenties there were frequent suggestions, especially from Reform supporters, that the Liberal and Reform Parties should form a united front against Labour. From 1919 to 1928 there was no significant difference between their programmes. Reform produced no new ideas, after its early emphasis on the freehold. In Parliament Liberals often voted for the Government, even against their own party, in order to keep it in office. In the electorates, however, the two parties competed for votes, and – since Labour had supplanted the Liberals in working-class electorates – for the same votes, those in the small towns, the countryside, and the more prosperous suburbs. The total Labour vote rose fairly steadily from 1905 onwards, though it was so concentrated that the party won few seats (in 1919 only a tenth of the seats with a quarter of the votes). There was a good case for the fusion of the anti-Labour parties, but they remained separate, partly because of the personal antipathy of Massey and Ward, partly because the Liberal Party was kept going by the increasingly feeble momentum of its tradition.

The triangular competition enhanced the importance of party organization and led to an increasing emphasis on the use of propaganda, hoardings, handbills, advertisements, canvassing and other campaign techniques. 'Vote for Coates and Safety.' 'Coats off With Coates.' 'HE CAN BE TRUSTED.' With such slogans, featured beneath enormous portraits of the new leader, Gordon Coates (like Massey, an Auckland farmer); with such implausible assertions of confidence and leadership; and under a clever campaign manager, Reform won its greatest victory in 1925. The same organizer, A. E. Davy, with similar boosting and ballyhoo, helped the Liberals to come back in 1928. Later the Labour Party, more efficiently centralized and with ranks more strictly disciplined than those of its opponents, was to profit by similar methods.

Labour learned other lessons from these two elections. In 1925, though it beat the Liberals and became the official Parliamentary Opposition, it lost votes and seats to Reform; in 1928 it lost seats to the Liberals. Though its total vote continued to rise, Labour realized that even in the towns its position was not impregnable. Forced to acknowledge that it could never win power without broadening its appeal, it was at the same time increasingly impatient for success. Thereafter there was less theorizing, more attention to adapting the Labour policy to changing conditions and immediate problems. Land nationalization was dropped in 1927; credit proposals likely to win the favour of farmers were added to the electoral programme. The formal party 'Objective', 'the socialization of the means of production, distribution and exchange', grew daily more remote, like a fiery comet receding in the political heavens.

To warn the timid employer of the dangers of a new 'Red Fed' visitation was still a useful trick for the conservative candidate. Massey seemed sometimes to imagine that the issue lay between the red flag and the Union Jack: the Union Jack formed an imposing backdrop for Coates's impressive figure on the electoral platform. But the real issues lay elsewhere. New Zealand parties, like those of the United States, were 'sectional alliances'. Politics were in part the rivalry of the regional and other economic interests, town versus country, importer against manufacturer, employer against employee, north opposed to south. There were also considerable differences of principle. The Liberal Party had set the pace: Labour was to take the baton from its failing hand and to continue in the same direction; the Reform Party, like the late nineteenth-century conservatives, was a 'party of resistance' against progress towards the welfare state.

This is not to say that Reform was quite hard-hearted towards the poor. In 1926, largely because of a clever Labour manœuvre during the previous election, Coates introduced a system of family allowances. They were, however, on a very meagre scale, two shillings a week being paid for the third and each subsequent child to families earning less than £4 a week. Children of unmarried mothers, of mothers of bad character, of aliens, or of Asians (whether naturalized or not) were not eligible. Reform also introduced pensions for the blind. In general, however, social legislation fell behind that in several other countries.

The Reform Party was not reactionary; nor was it conservative as a European would understand the term. It was predominantly an agrarian party and was obliged, to a considerable extent, to adopt whatever measures the farmers, and especially the North Island small-farmers, who provided its main backing, wanted. The farmers were in some respects conservative, for instance in their antagonism towards urban radicalism, an attitude which linked them with the urban business wing of the party. But, in a country still being developed, they were by no means opposed to all change. Moreover, they regarded the Government as a committee delegated to solve their problems. The Reform ministry found itself – not unwillingly – introducing radical extensions of state activity to promote the farmers' welfare.

The post-war depression coincided with the return to free marketing of primary produce. Many farmers, interpreting these phenomena as effect and cause, began to revive the demand, originally voiced before the war, for controlled marketing such as they had experienced under the wartime 'commandeer'. There was a general feeling that they were not getting a reasonable share of the price on the London market, and that 'some unfair power must be operating' against their interests. Guided by American anti-trust literature and laws, they looked for the source of their troubles not in their own land speculations, or in the fall of world prices, but in the machinations of 'meat trusts' in manipulating the London market. There was also a good deal of animosity towards shipping 'rings' or 'combines' and some talk of founding a state shipping line.

At the instigation of the Farmers' Union – though some sheep farmers were opposed to this – in 1922 the Government set up a Meat Board and, a year later, a Dairy Board. These Boards were made up chiefly of producers' representatives, though with a few Government members, and were empowered to control the export trade. They could negotiate storage, insurance, and freight contacts, conduct market research and advertising campaigns, and co-ordinate shipping and marketing. It was hoped that, by regulating supplies so as to prevent gluts in London, the Boards would be able to 'influence' the market. The Meat Board acted cautiously and effectively. The Dairy Board was more ambitious and attempted in 1926–7 to fix the London prices. Partly because of dissension on the Board, partly because, the market being over-stocked, British buyers were able to boycott the new season's supplies, it failed dismally. Thereafter it reverted to less comprehensive controls.

To the business community these measures and others like them (similar arrangements were made for selling fruit, honey, and kauri gum) were anathema because they interfered with trade. One Member of Parliament thought the Boards amounted to 'trusts and combines fathered by the Government', and as early as 1926, Coates was called a socialist by businessmen. The Labour Party was critical because marketing was not completely under state control. Its leader, H. E. Holland, said the Boards were 'a species of high-brow syndicalism'. They have also been called 'agrarian socialism'; but perhaps the best description anyone has hit on is 'compulsory co-operation'. The farmers were not too worried about labels.

In pursuit of increased production and exports, the Reform ministers did a great deal for the farmer. They reduced his taxes and subsidized his freight costs. They favoured him when building roads and bridges – which were still allocated on the principle of the 'pork barrel'. There could be no doubt which was the dominant section of the community. But still many farmers were dissatisfied. Most of them disliked the tariffs. Above all, they thought the Government's financial policy too grudging and orthodox. The trouble was that Reform was not exclusively a rural party. It could not ignore its business supporters – nor its economic advisers. But among the farmers there was a deep suspicion towards 'middlemen' which made it difficult for the Government to hold the farmer–business alliance together. Most farmers disliked the tariffs. But, above all, they thought the Government's financial policy too grudging and orthodox. The Farmers' Union demanded an agricultural bank – a land bank – whereas the 'city' insisted on orthodox finance. The Government passed a number of Acts to facilitate rural finance, but these did little to quiet the agitation. The bulk of the farmers' credit was provided by private agencies. The farmers thought this credit too dear and too scarce. In fact it was comparatively cheap; and, in the opinion of economists, the farmers were suffering not from too little but too much credit. The Government, deferring to the bankers, would go no further in encouraging its supporters to get into debt. Some of the farmers, dissatisfied with the 'sectional compromises' whereby Reform tried to satisfy its urban as well as its rural wing, at last, in 1922, formed a Country Party, which advocated free trade, agricultural banks, cheap credit and a farmers' co-operative shipping line. It contested four elections, with negligible success, but it increased the competition for rural votes.

In 1928 Sir Joseph Ward, now a very decrepit 'financial wizard', outbid all his rivals with one glorious last error. In a famous speech he promised a Vogel era of progress based on a £70,000,000 overseas loan. Later the party explained that he had meant to say £7,000,000 a year for ten years (which was no more than Reform had been borrowing), but the conservative Press, which persistently ridiculed his original grandiose proposal, kept that tempting 'seventy million' dangling before the voters' eyes. Droves of them, believing the newspapers' figure, returned to the Liberal (now called 'United') fold, hoping nostalgically that the pastures would be as lush as when Seddon had been the shepherd. United gained in town and country and country town, won as many seats as Reform, and with Labour's assistance, ousted the Government from office. But within a year a cold breeze blew from the direction of Wall Street; the green grass of the country's hopes rapidly withered in the worst economic crisis of the century.

New Zealand could scarcely have been worse prepared to face it, despite numerous warnings. Unemployment had been bad since 1926, though confined to a few industries, so that the Government had tapered off the substantial inflow of assisted immigrants. Prices for primary produce had been very uncertain, and the Reform ministers, who had been the most vigorous borrowers since Vogel, had felt obliged to restrict government expenditure – a fact which helps to explain Ward's victory in 1928. But, in general, the vibrations of the economy had been regarded, not as portents, but as a result of the last gales from the post-war depression. The future outlook seemed fair: in 1929 an economist wrote that the country was just emerging from the depression.

Politically, too, New Zealand's guard was down. There was a weak Government, kept in power by the Labour members, who were increasingly impatient as promised reforms failed to materialize, a sick Prime Minister, and an incompetent cabinet – some of the ministers had never before sat in Parliament. Then, when Ward resigned (and died) in 1930, he was succeeded by New Zealand's most improbable Premier, G. W. Forbes, a Canterbury farmer, and a good, honest man whose political merits will doubtless, one day, be uncovered by some dogged researcher.

Like that of the eighties, the depression led to a clarification of the party structure. For the election of 1931 the United Party at last entered a coalition with Reform and embarked on a journey from which it was not to return. The party of Grey and Ballance was dead, but the New Zealand variety of liberalism lived on in its rivals: the conservatives wore a liberal smile; the socialists spoke in soft, liberal tones.

In three years the national income was estimated to have dropped from £150,000,000 to £90,000,000; the value of exports fell forty per cent in three years. By 1933 there were about 81,000 unemployed, about twelve per cent of the work force. This figure included possibly forty per cent of adult Maori men, although it must be added that a high proportion of them had never been in full-time employment, but had partly lived by subsistence farming and fishing. In the New Zealand community as a whole there was a twenty per cent drop in the real standard of living. To alleviate the suffering implied by these impassive figures was one of the Government's main tasks. Another was to assist the farmers who were hit as hard as the working class. While the farmers' income declined by forty per cent in two years, his costs, including wages and interest, fell only perhaps ten per cent. Something had to be done to reduce the gap between external prices and internal costs.

The Government had a further problem, one which oppressed it even more than the others. From the previous century it had the heritage, to which the wartime Coalition and the Reform Government had added magnificently, of a national debt of truly awesome proportions. It was by 1933 one of the largest, *per capita*, in the world. Half of it was domiciled abroad. Because of falling prices, by 1931–2 it required twenty-six per cent of the country's exports merely to pay the interest, which in 1933 amounted to forty per cent of the total government expenditure!

For several years the Government appeared to conclude that, since the cause of these problems lay overseas in the faulty mechanism of world capitalism, on which New Zealand could have little influence, there was not much it could do. Certainly it contented itself with doing as little as possible. Its chief concern, by increasing taxation and reducing expenditure, was to balance the budget – a feat which could, like those of a gymnast on the Roman rings, be somewhat above the heads of the spectators: by severe economy it might have been possible, as Lord Keynes observed, to balance it at naught on both sides while the population was flat on its back. The Government cut pensions; it cut hospital and health expenditure; it cut education costs by raising the school entry age, lowering the leaving age, and closing two Teachers' Training Colleges; it cut Civil Service salaries; it cut down on public works and thus added to the unemployed: but it balanced the budget.

The Government's main prescription for the depressed conditions was an old one which offered little hope in the short term. It still hoped to increase the production and export of primary produce – at a time when the market was flooded, prices falling as the tide of products rose, and state-subsidized dairy produce was being dumped even on the British market. As one means of achieving this, the Government hoped to get men 'back to the land', thus incidentally relieving the dangerous concentration of unemployed in the towns. The economist, Colin Clark, who visited the country a little later, thought the conservative mind was a museum of economic errors, one of which was 'Physiocracy or the belief that it is essential to have more men on the land and fewer in the towns', a notion long abandoned by economists and contrary to the trend in New Zealand as in most other places.

A great many measures were passed for the farmers' benefit. Innumerable grants and subsidies, paid by the general tax-payer, were made to lower such farming costs as freight charges. For purposes of this sort government expenditure rose considerably. A series of mortgagors' relief acts reduced interest rates. The Government also succeeded in bringing about a considerable fall in wages. For some years the Industrial Conciliation and Arbitration Act had been the centre of a fierce dispute. Along with the banks and the allegedly over-paid and over-staffed Public Service, it was a favourite scapegoat of the farmers and business men. Whereas, in more prosperous times before the First World War, some of the workers had wanted to break out from the shackles of arbitration, while the employers insisted on keeping them confined, now the workers defended the system, which sheltered them from the full blast of depression, while the employers and farmers blamed it for the high wages. In 1932 the Government made arbitration voluntary but kept compulsory conciliation. In the event of conciliation failing, if the assessors representing employers and employees did not agree to submit to state arbitration, the employers could insist on the acceptance of their terms. One union after another was brought to its knees by this sort of conciliation, and wages fell rapidly.

No legislation to deal with mass unemployment existed until 1930, long after Great Britain and other countries had made provision for it. Even then, the sound principle of balancing the budget, which, in the circumstances, seemed to have become a fetish, was incompatible with a humane policy. The Prime Minister, G. W. Forbes, formulated the principle of 'no pay without work', for he believed the British 'dole' to be demoralizing. The unemployed were put to work draining swamps, making roads – or golf courses – planting trees, and were paid a miserable sum partly raised by special taxation. In many of the rural 'relief camps' conditions were extremely primitive; while important public works projects were abandoned, thousands of men were employed on unnecessary tasks which had the merit of requiring little capital and much labour. Each year of the depression the Unemployment Fund had a favourable balance.

J. G. Coates, the minister in charge of unemployment policy, was no stranger to large conceptions. At one critical stage of the depression he took the precaution of asking the army to draw up emergency plans for feeding hundreds of thousands in case of a complete collapse of the economy. But no more than Forbes did he believe in pensioning the unemployed. Rather he would have liked to help people to help themselves. Typical of his approach to the problem was his Small Farms Plan. The traditional solution, full-scale land settlement, was out of the question, but while spending Christmas 1931 on his own farm, he thought of a compromise. Near-by there was a family who owned a small section and lived in some comfort by subsistence farming together with their earnings from farm work in the neighbourhood. This example led him to introduce a scheme for settling unemployed on ten-acre sections, which might prove nuclei for larger holdings, and which would, in any case, provide a better living than starving in the towns. But it was not a success. Casual work was scarce – half the farmers were reported to be bankrupt – and only a few hundred families were settled in this way.

It is as hard now to recall New Zealand in 1932 as it was for people then to remember the hungry eighties: the ragged army of men 'on the dole' – as they called the payments for 'relief work'; architects, teachers, carpenters, chipping weeds on the footpaths; malnutrition in the schools – and children stealing lunches; ex-Servicemen begging outside a pub; the queue at the 'soup kitchen'; a rioter running up a back street, screaming hysterically, 'The "Specials" are coming!' Such sights were daily testimony of how far away was the fulfilment of the New Zealand dream.

Assisted migration was cut off, while the birth-rate declined. Was the young nation to have a stunted growth? Was it to be, in Wakefield's scornful words, 'rotten before it was ripe'? There was nothing like the turmoil in Germany, but even so, frustration and endless misery led to isolated outbursts of spontaneous violence. There was rioting and looting in Auckland and Wellington, ugly scenes elsewhere. 'Special police' were enrolled. The New Zealand Legion formed for its brief, inglorious hour. The Government passed repressive legislation annulling the traditional safeguards of personal liberty. Communists, liberal academics, outspoken public servants were alike penalized for their opinions. New Zealand had reached its nadir.

II: SOCIAL SECURITY

Government is a contrivance of human wisdom to provide
for human wants.

EDMUND BURKE, *Reflections on the Revolution in France*

THE Coalition Government, and especially the do-nothing
Liberals, seemed to have reverted not merely to the retrenchment policies followed by the Governments in the eighteen-
eighties, but almost to *laissez-faire* liberalism. But during 1932
and 1933 several circumstances, all connected with the depression, combined to strengthen the hand of J. G. Coates, the
chief advocate, within the cabinet, of stronger economic measures. One was the riots. Another was the increasing alarm of the
small farmers at the continuing fall of dairy prices (on the
London market butter fell from 183 to 66 shillings per hun-
dredweight between 1929 and 1934). Another was the gloom
which followed the imperial economic Conference at Ottawa.
The Government hoped to assure the farmers' market, first of
all by securing permanent exemption from the new ten per
cent British tariff. Secondly, it wanted a tariff preference on the
British market over the other Dominions. New Zealand's
tariff was only a quarter of Australia's and one of the lowest in
the world. Above all, both New Zealand and Australia hoped
to induce Great Britain to place quotas on imports of foreign
primary produce in the interests of the Dominions. Not 'rugged
individualism' but 'market planning' was the new slogan – and
euphemism. In July 1932, on board the *Aorangi*, which was
carrying the Australian and New Zealand delegations to Ottawa, a hot favourite at the ship's 'race meeting' was a horse
called 'Recovery' by 'Quotas' out of 'Quantitative Restriction'. The name of the winner is not recorded: it might well
have been 'Disillusionment' by 'False Hopes' out of 'Imperial
Unity'.

New Zealand gained from the Conference continued exemption from the British tariff – and on some produce, including
butter, a larger advantage – in return for increasing the New
Zealand tariff preferences on British manufactures. The plea

for a preference over other Dominions was ignored. Market restriction proved to be a boomerang. Great Britain could not afford to alienate the foreign nations who bought half her exports by adopting so discriminatory a policy as the Dominions advocated. But the British delegates arrived at the conference 'fully armed' with detailed proposals of their own. In the interests of the hard-pressed British farmers, Neville Chamberlain announced, Great Britain would regulate meat imports – Commonwealth and foreign supplies alike would be controlled. A few months later the British Government also made known its intention to restrict the importation of butter.

For nearly fifty years the Dominions had sought an imperial policy based on trading preferences and had granted preferences to Great Britain for thirty years. At last Britain had abandoned free trade and granted reciprocal benefits, only to speak in the same breath of market restriction. New Zealand had to recognize, Gordon Coates wrote, that the British market was not bottomless. But it was not merely the New Zealanders' faith in imperial trade which was shaken. The quota proposals were a blow to their larger and liberal view of international trade. They had taken for granted the interdependence of all countries and the soundness of natural specialization of production. Now, at a time when self-sufficiency was the aim of most European countries, a time of egotistic tariffs and restrictive trade practices – in which Great Britain proposed to join – it seemed that this faith in the brotherhood of nations had been naïve. All exporting countries were at a disadvantage, but New Zealand, which had a tiny local market and exported half its products, which had the highest *per capita* external trade in the world, was peculiarly susceptible to overseas conditions. Obviously the Dominion would remain at the mercy of every fluctuation in foreign trade and banking while she continued to be 'one gigantic cow-yard'.

British and New Zealand papers alike invoked the shades of George III and George Washington; but there is no need to discuss the recrimination and heart-burning which followed the Ottawa Conference. The war intervened before the regulation of New Zealand meat exports could do great harm.

Great Britain abandoned the proposed butter quota and also another proposal, to place a levy on meat imports. The chief influence of these events in New Zealand was to strengthen a resolve, which had been growing during the depression, to look to the Dominion's economic defences. Imperial co-operation had proved a broken reed. The only protection against nationalist economics, it seemed, must be economic nationalism. Within a few years New Zealand economic policy was to swing from an exaggerated devotion to imperialism and internationalism to a forlorn aspiration for autarchy.

Since January 1932 J. G. Coates had wanted to adopt one measure typical of nationalistic financial policies during the depression, to raise the exchange rate. A good many farmers and most of the economists were in favour of this move which, it was hoped, would improve the farmers' position by artificially raising his income, and stimulate industry by restricting imports. In the eyes of its advocates, exchange manipulation was the logical corollary of lowering the farmers' costs. The Prime Minister was, however, reluctant, and William Downie Stewart, the Minister of Finance, who was greatly in awe of bankers, would not countenance such political tampering with the rites of finance.

In January 1933 Downie Stewart resigned and Coates became the finance minister. The exchange rate (which had been raised by the banks in 1931 to £110 N.Z. to £100 sterling) was increased to £125 N.Z. to £100 sterling. The Government was at last trying to hit back at the Depression. In the same year the Government set up the Reserve Bank of New Zealand so that it could secure cheaper credit for the state (the banks had been charging an astonishing five per cent on treasury bills), and, more important, so that it could determine general monetary policy. Extraordinary as it seems today, until this time credit policy was determined by private banks, not public authority. Mortgages and state loans were converted compulsorily to a lower rate of interest. A National Mortgage Corporation, partly on the lines of the German land banks, was created in the hope of making cheaper credit available. In 1934 a Commission of Agriculture was formed to regulate the marketing and production of agricultural products. The Dairy Board was empowered to perform the same function for dairy produce.

All of these measures were designed to lower the farmers' costs or raise his prices, to provide the state with supervisory powers over financial policy, and to introduce an element of planning into production and distribution. In these respects, Coates's policy pointed in the direction which the Labour Opposition wished to take; but Labour was not pleased. Although Coates was regarded as financially unorthodox by the more conservative, although he gave budgetary considerations a secondary place, for instance in raising the exchange rate, his policy was formulated in accordance with economic and financial criteria which gave little scope to the humanitarian impulse of Labour. The new powers with which he invested the state were, moreover, incomplete. In the Reserve Bank and Mortgage Corporation private shareholders and directors representing them divided authority with the Government.

The differences between the Government and the Opposition may be illustrated by reference to the Mortgage Corporation. Coates hoped to provide cheaper credit for farmers and to write down existing mortgages; at the same time he wanted to avoid 'piling up' overseas debt. Whereas the old State Advances Department had raised money through government borrowing, the Corporation was to sell bonds which had no state guarantee. To Labour it seemed that a soulless business concern, aiming at profit, had replaced State Advances, which had been concerned with providing a social service. Moreover, loans for house-building were to be restricted in a way which would place great difficulties before the poor man who hoped to own his own house. Labour and Coalition were equally obsessed by economics: to the Coalition the success of economic policies was to be judged in economic terms, in terms of a healthy economy; but to Labour, economic policies must subserve a larger end. 'Social justice,' said Michael Joseph Savage, the Leader of the Opposition, 'must be the guiding principle, and economic organization must adapt itself to social needs.' Coates was grappling with fundamental economic problems, but the Opposition rightly felt that he had not done all he might to ameliorate the effects of the slump on the workers.

By 1935 Gordon Coates was, most unjustly, the most hated man in the country, detested by the unemployed and abhorred by the extreme conservatives. Much of his policy had obviously been shaped by his 'brains trust' of three economic doctors of allegedly socialistic views. A group of ultra-conservatives, alienated by his radical measures, and especially by his interference with interest rates in defiance of 'the sanctity of contracts', formed a highly undemocratic Democrat Party.

Coates had great political courage and quite enough energy to justify the election slogan of 1925, 'The Man Who Gets Things Done'; yet he was a leader who could carry neither his party nor Parliament nor the public with him. But had he been more of a politician – had he made more allowance for the views of his colleagues and his party; had he been more swayed by tactical considerations – he would have done less. When it is recalled that he was not the Prime Minister, that he had to drive from the back seat, his skill deserves all admiration.

The future lay with the Opposition. If the depression had temporarily strengthened Coates's position, it had improved the prospects of the Labour Party immeasurably more, for those measures which seemed to be demanded by the logic of events – or by the illogic of the electorate – were further to the left than he could go.

One effect of the slump was to unite the forces of Labour. In 1919 a new trade union federation, the Alliance of Labour, had revived the tradition of militant unionism, with all its scorn of Parliament (the 'national palaver'), its optimistic, syndicalist talk of 'One Big Union', and its dislike of industrial arbitration. The post-war slump had weakened the Alliance and forced it, by 1924, to modify its aims. Now, unemployment forced it to defend arbitration and support the Labour Party.

When the depression settled on New Zealand like 'a grey and ghastly visitor to the house' – as John Mulgan wrote in *Report on Experience* – a good many people wanted to know who had let him in. There was a quite extraordinary amount of speculation and controversy on economic questions. Marx, Keynes, the Russian Revolution, the 'New Deal', were scrutinized from every angle, not merely in academic institutions, but at trade union and farmers' meetings, and in the clubs and pubs. The correspondence columns of the press were filled with – to the historian – an appalling number of letters on High Finance. This analytical and intellectual approach to social questions tended greatly to the advantage of the party in opposition. Labour was plainly not responsible for the existing mess. It was radical, rational, in its attitude to society. Moreover, it could hum the popular tunes.

A great many voters, especially among the dairy farmers, were at this time attracted to the doctrines of Major Douglas. The social creditites held their first national meeting in 1932. The Auckland Farmers' Union, which had started the Country Party in the twenties, became their ally. Its journal, *Farming First*, helped to spread the gospel. The Banks were to Blame. Like the 'single tax' movement of half a century earlier, Social Credit was a reformist, not a revolutionary movement; many people, who would have been repelled by socialist doctrine, were led by this apparently less dangerous route to the Labour fold. In John Mulgan's novel about 'the bit in between the wars', *Man Alone*, a rural lorry-driver says:

That's what we want then, ain't it? Just the right to control our money. Take over our banks, we'd be all right then. Now I'm no politician, mind you, but that's the way it seems to me. Control the money, we'd be all right. Mind you I'm not one of these reds, don't go thinking that of me. I just want money to do its work the way it ought to do.

Many Labour politicians flirted with Douglas Social Credit, not always discreetly – but was there need for discretion? The Social Credit phrase, 'Deficiency of purchasing power', after all, sounded Keynesian to the untrained ear; and Keynes, to the Labour Party, appeared almost a Fabian. The cause of the present discontents, the Labour leader, M. J. Savage, announced in a pre-election speech in 1935, was 'the money system'; the cure was 'the intelligent use of the Public Credit'. 'Unless we get the equivalent in buying-power of the value of the things we are producing,' he proclaimed on another occasion, 'we shall never solve our economic problem.' The Labour programme, too, seemed by design to echo the sentiments of

Major Douglas. 'Politicians, my dear young lady,' the Major might have remarked, quoting Sinclair Lewis, 'are merely the middlemen of economics. . . . They take the Economic Truth and peddle small quantities of it to the customers, at an inordinate profit.' The emphasis on credit reform undoubtedly won over many farmers. If the use of the charmed phrase, 'social credit' by Labour politicians was often so much hocus-pocus, this was its strength. Credit, the farmers had long seemed to think, was a magical power – source unknown.

During the depth of the depression Labour Party meetings were revivalist gatherings where bitterness against evil times mingled with the most pure visions of tomorrow. In Auckland a radio station known as 'The Friendly Road' run by the Reverend C. G. Scrimgeour ('Uncle Scrim'), broadcast the same evangelistic message in a programme called 'The Man in the Street', which was tremendously popular in working-class districts. Of its theme song, once known to thousands, the author can recall little except its reference to the President in the White House; its exhortation, 'Brother, do your share'; and its comforting assurance:

> There's a new day in view,
> There's gold in the blue,
> There's hope in the hearts of men.
> All the world's on the way
> To a happier day,
> For the road is open again.

There were other respects in which Labour's prospects had improved. The Party had dropped many old socialist 'planks' from its 'platform'. Thus it ceased to alarm middle-of-the-roaders while, positively, it won their support by concentrating on immediate, urgent problems arising from the slump. It had another great advantage in its new leader. Harry Holland, who had died in 1933, though a great socialist 'fighter', was somewhat bitter and inflexible, a little frightening to moderates – he had been in gaol in Australia and New Zealand for his political activities. His successor, M. J. Savage, was a benign, political uncle, cosy, a good mixer, with a warmly emotional appeal. He smelt of the church bazaar and not at all of the barricades. He became one of the few Prime Ministers who were loved by their supporters.

Many left-wing writers have criticized the Labour Party for having no theory, but such remarks mean merely that it did not have the theory its critics expect. It had its own theory, a mixture of Keynesianism, socialism and Social Credit, with a dash of humanitarianism, internationalism and nationalism for flavouring. Its socialism was that of the Fabian Society, or rather, the 'state socialism' of Pember Reeves. Its aim, said a writer in *Tomorrow* (a periodical which, for a time, played *New Statesman* to the Labour Party), was 'to turn capitalism quite painlessly into a nicer sort of capitalism which will eventually become indistinguishable from socialism'. But the party was only two-thirds socialist. Its 1935 election manifesto spoke of taking over the central credit system; of controlling credit, the price level, and foreign exchange; of distributing production and services so as to guarantee 'to every person able and willing to work an income sufficient to provide him and his dependants with everything necessary to make a "home" and "home life" in the best sense of the meaning of those terms'. The influence of Walter Nash, an English Christian Socialist who had for many years been the Party's Secretary, and who wrote the manifesto, may be detected in these words. The Party would socialize the means of distribution and exchange; but there was nothing about nationalizing the means of production, which to a doctrinaire socialist would seem the fundamental issue. The problem, Labour considered, echoing Lord Keynes or J. A. Hobson, was not over-production, but under-consumption: the solution was to foster productive employment, increase the people's purchasing power; to apply fertilizing capital to the ailing plant of the economy. The present misery was due to faulty organization; the cure was to rationalize the economic framework of society by state planning, not to nationalize the productive sources.

'I am among those who believe that, in a fertile country, the standard of living of the people ... should not be influenced by any external factor whatever,' said M. J. Savage in a parliamentary debate in 1935. Obscurantism? *Naïveté?* The declaration pointed, in an exaggerated gesture, to one of the major objectives of the Labour Party: Insulation. It wished to 'insulate' the economy against overseas price changes, against financial influences from abroad. Economic nationalism could hardly go further; economically, it was going too far. An exporting country could not, by definition, close itself off from the outside world. Nevertheless, it did not seem vain to hope at least to mitigate the effects of unfavourable movements in the terms of trade and to shelter New Zealand from their direct onslaught. Much of the Party's 1935 election programme is to be understood in the light of this ambition. For the farmers there was to be a 'guaranteed price'. The state would purchase the farmer's produce, pay him a price based on average prices over a period – thus abolishing the element of speculation in his income – and sell it abroad. Sales in a good year might yield a reserve to be drawn on when prices fell. It was also intended that the 'guaranteed price' should take into account the farmer's costs and the general standard of living in the community; but whether a socially 'just' price would prove to be the same as an average market price remained to be seen.

Labour was also to have its guaranteed price, a statutory minimum wage, and to be protected once more by compulsory arbitration. Finally, by encouraging secondary industry, in order to create a more 'balanced' economy, Labour hoped in the long term to place the country in a better position to withstand economic tremor or shock. For the rest, the Labour Party election plan spoke of utilizing 'to the maximum degree the wonderful resources of the Dominion'; it listed a national health service, educational improvements, the forty-hour week, better pensions. The most profound observation on Labour's intentions was made by 'Micky' Savage: 'We intend to begin where Richard John Seddon and his colleagues left off.'

Labour had recaptured the New Zealand Liberal tradition of state humanitarianism. There were many resemblances between the tasks and actions of the two parties. Both came to office towards the end of a severe economic depression, a time of fervent economic and political soul-searching. Both hoped to diversify the economy, to encourage manufacturers, to improve the lot of the working man. For both the mountain of overseas debt was a dominant feature of the economic landscape. In office, Liberal and Labour alike tried to extend the country's political influence abroad. In office, both were helped by rising prices. But their problems were not identical. In 1890 the major aim of the Liberals was to encourage small farmers, to get men on the land and get the country's dairy products on the world market. By 1935 Labour wanted to protect the small farmer – and the country – from exposure to world market conditions.

At the election of 1935 Labour easily defeated its opponents. It managed partially to revive the old Liberal combination of trade union, small farmer and manufacturer, and to win, as well as its working-class strongholds, a number of middle-class suburbs and rural or semi-rural seats, notably in the North Island, where Social Credit was strong. With fifty-three out of the seventy-six European seats, it had the second largest majority in the country's parliamentary history. The Coalition, now calling itself 'National', offered a moderately progressive policy, but was quite outbid by Labour. The number of its seats fell from forty-two to seventeen. The extreme right-wing Democrat Party was slaughtered. Its programme, anti-socialist, offering to abolish both unemployment and obnoxious taxation, was not sufficiently plausible to win a majority of voters in a single electorate.

The Labour ministry consisted of six ex-Australians, five New Zealanders, and an Englishman and a Scot who had emigrated in their youth. Seven of them had been members of the 'Red' Federation of Labour; six had been on its executive; several had been imprisoned during the First World War for opposing conscription. The Australian influence in the Labour movement, noticed earlier among the 'Red Feds', is worthy of remark; twentieth-century radicalism could be put into practice more easily in New Zealand than in federal Australia, just as, in the late nineteenth century, radicals met less resistance in New Zealand than from the powerful vested interests of conservatism in England or the United States.

The Labour ministers formed a combination of considerable administrative ability. Walter Nash was one of the ablest Ministers of Finance the country had had. The Minister of Health and Education, Peter Fraser, has never been excelled in his management of the Departments. In 1916-17 he had served a prison term for protesting against conscription; but in 1940, when he succeeded Savage as Prime Minister, he proved an admirable war-time leader. He did not win Savage's popularity, but as a politician, and as a parliamentary technician, he was probably the equal of Seddon and Massey. Most of these Labour men were self-educated at the Workers' Educational Association. They had not tired of reading or learning, like so many of the forcibly-educated. Fraser and Nash, in particular, had a breadth of intellectual interest rare in political leaders since the nineteenth century. Other members of the cabinet deserve mention, especially Bob Semple, the irrepressible Minister of Public Works, who added a number of colourful expressions to the language – 'snivelling snuffle-busters', for instance, as a term of abuse.

In a tremendous burst of legislative activity in 1936–8, and another in 1945–6, Labour transformed the State into the Welfare State. Part of the task was to recapture territory lost during the slump. The cuts in salaries were restored, the compulsory arbitration system was re-erected, and the Court was directed to fix a basic minimum wage for all workers. A large public works programme was commenced to provide employment on full wages instead of 'relief'. But Labour went much further than its predecessors could have ventured.

Soon after coming to office, the Government increased existing pensions, introduced invalidity pensions and payments for deserted wives. It began to build state houses, which were let at a low rental. In 1938 the Social Security Act again increased pensions, extended family allowances, and introduced a national health service providing medicines, medical treatment and maternity benefits. Virtually free to the recipient, these services were paid for by a special tax on income. It was, an authority on the subject has written, the first comprehensive and integrated system of social security 'in the western world'.

In 1946 came an equally revolutionary reform. 'Family benefits' were in 1938 paid only for the second and subsequent children of poor families; in 1941 they were given for the first child as well; in 1946 the means test was abolished and the – then – large sum of ten shillings was paid to the mother or guardian of every child under sixteen (or, in some cases, under eighteen) in the country. The number of families receiving these payments leapt from 42,600 to 230,000 – nearly a quarter of a million families partly dependent on the state. Was not the doctrine of 'payment according to need' somewhere on the horizon? Family men paid less income tax, because of deductions for dependants, and received more benefits. The cost rose from £2,000,000 to £12,000,000 in a year. In 1949 social services absorbed 16 per cent of the national income, as compared with 3·3 per cent in 1928; 31·7 per cent of total government expenditure as compared with 19·1 per cent.

It was all very expensive; but it was worth the cost. The state had abolished the fear of destitution, which made a large family seem a misfortune. It had abolished the economic corollary of illness – the fear of not being able to afford a doctor. Men stood now as equal before disease as before death. It was Labour's greatest achievement, the greatest political achievement, indeed, in the country's history. What Caesar has had a more splendid triumph?

New Zealand's social security system was shaped by the ideal of equality; it made men more free. Only a fortunate country could have afforded it, but it was not merely a by-product of reviving prosperity. It was created by the general will – a will which had sought expression from the earliest days; which had been inspired, in the colonial cradle, by the humanitarianism of the missionaries and by the utilitarian creed, 'the greatest good of the greatest number'.

The moral and social effects seem plain: they were almost entirely beneficent. Of the economic effects it is harder to speak. The whole system of social security, taken in conjunction with progressive taxation, has undoubtedly involved some redistribution of income from the rich to the poor and from the single to the married. From another viewpoint, it has been argued that social security has encouraged economic development despite the higher taxation of high incomes. Certainly the volume of production per worker rose remarkably, though many factors were involved in this improvement. Social Security is, however, clearly an investment in the future personnel of industry as well as in the happiness of the citizenry.

The Maoris shared in the benefits dispensed by the Government. The Labour ministers, especially Peter Fraser, endeavoured by every means at their disposal to raise the living standards of the Maoris to the European level. The task they faced was formidable, not merely because of the extreme poverty and bad housing of many Maoris, but for a reason explained in a remarkable minute written by F. D. Fenton, then the Native Secretary, in 1856:

It has been observed by some, that the British power, having bestowed upon the Maories every right to which a white citizen is entitled, is free from any further claim for extra assistance. . . . But, in reality, this is a very unfair argument. When the uneducated Maori is placed side by side with the intelligent and highly cultivated member of an elaborate civilization, he is at once subjected to an amount of competition which first astonishes and ultimately disheartens him. In the great contest for livelihood, for which every member of a civilized community is educated . . . the bewildered Maori clearly distinguishes nothing, beyond an all-absorbing eagerness to acquire property, and suspects the professions which are made to him, that the success and advancement of his own race is an object that interests every European. Unable to endure the social attrition to which he is subjected, he abandons the contest, or pursues it in a listless and indolent manner that can never result in any great measure of success. It is therefore the duty of the governing body, either to relieve him from the liabilities to which he is subject, as one of a civilized community, or by rendering him assistance which the educated member does not require, place him in a position in which the general conditions of success may be equalized.

If the Maoris were ever to enjoy effective equality of opportunity with the Europeans, they needed more than equal assistance. Governor Grey had realized this; so had some of the missionaries; but since the Maori wars, the Maoris had never received as much government aid as the Europeans.

There were definite but unspectacular signs of improvement in the early twentieth century, many of them inspired by the Young Maori Party leaders, Maui Pomare, who was a minister in the Reform cabinets, and Apirana Ngata, a minister in the years 1909–12 and again in Ward's government, 1928–30, and under Forbes. More attention was paid to Maori health and education. Some effort was made to consolidate the scattered land holdings of families or groups of Maoris into compact farms. A system was developed of legally 'incorporating' the owners of a tract of land, who would then elect a committee to supervise the farming. In this way it was possible to follow European agricultural methods while retaining communal ownership. But such experiments seem to have had relatively little effect in the twenties except among Ngata's people, the Ngati-Porou tribe of the East Coast, who began to engage in extensive sheep-farming and, later, dairying.

Whereas everything was done to help the European farmer, since Grey's governorship next-to-nothing had been done to encourage the Maori to become an efficient farmer. The main European aim, as always, had been to get his land. Between 1911 and 1929, despite their Land Councils, the Maoris had sold over 3,500,000 further acres. After that date sales almost ceased, but 65,000 Maoris had only 4,300,000 acres left, at least half of it very poor land, while 1,500,000 acres were leased to Europeans.

At last, in 1920 a Native Trust Office was established and authorized to lend money (from various Maori trust funds) to assist Maori farmers, but it lent relatively small sums. Then, in 1929, for the first time the Government decided to finance Maori land development from public funds. Unfortunately this decision coincided with the beginning of the depression, so that expenditure was necessarily restricted. Nevertheless, it was plain that there was a new spirit among the *pakeha*. In the nineteen-twenties several Royal Commissions had considered Maori grievances. The Government had agreed to pay financial compensation for unfulfilled promises (for example, to grant reserves, or to build schools) made in earlier days in connexion with land purchases. Most important of all, one Commission had reported that, in the case of most of the tribes concerned, the confiscation of Maori lands during the wars of the sixties had been unjust. Substantial compensation was paid to the injured tribes.

Ngata's inspiring leadership in this period was weakened by an irresistible inclination to favour his own tribe and electors.

In 1934 a Commission reported unfavourably on his administration of funds and he resigned. But the Young Maori Party was, in any case, being by-passed by a new Maori movement.

As well as new-style politicians the Maori still had their prophets. One of these, Kenana Rua, led a movement in the Urewera. He claimed to be the Messiah whose coming had been prophesied by Te Kooti and many of the Tuhoe tribe believed him. They called themselves Israelites and followed a religious service like that of *Ringatu*. Rua prophesied that King Edward VII would come and give him money to repurchase all the lost Maori lands. The Europeans would be deported. Even the failure of the King to arrive on the appointed day did not disillusion the faithful. Rua came into conflict with the European authorities over various issues. Although he taught his people not to smoke or drink, he was twice convicted for sly-grogging. In 1916 he was arrested by armed police after a gun battle in which two Maoris were killed. Many people believed that the real motive for his arrest was the suspicion that he was dissuading the Tuhoe from volunteering to go to the war.

Of more lasting importance was the Ratana church, founded by Tahupotiki Wiremu Ratana. In 1918 the Holy Ghost appeared to him in a vision and appointed him the *mangai*, the mouthpiece of God. He gained a reputation for faith-healing and Maoris flocked to join him. His church, Christian but unorthodox by the standards of the others, became (and remains) the largest specifically Maori one. Like other similar Maori leaders he gave his people comfort, hope and ambition. His friends, he said, were 'the shoemaker, the blacksmith, the watchmaker, carpenters, orphans and widows'. Soon, he said they would be in power, 'and I will be the government'.

In 1931 a Ratana candidate, Eruera Tirikatene, captured a Maori seat in Parliament. By 1943 Ratana members held all four Maori seats. During the years 1946–9 Labour held office only by virtue of the support of the Maori members. They were jokingly called 'Labour's mandate'.

Labour and Ratana sought to speak for the underprivileged and to improve their lot. Their alliance was a natural one. And, with the return of prosperity under the Labour Government, the Maoris entered a new era. Now they received some of the extra help they needed. There was a higher expenditure on Maori primary schools, per pupil, than on European schools; particular attention was paid to Maori housing, as part of an ambitious scheme of Maori welfare. In the past, Maoris had been given smaller pensions than the *pakeha* on the specious ground that their needs were less. Labour gradually brought their pensions up to the European level. Similarly, after Labour was elected, Maoris were given the same unemployment payments as the *pakeha* – previously they had been paid on a lower scale. Land development schemes, which had been frustrated by the slump, were pushed ahead and the area being developed was greatly extended. By March 1939, £4,300,000 had been spent on Maori land development. 253,000 acres were being farmed or 'broken in'. By 1946 this area had been increased to 559,000 acres, on which 1,800 Maori 'settlers' were established. Including their labourers, families, and other dependants, it is estimated that 20,000 Maoris (about a fifth of the Maori population), derived at least part of their livelihood from the state schemes.

The Labour Government did not altogether succeed in equalizing the living standards of the two races, but its measures contributed to a marked improvement in Maori conditions.

How were all these gains in human welfare to be safeguarded? By 'insulation'. To protect the farmers against the effects of price fluctuations abroad, Labour introduced state guaranteed prices for dairy produce and assumed complete control over the marketing of butter and cheese exports. At first there were difficulties over setting a price, but during the second World War and for some years after – from 1939 until 1954 – a bulk purchase agreement with the United Kingdom provided prices agreeably high, though below world market prices. By 1949 there were £12,000,000 in the Dairy Industry Stabilization Account; a reserve fund to cushion future falling prices. During the war the system of state marketing was also, in effect, extended to all primary exports, while, from 1937 onwards, the Government also took charge of the internal marketing of dairy and agricultural produce.

In the interests of economic safety, manufacturers had to be encouraged and protected from overseas competition. In 1936 a Bureau of Industry was set up to plan new industries and reorganize existing ones by a system of licensing. This attempt to rationalize the structure of industry had little effect, but, for several reasons, industry expanded rapidly. In 1938 there was a serious financial crisis, due to over-importing and to the flight of frightened capital from the threat of socialism. Severe import restrictions were imposed which, in conjunction with the shortage of imports during the war, gave great stimulus to local manufactures. In 1938–47 the volume of production of secondary industries rose forty-seven per cent while the number of people engaged in these exceeded the number of those farming. The days when the small farmers alone could dictate government policy had passed.

In banking policy, as well as in its control of marketing, the Labour Government went further than Gordon Coates, but along the same road. In pursuit of financial autonomy, it nationalized the Reserve Bank which became purely an instrument of government policy. Thus, Sir Keith Hancock wrote, 'It was New Zealand, traditionally the most dutiful of the Dominions and the one most economically dependent upon Great Britain, who armed herself with the most formidable weapons of monetary self-help.' In 1945 the chief trading bank, the Bank of New Zealand, was also taken over by the state. High trading prices during the war and after enabled the Government to reduce the overseas debt considerably, a step which was thought essential to 'real self-government'. By the end of the war most of the national debt was domiciled in New Zealand. The overseas sterling balances were so favourable that New Zealand was able to make the United Kingdom a gift of £10,000,000 ($20,000,000).

'Welfare' – 'insulation' – meant the State. Perhaps that is the most striking feature of New Zealand history. From the beginning the settlers have sought to achieve their aspirations through the medium of government activity. Farmers' governments or workers' governments alike have extended their sphere of action. Slumps and wars alike have led to further centralization of power. The Second World War, as in many other countries, encouraged what was already the chief tendency of the Labour Government, and speeded the progress towards a 'planned economy' via 'price control' and 'stabilization'. Broadcasting, internal airways, the linen flax industry, were added to the long list of state monopolies; but, in general, the Government contented itself with control over credit and marketing and made no attempt to nationalize production. Though George Bernard Shaw persisted in calling the country 'Communist' when he came on a visit in 1934, it could not, even after the war, be described accurately as 'socialist'. Like Great Britain after 1945, it had a 'mixed economy'. In both countries Labour aimed, in Lord Beveridge's phrase, at the 'socialization of consumption'.

'Insulation' – but not isolation. The weapons of economic nationalism were, in world politics, to be supported by the instruments of internationalism. The Forbes Government had drifted reluctantly into supporting the League and obligations under its Covenant, in the wake of the British Government during the early phase of the Abyssinian crisis in 1935. Now, with the election of Labour there came a transformation of the country's foreign policy and a refreshing willingness to take the initiative. New Zealand at last played an active role in the League of Nations. In 1936 the Dominion was elected to the League Council and, thereafter, supported the proposals of the U.S.S.R. for 'collective security'. In the uneasy years of freedom for Fascists, New Zealand persistently favoured the enforcement of the 'sanctions' against aggressors provided for in the League Covenant, a policy which necessarily involved frequent open disagreement with Great Britain, especially during the Spanish and Abyssinian crises. Of Commonwealth countries, New Zealand alone refused to recognize the Italian conquest of Abyssinia. The idealism was admirable, though often, in the speeches of Labour politicians, 'the League of Nations' seemed a new mystic phrase, with no obvious objective correlative, like 'the Empire' on the lips of the Reform ministers.

In 1939, the pro-British sentiments of old-fashioned 'imperialism' and the anti-fascism of new-fangled internationalism met. When he followed Britain in declaring war on Germany, Savage was able, consistently with Labour's foreign policy, to make the traditional appeal to loyalty to Britain; to declare, what had recently been so demonstrably untrue: 'Where she goes we go; where she stands we stand.'

In 1940 the Dominion of New Zealand celebrated its centenary. In a hundred years the islands had been transformed from a rugged wilderness to one of the most productive parts of the world. There had been loss in the process, wanton destruction of the bush and spoliation of the soil, which had led to erosion; but most of the pioneers and their descendants were willing to spend beauty to buy progress. In 1940 there was no other people so prosperous or so fortunate. Migration, they could say, had been a success. The material and social ambitions of their fathers had been realized in generous measure. In 1939 the economist, Colin Clark, estimated that they had the highest level of real income per head in the world.

To celebrate the event the Labour ministers turned back, not to the 'common colonist', but to Wakefield, Godley, Featherston, FitzGerald, to the cultural ambitions of the systematic colonizers and the colonial gentry. In addition to the customary festivities and exhibitions, the Government arranged for the publication, under the editorship of E. H. McCormick, of a series of surveys of New Zealand life. Among the most able were McCormick's own *Letters and Art in New Zealand*, a work of such discrimination and scholarship as at once to establish the author as the first of his countrymen entitled to be called critic; F. L. W. Wood's *New Zealand in the World*; Helen Simpson's *Women of New Zealand*; and Oliver Duff's urbane description of *New Zealand Now*. At the same time a series of literary competitions brought before the public more worthwhile work than is usually the case with such contests. One of the prize-winning entries was Frank Sargeson's story, 'The Making of a New Zealander'; another was M. H. Holcroft's essay, *The Deepening Stream*, the first of a series of discussions of New Zealand life which, though much criticized since, were at the time immensely stimulating.

To erect a literary monument was an unexpected choice, but, what was more surprising, one which was now possible. During the nineteen-thirties literature had at last found its feet, or at least a foothold, in the new land, after endless, disheartening stumbling. At last there was a small body of work of real merit in its own right and not merely, as is true of most previous writing, of interest to the literary historian. The first significant scholarly monographs on New Zealand history and anthropology had appeared in the early works of J. C. Beaglehole, W. P. Morrell, J. B. Condliffe, and Raymond Firth in about 1930. The new impetus in prose to fiction was to be seen, for instance, in John Mulgan's novel, *Man Alone*, in the novels of Robin Hyde, in the autobiographical writings of D'Arcy Cresswell, but above all, in the short stories of Frank Sargeson, a master of his craft. In the slight sketches for which he first became known, many influences have been detected, notably that of Sherwood Anderson, but the product is entirely Sargeson. The cadences of New Zealand speech have somehow become part of the texture of the general prose and not merely of the dialogue: 'When I called at that farm they promised me a job for two months so I took it on, but it turned out to be tough going.' Something of New Zealand had entered into English writing, instead of being stuck on to it, like a Maori carving over the entrance to a museum – a not unfair description of the work of many earlier writers, who expressed time-worn sentiments in outmoded forms and styles, embellishing them with references to the *kowhai* tree and the Maori.

The 'rebirth' – it has been called – of verse is usually associated with a group of Auckland students and their friends who, in 1932–3, published *Phoenix*, one of those iconoclastic periodicals with which university – though more rarely, literary – history is studded. It was remarkable chiefly for the contributions of R. A. K. Mason who, since 1924, had been publishing a few poems of an intensity and precision previously unequalled. Within a few years, however, A. R. D. Fairburn, Allen Curnow and Charles Brasch, all contributors to *Phoenix*, had established their right to speak as poets. At the same time, the names of J. R. Hervey and Denis Glover, of Canterbury, became known to discerning readers of verse.

Never before had there been more than one or two writers deserving of serious attention; never had there been so many publications of literary merit as in the years 1938 to, say, 1943. Very little verse which today seems worth reading had been published since the age of Seddon. Perhaps the 'Great War' was partly responsible for this: few poets or writers arose from the generation which fought in Flanders fields. What accounted for the change in the nineteen-thirties?

It was scarcely possible to pretend that a demand for poetry had evoked the supply. Ever since the mid nineteenth century there had been endless, idle chatter about the need for a national literature and confident assertions that New Zealand was likely to inspire it. In one of his apostrophes to 'God's Own Country', after surveying the scenery from the Bay of Islands to Lake Wakatipu, Thomas Bracken had reached the popular verdict that

> Here the poet soon might gather subject for a
>   thousand lays,
> Here the artist might discover rich employment
>   all his days.

In fact New Zealand did not want artists and poets; there was no place for them; or, rather, there was no place for them if they were men. If the male poet found 'rich employment', as Domett and Reeves did, it was by serving the state in practical affairs. It was not by accident that the task of tending the arts had been borne chiefly by women such as Jessie Mackay and, succeeding her, Eileen Duggan and Ursula Bethell. There was room only for the artist considered as a young gentlewoman. The male poet, if he were more than an entertainer of the stamp of Thomas Bracken (whose effusions were in the late nineteenth century declaimed on such occasions as 'the O'Connell Banquet' or 'Alice May's Benefit'), was bound to be a rebel. This was as true of Reeves as it is, now, of R. A. K. Mason and his fellows.

The most important fact was that the chief positions offered by the state in the early thirties were on unemployment 'relief works'. The depression preserved young writers, temporarily at least, from safe posts and comfortable domesticity. It accounts in part for the Marxist note in much writing of the time. As in the eighteen-eighties, the failure of society prompted critical writing as well as thought. That New Zealand should appear in Sargeson's stories as a 'rural slum', inhabited by waifs and strays, was by no means inappropriate. On this occasion, however, the literary movement, stimulated by poverty, did not die out when prosperity returned.

The writings of W. B. Yeats, T. S. Eliot, W. H. Auden and other poets in Great Britain were a constant stimulus to the New Zealand poets. These were not, however, merely distant imitators. For the first time since New Zealand was settled, English poets were dealing with issues real to the New Zealanders. The viewpoint of writers in both countries had been influenced by a common experience of war and slump. The example of the greatest British poets incited New Zealanders to write about what they knew – and to write about it in vigorous, everyday language. Consequently New Zealand verse acquired an immediacy, a relevance to the island condition, which it had rarely had before. 'Poetry' had been a subject studied at school: it had evoked Christmas snow when children were sunbathing in their antipodean December; it had called up the nightingale, while a tui croaked and chimed outside the classroom. Certainly it had had nothing to do with life. Local writing had generally been as remote.

Poetry came home; and so did the poets. Many of the writers of the thirties visited Europe and returned. Several testified, on some occasion or other, that the process of becoming New Zealanders had been slow and awkward; some discovered their sense of nationality when they arrived in Europe; others on returning to New Zealand. Of them could be said what the American critic, Leslie Fiedler, wrote: 'the end of the American artist's pilgrimage to Europe is the discovery of America.'

As E. H. McCormick observed of Robin Hyde, the writers of the thirties in general 'reached a stage of equilibrium between paralysing subjection to the prestige of England and strident nationalism'. 'Remember us for this, if for nothing else,' Robin Hyde had written; 'in our generation, and of our own initiative, we loved England still, but we ceased to be "for ever England". We became, for as long as we have a country, New Zealand.'

That 'paralysing subjection' was not too strong an expression; and that a declaration of intellectual independence was a necessary step, may be gauged from some comments written in

1937 by J. N. Findlay, a British philosopher who was then a professor in Otago – not one of the centres of the literary revival. In an article on 'The Imperial Factor in New Zealand', published in the periodical *Tomorrow*, he remarked on the 'visionary and idealized England, which absorbs the emotional energies of New Zealand, and which keeps it permanently in a state of feeble-mindedness and infantilism'. 'At present anything less English than the "loyal" New Zealander's notion of England,' he wrote, 'can scarcely be conceived.' It was, in his judgement, these 'spurious loyalties, not in any way culturally significant or fruitful, which prevent [New Zealand] from facing her individual destiny.'

Much of the writing of the thirties was very conscious of 'becoming New Zealand'. As in the United States and other European countries of the New World, there was an intimate connexion between national sentiment and the development of a local literature. It was only a phase, but a necessary one. To revolt, to stand some distance off from ancestral tradition, was an essential preliminary not merely to *New Zealand* writing, but to good writing in New Zealand, to writing from a New Zealand experience. The intellectuals were bringing up the rear, a long way behind most of their countrymen; but the fact that they had at last, somewhat reluctantly, and not without nostalgia for their cultural 'Home', accepted the facts of geography and history and had begun, as Allen Curnow wrote, to make 'a new discovery of their country', was a hopeful sign for the future. Whatever the ultimate status of the writers of the thirties may be, they have an important place in the history of New Zealand.

III: THE 'COLD WAR' BOOM

... the ideals of New Zealanders: to live in a country with
fresh air, an open landscape and plenty of sunshine; and to
own a house, car, refrigerator, washing machine, bach,
launch, fibre-glass fishing rod, golf-clubs, and so on. These
aims are relentlessly pursued, and widely achieved ...

C. K. STEAD

NEW ZEALAND history changed dramatically in a few days in
December 1941. Previously European New Zealanders had
often acted as though their country lay somewhere near
Europe. They had given little thought to the Pacific. There had
been a vague anxiety about Asia, uneasy talk about 'the yellow
peril', but these were remote fears, wraiths disturbing the
fretful sleeper. A British naval base being built at Singapore
would, conservative New Zealand governments between the
wars believed, keep potential Asian aggressors at bay, even
though there was no British Pacific fleet to station there.

On 7 December the Japanese attacked the American base at
Pearl Harbor, in Hawaii. Three days later two powerful
British warships, H.M.S. *Prince of Wales* and H.M.S. *Repulse*,
which had been sent out instead of the promised fleet, were
sunk by the Japanese. The supposedly impregnable Singapore
base surrendered in February 1942 after a brief campaign. New
Zealand was almost defenceless. Most of the New Zealand
forces were in the Middle East. As the Japanese steamed
southward a force of 'territorials' – eighteen-year-olds and
veterans of the First World War – stood guard in slit-trenches
along the coast, armed with ancient weapons, knowing their
resistance would be hopeless. But it was not the Japanese who
invaded New Zealand. One day in mid 1942 the coastal forces
saw a grey ship slipping down the Hauraki Gulf, then two,
then ten. The United States Marines had arrived, a century
after the New England whalers had sailed away.

The consequences of the rise of Japanese and the decline of
British power in the Pacific and of New Zealand's new dependence on American protection were far-reaching. The first
task was clear, to win the war. New Zealand established a

division in the south-west Pacific, but, unlike Australia, left her main forces to fight in the Middle East and Italy. Only Russia, of the allies, called up a larger proportion of her citizens for armed service.

Even before Japan was defeated, Australia and New Zealand became uneasy about seeing the Pacific become an American lake, and unhappy about the failure of their great allies to admit them to their counsels. The result was a kind of Monroe Doctrine against outside interference in the South Pacific, the Canberra Pact of 1944, a product principally of the chauvinism and conceit of the Australian Minister of External Affairs, H.V. Evatt. The 'Anzacs' agreed to continue to co-operate in war and peace. They asserted their claim to a voice in any armistice or post-war settlement. They spoke of the need for a regional zone of defence in the South and South-West Pacific. They served notice on an unnamed 'power' that the possession of war-time bases in the Pacific afforded no rights to post-war sovereignty. This agreement, which Robert Menzies called 'only isolationism with a slight territorial extension', produced no results except the South Pacific Commission.

In the long run the war forced the Government to formulate a policy more closely related to the facts of power than the internationalist idealism of 1935–8, and immediately impelled it into diplomatic activity. In November 1941 Walter Nash was appointed New Zealand's first diplomatic representative (that is if we ignore the High Commissioner in London). He was sent to Washington as Minister. In 1943 the Department of External Affairs (now Ministry of Foreign Affairs) was set up. In 1947 the Statute of Westminster was at last adopted, giving legal fulfilment to the fact of sovereignty. New Zealand was now a fully independent state, though owing allegiance to the British King.

During the Second World War the New Zealand casualties, 11,600 dead and 15,700 wounded, although terrible enough, were not as severe as in the First World War. On 'the home front', the economy boomed in some ways. Although by late 1942 nearly a third of the male labour force was in the armed forces, both manufacturing and farm production had actually risen since 1939. Economic 'stabilization' of wages and prices, introduced with the co-operation of the unions, was remarkably effective. During the war prices rose only fourteen per cent, which Nash boasted was about the lowest war-time rate of inflation in the world. Because of the shortage of imports, New Zealand's sterling balances rose to unprecedented heights. The Government was able to redeem London debts and, in 1948, Nash revalued the £N.Z. once again to parity with sterling.

During the Second World War there was no coalition government like that during the first. A War Administration, in which both parties were represented, broke up amidst mutual recriminations after three months. Two members of the pre-Labour Coalition Government, Coates and Adam Hamilton, served as individuals in the War Cabinet. The National Party, which replaced the Coalition in 1936, continued in Opposition, with a new leader, S. G. Holland. It sought successfully to collect a mass membership and to rid itself of the 'depression' or 'Tory' image attaching to Coates.

Both parties had their domestic difficulties. In 1940–41 National faced a right-wing threat from the People's Movement, which regarded the two leading parties as socialist. In 1941 National absorbed some of its leaders. The rest were massacred in the 1943 election. Labour had a more formidable enemy. In 1940 John A. Lee, a war hero, novelist, dynamic orator, irrepressible dissenter and altogether one of the most dramatic figures in New Zealand politics, was expelled from the party. He had been fighting the leadership chiefly over its financial policy, which he thought too orthodox – his own talk of 'debt-free loans' had a social credit resonance to it. He also advocated more industrialization, a policy later given greater emphasis by Labour. But his unforgivable sin was to denounce Savage, who was dying, in an article on 'Psycho-Pathology in Politics'. He founded the Democratic (Soldier) Labour Party which received four per cent of the votes in 1943. It won no seats but cost Labour a few by vote-splitting.

The Labour Government faded away. Although, in 1938, it won over half the votes in the first majority victory since 1908, it began to lose rural seats. Then the country towns fell away. In 1945 the Government abolished the twenty-eight per cent 'country quota', which gave that much extra representation to the rural population, but in 1946 it lost three more seats, retaining a majority only by virtue of the four Maori members. As the country voters deserted Labour for National, as they had once left the Liberals for Reform, Labour was forced more and more to appeal to the 'floating vote', which consisted, supposedly, of people of moderate means and moderate opinions, particularly 'white-collar workers'. As a result it continually offended the left wing of the Labour movement. During the war and immediate post-war period Peter Fraser met the fate of all Labour leaders: he was affronted by frequent strikes which, to him, seemed blows aimed not at the employers but at the Government. The more militant unionists were unhappy about their regimentation in the Federation of Labour, which was formed in 1937, or the restriction of their action by compulsory arbitration and the Government's 'stabilization' policy. The Government wanted the unions to act as though industry had been nationalized and socialism had arrived. When they struck – illegally – on several occasions the Government 'deregistered' them (that is, struck off their registration under the Industrial Conciliation and Arbitration Act) and took stern measures against the strikers. It alienated the radicals without satisfying the strong body of opinion, even within the trade unions, which was impatient with the frequent industrial stoppages, and especially hostile towards the waterside workers.

The Government was also damaged by the internationalist leanings of its leaders. During the war Fraser and Nash had become 'Commonwealth men': they thought in British Commonwealth terms. After the war they did everything possible to help Great Britain, which was, after all, New Zealand's chief market. For instance, food rationing was continued so as to maximize exports to Britain. Imports were rigorously restricted and petrol rationing was continued so as to conserve American dollars and assist Britain, which was suffering from a severe dollar shortage. These policies, although they could be defended, alienated voters who were tired of war-time shortages and controls and wanted to 'let their hair down' a bit after the war. It was easy for the National Party to describe these continuing controls as socialism.

Labour received another self-inflicted wound. Fraser was convinced at Commonwealth Prime Ministers' conferences in 1948 and 1949 that Russian Communism threatened the world and he became an early 'Cold War' warrior. He came out in favour of peace-time conscription, contrary to Labour's traditional policy. He held a referendum, spending public money to ensure a 'yes' vote, and got his way, but severely damaged his party's branch organizations. Old Labour men saw his actions as a betrayal.

The National Party promised to 'make the £ go further', consumer prices having risen some 4·5 per cent annually in 1946–9. It would deal with militant unions. It would defend private enterprise and would abolish socialist restrictions and controls. In 1949, after fourteen years in office, Labour was swept aside. National won a majority of twelve seats.

Within two years the Government had wrecked the militant unions, after a prolonged strike (or 'lock-out'), by employing 'deregistration', 'arbitrationist' labour, the armed forces, and police, and some frightening 'emergency regulations' based on war-time decrees. It was a time of violent emotion. The wharf leaders were generally regarded as Communists (which the most prominent were not). The Prime Minister, 'Sid' Holland, claimed that there was a 'very determined effort . . . to overthrow orderly government by force' and said that the country was 'actually at war'. The strike was 'part of the Cold War, engineered by Communists to advance their cause and the cause of Russia', another Minister declared.

Though several unions struck, once again, as in 1913, the militants received scant sympathy from the majority of unions. The Federation of Labour actively opposed them. The bigger unions had often played an important role in leading the way to better wages or conditions of employment by means of direct action or negotiation with employers; but the weak unions, whose influence, and even existence, depended on the arbitration system, had inclined to be resentful and to regard strikes as blows against arbitration. Consequently, they had tended to support the Government and the employers in forcing militants back into the state fold. In 1951, as in 1913, the strong unions were not as strong as they imagined. The leaders of the waterside workers unwisely and arrogantly led their followers to disaster. That there was widespread approval for the Government's blows against industrial 'wreckers' and Communists was revealed in a surprise election in 1951 when Holland's party won an increased majority.

The £ did not 'go further' but further away. The wharf dispute coincided with the Korean War boom – in New Zealand's case a wool boom – and inflation rose to over ten per cent. (The only other occasion when it had reached that level was just after the First World War.) There followed over twenty years of prosperity, a prolonged boom which had its interruptions, notably in 1958 and in 1967, but which continued into the early nineteen-seventies. New Zealanders continued to enjoy one of the highest standards of living in the world, measured by any of the popular indicators, such as the number of automobiles or telephones per thousand people. The 'real standard of living' was always among the top half dozen in lists of comparative standards.

In the years 1950–68 prices doubled, but the annual increase was generally below four per cent. This level of inflation seemed beneficial to many, probably most, people. It was accompanied by fairly steady economic growth (the Gross Domestic Product grew at over four per cent per annum in the period 1955–73). This prosperity was the all-pervasive fact in New Zealand life for the first two post-war decades; it was the dominant influence on social attitudes and on politics alike.

New Zealand for long enjoyed a name for radicalism which disguised the generally conservative outlook of both leaders and voters. That reputation rested on two brief periods of radical legislation, 1891–8 and 1936–8, when the Liberals and then Labour established the framework of the interventionist and welfare state. But for most of New Zealand's history, politics have been about economic development, which has been needed to pay for the gains in education, pensions and health. The typical New Zealand leaders have seen their chief task as to initiate and administer development, an observation as true of Vogel and Seddon as of Nash and Holyoake; as true of the Liberals as of Reform, of Labour as of National. Only when economic progress has been halted by depression and their high living standards have been eroded, have the voters sought sweeping political reforms. In the period since 1939 the left wing has been a tiny minority. Communist voters in elections, if a party whose chief programme was to support Russian foreign policy may be regarded as 'on the left', have been no more than 0·1 per cent. There has been little demand for revolutionary change in the economic structure. There have been radical causes, in foreign policy, women's rights and racial equality, which will be considered presently, but they have not notably affected voting preferences. Elections are decided on economic issues: indeed, two political scientists have recently argued that they may be explained almost entirely by reference to a few aspects of the economy.*

Up to 1938 there were big differences between Labour and its opponents, but since then Labour and National have, in general, become alternative conservative parties. Labour has sought to conserve the gains it had made in welfare. National, on the other hand, has come to accept the social security system. Party propaganda seeks to exaggerate the differences between the parties, but there has been a consensus over the basic domestic issues – social security and full employment – and also, usually, over foreign policy.

Both parties inherited the Liberal tradition. The Liberals were absorbed in the National coalition with Reform; M. J. Savage claimed to begin where Seddon left off. Are there any substantial differences between the parties? National accepts the welfare state but puts more emphasis on the free enterprise side of the 'mixed economy'. For three decades, after 1935, Labour placed rather more stress on welfare legislation and paid more attention to the needs of the Maoris and other minority groups. It was always more responsive to the views of trade unions. Certainly the two parties had different appeals. Most unskilled workers and skilled manual workers vote Labour; most professional and business people vote National. Few farmers vote Labour; few Maoris vote National. And it could be argued that there has been another difference.

* E. A. Hudson and M. L. Wevers, *Political Science*, vol. 29, no. 1, July 1977.

National appears to have had a greater drive to secure and keep power. National leaders see it as their role to administer the system – to administer, not to change it. When asked what was his political goal Mr R. D. Muldoon, Prime Minister in the nineteen-seventies, said that it was to leave New Zealand 'no worse than when he took it over'.

National not only sought power, but kept it. Labour was to be in office for only six years in the three decades after 1949. Any full explanation of this dominance would be complex, but there is no doubt that prosperity was a principal reason. New Zealanders are a property-owning democracy. Their chief ambition has for long been to own a house – on its own 'section'. The number of houses owned by their occupants rose from sixty per cent in 1950 to over seventy per cent in 1976. And the National Party represented property owners.

After initial struggle which exacerbated social tensions, the government of Sid Holland from 1949 to 1957 largely exemplifies these generalizations. National did try to give a greater emphasis to individual and private enterprise. State control of urban land prices was lifted; petrol and butter rationing ceased; power restrictions were ended. The tenants of state houses were enabled to buy them on very reasonable terms, which seemed wicked to old Labour leaders. Labour's Internal Marketing Division was abolished and its functions, including the sale of eggs, fruit and honey, were handed over to producer boards, on which, however, the Government was represented by nominees. This process had begun under Labour. Since 1947 the marketing of dairy produce, for instance, had been controlled by a Board representing the Government and the industry. National gave the majority to the producers. There was no suggestion, however, of a return to competitive marketing. As with other agricultural marketing there was still control by the producers.

The National Government did not bring about a return of free competition. For instance, it began by freeing many imports from direct licensing control. But as early as 1952, balance of payments difficulties forced it to introduce 'exchange allocation', a form of disguised import licensing which rationed overseas exchange instead of imports of goods. To the community the effect was much the same. (A licence is still required in the late nineteen-seventies for certain classes of imported goods, so that the system has lasted for forty years since Walter Nash introduced it in 1938.) In 1955 inflation led to a credit squeeze and further controls over building and hire purchase.

Under National, New Zealand was not noticeably nearer to free enterprise; the benefits of competition were not much in evidence, at least not to the average citizen. He found – and still finds – that the Government or retailers' associations or manufacturers fix the price of a wide range of commodities. Strenuous competition between rival stores is a rare phenomenon. In comparison with Australian, European or American stores, the buyer finds relatively little choice between varieties or brands of foodstuff. The housewife goes shopping in a market owned neither by the community nor subject to free competition – the market-place of a 'mixed economy'.

In 1957 the National Party published a small book, *A Record of Achievement: The Work of the National Government, 1949–57*. It was able to stress some significant changes: for instance, it boasted that as a result of its 'firm handling' of the 1951 strike, and its subsequent tough industrial legislation, there were very few strikes. The number of working days lost as a result of industrial disputes in 1955 was only a quarter of the total for 1949. There were other changes too, some of which have been mentioned. But mainly the publication consisted of long lists of goodies which had increased under National. People had more money, pensions, sheep, cattle, telephones, motor vehicles, houses, electric toasters, vacuum cleaners, washing machines, radios, overseas trips, university scholarships and aircraft for aerial top-dressing. The 'rabbit menace' had, however, declined. 'New Zealand,' the Prime Minister proclaimed in a foreword – and with every justification – 'is a happier, healthier and more prosperous nation.' It was a materialist's paradise.

Perhaps the most surprising change introduced by National was the abolition of the Legislative Council in 1950. This reform was largely the personal responsibility of the Prime Minister. Not all his ministers agreed, but the Council had become redundant. Its contribution to legislation was almost nil. Conservatives have from time to time since then lamented the absence of a delaying – or reviewing – upper house and, indeed, the Holland Government itself set up a parliamentary committee to consider alternatives. But New Zealand has remained that unusual polity, a state with a uni-cameral legislature.

Sid Holland had immense self-confidence, determination and energy, but very limited intellectual horizons. He has been described as 'jaunty', 'ebullient', 'bouncy', 'aggressive'. He was notorious for a cheerful vulgarity which made sensitive citizens shudder, but was not disliked by the average voter. Although he ruled the country for eight years, he developed no great personal following. He was detested by his enemies while his party supporters failed to love him.

After 1951, he survived one more election, in 1954. Although politicians proclaimed that National would oppress the workers or Labour would destroy private enterprise, few voters believed them. The main surprise was the success of the Social Credit Political League. Douglas Social Credit groups had existed since just after the First World War, but did not form a political party until 1954, when they won eleven per cent of the votes, though no seats. Then the party declined until the 1966 election, in which it won over fourteen per cent of the votes and its leader, Vernon Cracknell, won a seat in the House. Social Credit receives support among farmers and in country towns, and it receives a 'protest' vote from those tired of Labour or National and probably from new voters. It benefits from the persistence of widespread suspicion of banks and orthodox finance, which is usually accompanied by innocence in matters of economic theory. But it seems a long way from becoming a rival right-wing party.

In 1954, fifty-five per cent of the electorate voted against the Government, but it still won a majority of seats, losing only five to Labour. In 1957 Holland reluctantly resigned, to the relief of his party, but not soon enough to please his successor, Keith Holyoake, who was not able to form his own ministry until just before the election. He had lived long in Holland's shadow and was in any case a reserved man who had not established any clear popular image. Walter Nash, Peter Fraser's successor, was, by contrast, one of the best known people in the country. He was old, but he seemed tireless. Many people thought that he should have a chance, that it was 'time for a change'.

A political scientist has described the election in these words: 'there was no intricacy or subtlety about what the parties were doing. They were conducting an auction for the electors' votes. The Labour Party's final bid was engagingly direct – "Do you want £100 or not?"' Labour offered this rebate when Pay-as-you-earn income tax was introduced. National, by contrast, offered only a £75 rebate. In this election of promises the voters decided that Labour's were worth two seats more than National's.

Since 1949 Labour has established an unfortunate reputation for lacking staying power: National rules the country while Labour occasionally intervenes for three years. So it was for Walter Nash in 1957–60. No sooner had he taken office than he learned that Labour had inherited a major balance of payments crisis, which the Government had ignored and had concealed from the voters during the election. Because of falling export prices, the deficit in the balance of trade in December was £30 million. Overseas reserves had fallen from £83 million in early October to £45 million by Christmas: they would now pay for only six weeks' imports.

The Minister of Finance was Arnold Nordmeyer, a very able and intelligent administrator who was much respected but inspired little affection. He was a Presbyterian minister and in manner somewhat austere. He and the Cabinet were prepared to impose heroic sacrifices upon the nation. Rigorous import controls were introduced. Then came the famous 'black budget' of 1958. Income tax was raised very substantially. Duties on beer, spirits, tobacco and cars were doubled. The tax on petrol was nearly doubled. It was a puritan's budget, and cynics noted that neither Nash nor Nordmeyer smoked, drank alcohol or owned a car. It contrasted very greatly with Labour's lavish promises at election time. Not that they were forgotten – age benefits and other pensions and the family benefit were raised, but these improvements made little impression.

Hitting the working man's fags, beer and petrol was not what the unionists expected or wanted. Some of their leaders denounced the Government. The effect of the budget on party branches was disastrous and there was a precipitous decline in membership. In Auckland nearly a third of the branches closed down. The budget was honest but, as it turned out, an over-reaction to the crisis, for the terms of trade began to improve almost at once.

The Nash Government was responsible for some noteworthy policies. Its principal drive was to speed up industrialization. What was needed, the Government proclaimed, in the words of Dr W. B. Sutch, the country's leading economic nationalist and head of the Department of Industries and Commerce, was 'Manufacturing in Depth'. The aim was to make the country less dependent on imports – a return to the 'insulation' policy of 1935. Negotiations were begun – or continued – to set up a number of major industries, including a steel-rolling mill, glass works, a gin distillery, an oil refinery and an aluminium industry. For the last of these the Government was to sell very cheap power from a huge hydro-electric project at Lakes Manapouri and Te Anau. Almost at once protests began from conservationists against raising the level of the lakes. This was the first sign of what was to become a major environmental protest movement. Nash also took steps to set up a cotton mill in Nelson. There was widespread public criticism at this proposal, which guaranteed to an English company a major share of the New Zealand market. The next government cancelled the contract.

The Nash Government introduced equal pay for equal work, regardless of sex, in the public service. It abolished compulsory military training. Families were enabled to 'capitalize' the family benefit payments for children in a lump sum to pay a deposit on a house or pay off a mortgage. This step, plus new three per cent housing loans, greatly increased the prospects of the not-so-wealthy purchasing a house. But it was not to be forgiven for the draconian policies of 1958.

Nash's greatest achievement was entirely a personal one. He travelled extensively round the world to meetings and talks with Harold Macmillan, Nehru, Hammarskjöld, Khrushchev,

Eisenhower and others, discussing the great issues of the day, notably disarmament, as well as an Antarctic treaty, the fighting in Laos and other subjects. Alone of New Zealand leaders, except for Peter Fraser, he had achieved a certain international status which enabled him to talk on equal personal terms with the world's leaders. This was not, however, appreciated by the voters, who noticed his constant absences.

In the 1960 election Nash travelled about repeating, 'You've never been so well-off in New Zealand as you are today', 'everyone, everywhere will again be better off.' The message was the same as Harold Macmillan's winning slogan of the previous year, 'You've never had it so good.' But the Government was thrown out. It lost seven seats. National won forty-six seats to Labour's thirty-four.

The long Prime Ministership of Keith Holyoake now began. It was to last twelve years. It is (in 1979, while he is Governor-General) still too soon to attempt any final assessment of his political career. But some observations may be made. He kept his cool, did not panic in a crisis. He was master in the House and, it is said, in cabinet and caucus. If so, he must have been a very good chairman, for he had some ministers not easily controlled, notably the pugnacious Tom Shand and the obstreperous R. D. Muldoon.

Holyoake's view of the role of a Prime Minister was that he was chairman of the board of directors of the biggest business in New Zealand. He saw his duty to be 'leadership by consent'. Similarly, in the country at large, he sought 'consensus politics'. Although he was re-elected as national leader four times, he never possessed any great personal mana: he lacked much gift for spontaneous rapport with ordinary citizens; he seemed aloof and sounded pompous. His political nous was remarkable. He was widely trusted.

Much of the Holyoake Government's great anxieties and work concerned foreign relations, notably economic foreign policy, as Great Britain came nearer to joining the European Economic Community (E.E.C.). These policies will be considered later. They included the decision in 1961 to join the International Monetary Fund, which met with hysterical opposition from some leftists and a wide array of funny money men, who believed that the country was being handed over to 'alien control'. New Zealand was almost the last country outside the Soviet bloc to join.

Some of the notable reforms made under the Holyoake Government were the work of other ministers. Ralph Hanan, Minister of Justice, working closely with the Secretary, John Robson, introduced a notable liberalization of criminal and divorce law. Hanan was responsible for the abolition of capital punishment for which he had crusaded, especially against many of his own party. In 1962 the office of Ombudsman was created and a leading former public servant, Sir Guy Powles, was appointed the first Ombudsman. His task was to investigate on complaint or on his own initiative any actions or inactions of government departments, and to make recommendations to the Government. These powers have since been extended to investigating the actions of local governments. This innovation has given citizens a very real protection against unjust authority. In 1976, for instance, the Ombudsmen (now plural) investigated 1,504 complaints and held 134 of them justified (513 being outside their jurisdiction).

Two other reforms deserve special mention. One was the Equal Pay Act of 1972, which prohibited discrimination in incomes and salaries on the basis of sex. Another was the Accident Compensation Act of 1972, which provided compensation for all members of the work force suffering personal injury from accident. A year later a new Labour Government extended this to cover everyone, whether working or not. It covered all accidents – automobile, domestic, industrial and sporting. On the whole, however, the politics of prosperity were not very fertile in legislative innovation. The Government's main job was managing the economy. After 1949 it had wanted to reject that responsibility, which Labour had accepted and which National regarded as socialist, but it was increasingly drawn in, as it was over import controls. The welfare state implies a very high degree of state intervention. National could not have one without the other.

Although the country was very prosperous, the Government was given little credit. Economic planning seemed to follow rather than precede the crises, as in 1957 and 1966. The reports of the Monetary and Economic Council, set up in 1961, sounded like the periodic lamentations of Cassandra. Each report regretted excessive spending, economic instability, over-importing, unrestrained internal demand. The Council consistently thought the economy 'over-extended'. It regretted the relatively slow rate of increase in productivity per person – most western countries had greater growth. Nor was it alone in its views. A satirical article in the *Economist* in 1963, entitled 'How to Progress Backwards', argued that the main aim of New Zealand economic policy was to regress from 'the age of high mass consumption to a traditional society' by, among other techniques, removing economic growth from politics. In 1962 the Monetary and Economic Council gave its preliminary verdict that 'Government policies in the past decade had not made the contribution which they should to the achievement of greater stability and to the promotion of growth.'

One of the worst features of the economy was that some of its crises had been democratically induced. The Monetary and Economic Council dryly observed that the coincidence of triennial elections and triennial economic crises appeared not to be a coincidence. There were balance of payments difficulties of varying severity at the time of each election from 1946 to 1966. A political scientist, R. M. Chapman, sombrely wrote that 'politicians had correctly concluded that the voters demanded more than economic effort had earned.' In each election year, ignoring evidence of declining overseas earnings, successive governments catered to this demand by lowering taxes and especially by permitting an import spree, despite repeated warnings from their economic advisers. National Governments were the worse offenders only perhaps because they had more opportunities.

In 1967 the Government faced the worst balance of payments crisis since the Second World War, the first really severe economic quake for nearly thirty years. The deficit on current account was about $135,000,000 in the year ending in October 1967. The crisis forced a devaluation of the currency into line with the Australian dollar. (From 1948 to 1967 the New Zealand pound – now two dollars – had been on a parity with sterling.) The Government asked the World Bank to send a team of experts to write an independent report. That report stressed New Zealand's over-dependence on the export of a few primary commodities and the need for diversification, and said that 'the balance of payments is the Achilles' heel of the New Zealand economy.' It concluded that the country lacked effective instruments for long-term economic planning. The trendy new term became 'indicative planning' – *'le planification indicatif'*. No one knew quite what it meant but it sounded impressive.

National's principal effort to provide long-term economic strategy was through the National Development Council, set up after a National Development Conference in May 1969, which made over 600 recommendations for future policy. The Council co-ordinated a host of lesser councils. It was supposed to set targets for 'indicative planning'. The Government obviously hoped to involve many people in planning and in contributing to decisions; to build up confidence in its management; and, above all, in the Holyoake style, to create a wide consensus. Planning – but not socialist planning – had now become acceptable to National. Not, however, in this form, to Labour. The next Labour Government dissolved the Council and its functions were taken over by a cabinet committee and, no doubt, by the Treasury.

Despite the faults of a 'stop-go' economy, and however insecure the foundations would prove to be in the next decade, the country's economic achievements were still remarkable, both in maintaining one of the highest average standards of living in the world and in maintaining full employment to an unrivalled degree. For over twenty years after the Second World War the number of registered unemployed was so small – a few hundred – that it was jokingly said that they were all known by name to the Prime Minister. Even during the economic difficulties of 1968 the rate of unemployment, though a shock to local opinion, was less than one per cent of the work force, which seemed extraordinarily low elsewhere.

There were, under National, no dramatic legislative innovations changing the shape of society, like social security in 1938. Nevertheless, during the prolonged post-war economic boom National presided over, sometimes guided or assisted and sometimes merely observed, very great changes in society. These changes may be broadly summed up by saying that New Zealand society became more complex and much more sophisticated. Most of them were a function of size – population growth and urbanization – or products of prosperity. They were underpinned by economic development.

After the Second World War greater mechanization, aerial top-dressing on a unique scale and other modern techniques caused an agrarian revolution. The volume of farm production (ignoring forestry) rose nearly a hundred per cent in the years 1938–66. The proportion of the labour force in primary industry fell, from 1936 to 1966, from twenty-seven per cent to thirteen per cent – a figure that should be noted by those who think of New Zealand as an extensive farm.

The war greatly stimulated industrial development. The engineering factories led the way – encouraged by farm mechanization and the rising demand for motor vehicles – but there were some notable new industries. Chief of these was the pulp, paper and particle-board industry, based largely on the enormous man-made pine and other exotic forests. By 1970 the steel industry began using the local ironsands, instead of imported iron. The aluminium industry went into production in 1971. The electronics and plastics industries, the glass industry and the carpet industry were all of growing importance. By 1966 thirty-seven per cent of the workers were engaged in secondary industry.

The rate of population increase was one of the highest among the 'developed' countries. The cities grew very rapidly. In 1971 the population was classified as eighty-two per cent urban: in 1936 it had been sixty-seven per cent. The main industrial centre and the biggest city, Auckland, contained over 700,000 people by 1972. Although very large in area, because of the relatively large 'sections' on which houses were built, it was not a really big city by world standards. But life in Auckland and the other cities had become more urban in tone, in some ways more cosmopolitan.

One change cannot be understood by the young. From the First World War until 1967 all bars closed at six o'clock. This law, imposed by those who opposed the consumption of alcohol, led to the 'six o'clock swill' – the most barbarous drinking custom in the world – whereby people got as drunk as possible as quickly as possible after work between five and six o'clock. In 1967 every electorate voted overwhelmingly in a referendum for extending drinking hours to 10 p.m. The facts that in 1967 twenty-seven per cent of first babies of mothers in the age group sixteen to twenty-five were illegitimate, while some forty per cent of first babies of married women in that age group were born less than eight months after marriage, may be regarded as further evidence that colonial puritanism was being undermined, or at least that there are carefree and careless attitudes.

Another change which would surprise younger adults is that, even in the early nineteen-fifties, there were scarcely any licensed restaurants, other than in hotels, in the country. By the end of the sixties dining out was a rapidly growing custom. So, too, was drinking wine. The wine industry had made rapid progress, producing good quality wines from cabernet sauvignon, pinot, riesling and other 'varietal' grapes. The acid and 'foxy' 'Dally plonk' of the nineteen-thirties and forties was almost forgotten. An Australian model, returning to Sydney after a week in New Zealand, when asked what it was like, replied: 'I don't know: it was closed.' Perhaps the joke had less point in the nineteen-seventies than it had a decade earlier.

The New Zealanders were now, on average, better educated and better informed than a generation ago. In the nineteen-thirties most people did not go to secondary school, but since 1944, when the school leaving age was raised to fifteen, everyone did. The Prime Minister in 1972–4, Norman Kirk, who (like Sir Keith Holyoake) left school at the end of primary school, once said that he would be the country's last uneducated political leader.

The overwhelming majority went to the state schools, which provided a sound, general and secular education academically more advanced than in most American high schools or English secondary moderns, though not as good as the upper forms in English grammar or public schools. A high proportion of school leavers (some twelve per cent in 1970) went to university. The universities expanded very rapidly after the Second World War. By 1972 there were 35,000 students enrolled at the six universities and one agricultural college. The largest university, Auckland, had 9,500 students. University fees were very low so the universities had none of the élitism associated with Oxford or Cambridge. They provided a respectable undergraduate education, similar to that in British provincial or in American state universities. They had rapidly growing postgraduate schools, in which a master's degree was much more common than a doctorate. In 1971 about 4,700 people graduated.

A number of other facts justify the assertion that the population was becoming better informed. An astonishing number of people travelled abroad. In 1972, for instance, 134,000 people went on overseas trips. That was one in twenty of the population. In addition a great proportion of the older men had been transported abroad at public expense during the World Wars. New Zealand is a major book-importing country. People buy and borrow books much more frequently than in most countries. By 1972 eighty-three per cent of homes had television sets. Another important fact which militated against insularity was that, because of the country's brief history, education was largely directed towards the history and literature of the outside world.

One result of the growth of cities was an increase in professionalism. In earlier days the intellectual and artistic life of the community was mainly sustained by amateurs – the early historians and ethnologists, for instance, were all amateurs – often journalists or public servants, admirable men like Elsdon Best or Edward Tregear or G. W. Rusden, but rarely trained to evaluate critically the data they collected. Much the same could be said of the arts. By and large they were the preserve of the amateur, large numbers of people participating in the productions of amateur theatrical groups and choral societies. Most of the painters were 'Sunday painters'.

By the seventies this had begun to change. Valiant efforts had been made to create and sustain orchestras, opera and ballet companies and companies of professional actors. Some of these groups collapsed for want of a large enough public, but there was a new and indigenous professionalism. The same was true of the public art galleries. Several galleries had begun to build up worthy collections. It could not, however, be said that the theatre had achieved West End standards or that the art museums rivalled those in Melbourne or Europe or the U.S.A. They did not have enough money.

There was an extraordinary proliferation of painters and small galleries. In the nineteen-sixties painting seemed to have replaced writing as the form of expression preferred by a new generation. The leading painters were highly professional. Don Binney, Ralph Hotere, Michael Smithers and many other new painters joined the older Colin McCahon, Toss Woolaston and Louise Henderson, who were still painting.

The literary movement of the thirties, unlike that of the nineties, survived and flourished. The leading writers continued with their work and some of them, like Charles Brasch, greatly enlarged their range and reputation. In the late nineteen-forties and fifties there were a surprising number of poets to the urban acre. Of these at least James K. Baxter and Kendrick Smithyman, in very different ways, secured a permanent place in the anthologies. There were also at that time a number of new prose writers, including Maurice Duggan, Janet Frame, John Reece Cole and David Ballantyne, who were extending the span of New Zealand fiction. The late fifties and sixties saw the appearance of a quite unprecedented number of successful novelists and short story writers, notably Maurice Shadbolt, Ian Cross, Sylvia Ashton-Warner, Maurice Gee and Noel Hilliard. New Zealand literature was, by about 1970, not merely a national aspiration but a substantial body of work.

Professional standards had been adopted in activities too numerous to list, but of great importance in cultural growth. Articles in scholarly journals and research in general increased enormously in volume after the pioneering work of a handful of trained scholars and scientists between the wars. The standards of literary criticism had risen remarkably, because of the growth of university English departments and because of the establishment of a literary quarterly, *Landfall*, by Charles Brasch in 1947. A little solemn, a little academic, it had immense influence in stimulating young writers and in raising the standards of reviewing.

Most of this intellectual and artistic growth received, in one way or another, state aid. A State Literary Fund had been established in 1946. At least one literary figure, the poet A. R. D. Fairburn disapproved. He wrote:

> Here is a piece of wisdom
> I learnt at my mother's knee!
> The mushroom grows in the open,
> The toadstool under the tree.

Nevertheless, it helped writers and publishers a great deal with scholarships and subsidies. In 1964 the Government set up the Queen Elizabeth II Arts Council, which subsidizes the musical, theatrical and visual arts.

Writers had not become rich, but they received much more encouragement by the nineteen-seventies than ever before. They could get subsidies, scholarships, bursaries, fellowships and awards. Norman Kirk set up an authors' lending fund, among the first in the world, to compensate writers for the use of their books in libraries. The literary scene was changing rapidly for another reason. In the nineteen-fifties there were only two or three New Zealand firms which published serious literature. New Zealand authors had to seek English publishers. But by the early seventies there were a number of local publishers. In 1974 1,400 books were published in New Zealand.

To write about urbanization, professionalism and sophistication in New Zealand is inevitably to risk giving a false impression. For, more than almost anywhere else, the towns were not *urbs* but suburbs. In their towns the New Zealanders had managed to retain many rural advantages. The quarter-acre 'section', once ubiquitous, was shrinking by 1970, but nevertheless most houses had sections large enough to contain fruit trees, flower and vegetable gardens, and lawn. Within the growing cities there could still be found many features of a simpler life. Life in New Zealand was, and indeed is, still largely lived out-of-doors. Almost everyone lives near the sea, or mountains, or the bush, perhaps all three. A temperate climate encourages the people to take advantage of what nature so generously offers.

The post-world-war boom began with the Korean War boom. Throughout the long, affluent years the Cold War remained an ominous, sometimes lurid, backdrop. When North Korea invaded South Korea, and the United Nations, in the absence of the U.S.S.R., declared the former an aggressor, New Zealand sent 2,000 troops, as part of a (British) Commonwealth brigade, in the defence of 'collective security' and to fight Communism. The Americans were anxious to conclude a prompt and generous peace treaty with Japan, which made Australians and New Zealanders nervous at the possibility of renewed Japanese militarism. On earlier occasions when Australia and New Zealand leaders wanted a Pacific pact, the Americans had not been interested, but the Korean War led to a reassessment of the dangers of Asian Communism and the Americans now agreed to a mutual defensive pact, A.N.Z.U.S. (Australia, New Zealand, U.S.A.), which was signed in 1951 a few days before the peace treaty with Japan. The three allies agreed, in the event of an attack on any of them, that each should 'meet the common danger in accordance with its constitutional processes' – a phrase which has caused some misgivings among the 'Anzacs', because it presumably meant that American aid would require the consent of Congress, whereas no constitutional process need delay them in helping the United States. Still, the treaty provided the best guarantee they could hope for against non-nuclear attack: in a nuclear war 'defence' may not be a meaningful term.

The southern members of the Commonwealth also joined John Foster Dulles's South East Asia Treaty Organization. This pact arose out of the Americans' fears of a Communist take-over in Vietnam, Cambodia and Laos. These states, although not signatories, were specifically guaranteed in a protocol to the treaty. S.E.A.T.O. provided against 'subversive activities' as well as armed aggression in the area. An 'understanding' appended to the treaty explained that to the United States 'aggression' meant only 'communist aggression'. The signatories were the U.S.A., France, Great Britain, Pakistan, the Philippines, Thailand, Australia and New Zealand. This treaty was the object of some criticism in New Zealand. It was not plain that it added anything to the country's security not provided by A.N.Z.U.S. Influential Asian states such as India and Indonesia were conspicuously absent. The Government was probably pleased, however, at the inclusion of Great Britain, for it had not been happy at Britain being excluded from A.N.Z.U.S. The New Zealand leaders, Peter Fraser as well as Sid Holland, habitually thought of defence in Commonwealth terms. New Zealand's wide range of interests in international affairs largely arose from the Commonwealth connection. There was Commonwealth defence planning in the Middle East, the Pacific and South-East Asia, as well as a Commonwealth army in Korea. Commonwealth Prime Ministers' meetings and a Commonwealth 'bloc' in the U.N. provided further links. The New Zealand Government acknowledged that its defence relied mainly on the U.S.A., but Britain still seemed an important power – one of only three armed with nuclear weapons, and an Asian power at that. The real extent of Britain's decline was not yet obvious, least of all to the British.

New Zealand's comfort and security rested on Anglo-American accord. Any rift between the allies would gravely embarrass the New Zealand Government, as was shown during the Egyptian crisis late in 1956. When the British and French intervened in the war between Israel and Egypt by attacking the latter, the Prime Minister, Sid Holland, expressed 'grave concern' at the difference of viewpoint between the United States and Great Britain. Although he expressed 'full confidence in Britain's intentions', there were, he added, 'disturbing features', which, he hoped, would be explained. His initial statement, which was widely quoted as signifying support for Sir Anthony Eden, was in fact a thickly sugared pill. A large section of public opinion regarded the Anglo-French action as aggression. Though the Prime Minister's subsequent statements were unequivocally 'loyal', and though New Zealand supported Great Britain in the United Nations, the Government was plainly most unhappy. The decision to establish an international force to supervise a ceasefire in Egypt was 'welcomed with considerable relief'. The Government promptly volunteered to contribute, thus reviving two traditions – that of being the first to offer troops (in the past always to aid Britain) and that of advocating that the League of Nations should be fitted with teeth. The offer was quietly snubbed, and the public and the newspaper press gladly turned their attention to the Russian intervention in the Hungarian revolution and to welcoming Hungarian refugees.

It might be thought that A.N.Z.U.S. and S.E.A.T.O. signalled New Zealand's thorough involvement in Asian affairs, but such was not immediately the case. Indeed, the Government's intention was that New Zealand's main defence commitment should be part of Commonwealth strategy in the Middle East, and the A.N.Z.U.S. pact was regarded as freeing New Zealand from fears in the Pacific so that it could contribute to the defence of the Middle East. An R.N.Z.A.F. fighter squadron was promptly sent to the Middle East. But A.N.Z.U.S. and S.E.A.T.O. did indicate that the Government considered that the defence of New Zealand itself lay in Asia. The logic of that conclusion was at last recognized in 1955 when New Zealand gave up its Middle East interest and agreed to contribute to a Commonwealth force, with British and Australian armed forces too, in Malaya. This was New Zealand's first decision to station ground troops abroad in peace time. The name A.N.Z.A.M. (Australia, New Zealand and Malaya) was coined for the defence agreements made after the Second World War for the Malayan region.

New Zealand's treaty and defence commitments now were all related to South-East Asia. There followed a period of South-East Asia mania. New Zealand concentrated its diplomatic activities in that area having, by 1966, embassies and other diplomatic offices in Singapore, Malaysia, Laos, Thailand, Vietnam, Indonesia and the Philippines, but none in Eastern Europe, Africa or South America. New Zealand troops took part in several campaigns, in Malaya against Communist terrorists in the late fifties and during the 'confrontation' of Indonesia with Malaysia in 1964–5. A cabinet minister, though not one of the cleverest, was heard to declare that New Zealand was part of South-East Asia – oblivious of the fact that its nearest Asian neighbour, Indonesia, was nearly 4,000 miles away or that North Vietnam was as near to Western Europe as it was to New Zealand.

When, in 1964-5, the civil war in South Vietnam expanded, and North Vietnam units intervened to help the Viet Cong, the southern government asked New Zealand for military assistance under S.E.A.T.O. Keith Holyoake's Government decided in 1965 to send New Zealand combat troops to help the non-Communist, hopelessly corrupt government of South Vietnam.

These units, infantry and artillery, never exceeded more than about 500 men: so small was the contribution indeed, that it sometimes seemed that the Government secretly agreed with its critics, who opposed sending troops. Certainly the Government did not want a heavy commitment and must have to some extent welcomed the prolonged protest which now arose, as providing evidence that the public did not wish to enlarge the military contribution.

The Vietnam War led to the greatest public debate on foreign policy in New Zealand history; indeed the first in which any significant section of public opinion opposed government policy. New Zealand had its 'teach-ins' and its demonstrations. An active and numerous minority, including a wide sector of people and opinions, persistently denounced the sending of troops. Eventually the Labour Party came out in opposition and the military involvement became an issue in the 1966 election – an issue which certainly cost Labour votes. National won that election. By the 1969 election probably most people opposed the war and it was scarcely an issue.

Keith Holyoake and his Government had accepted the superficial 'domino theory', that if one South-East Asian state turned Communist the rest would follow. They spoke of 'forward defence' – New Zealand was to be defended on the Mekong. But the carpet was pulled from under their political feet when President Nixon went to Peking in 1972 and the U.S.A. pulled out of Vietnam. The Holyoake Government withdrew some of the New Zealand forces in 1971. The last were pulled out by Norman Kirk's Government in 1972.

IV: THE UNCERTAIN SEVENTIES

New Zealand the way you want it.
NATIONAL PARTY election slogan, 1975.

KEITH HOLYOAKE gave up the leadership of the National Party early in 1972 and J. R. Marshall ('Gentleman Jack') became Prime Minister until a general election in November when Labour was elected to power with a large majority, fifty-five seats to National's thirty-two. Labour's leader was now Norman Kirk. For a time the economic boom continued and, indeed, expanded. New Zealand built up a huge surplus in its balance of payments. There were two revaluations of the New Zealand dollar. It seemed that New Zealand was economically strong and that the Government could go full steam ahead to implement its very numerous promises. But, in fact, major changes in the world scene, some of which had been occurring over a long period, were becoming effective all at once, and altering both New Zealand's position and its capacity to control its destiny. In the fifties world affairs had seemed 'quite straightforward': New Zealand belonged to the British Commonwealth, the junior partner, 'and not too junior either', of the United States, which was the leader of the 'free world' in the struggle against Communist expansion. So said Brian Talboys, Minister of Foreign Affairs, in a speech in 1977. Now the simplicities of the Cold War had given way to the complexities of détente.

The Commonwealth, no longer 'British' after 1949, when India and Pakistan became members, had been declining for a long time, receding like the Cheshire cat, leaving behind a pleasant British smile. From the late nineteen-fifties the possibility that the United Kingdom would join the E.E.C. had been the greatest threat hanging over New Zealand's future. After two British applications were vetoed by the French, Britain did join in 1972. New Zealand claimed to be a 'special case', and J. R. Marshall succeeded in negotiating arrangements giving access to the British market for specified quantities of New Zealand butter and cheese up to 1977. But the future looked ominous. New Zealand was already making efforts, sometimes strenuous, to diversify her production and markets. But what markets were there to absorb the huge quantities of high-grade protein that Britain traditionally imported from New Zealand?

At the same time the U.S.A. disengaged its forces from Vietnam and, substantially, from Asia. The superpower adopted a 'lower posture'. President Nixon told his allies to stand more firmly on their own feet. 'Alliances are not as strong as they used to be in the fifties and sixties,' Mr Talboys confessed. The future of S.E.A.T.O. was at once a question-mark and it was to be completely 'phased out' by 1977. These changes marked the end of 'forward defence'.

New Zealand's Commonwealth role in South-East Asian defence was undermined simultaneously. The British had begun to pull their armed forces out of Asia in the late nineteen-sixties. The timetable was revised several times. A new defence arrangement in 1971 postponed what the New Zealand Government, at least, saw as an evil hour. But the Australians pulled their troops out of Singapore and then, in 1976, the British did so too. By 1977 the British Empire in Asia had shrunk to Hongkong, Gan, an island in the Indian Ocean, and Masirah, an island off the southern coast of Arabia. Some New Zealand troops remaining in Singapore, and some Gurkhas in Hong Kong, were about the last relics of British imperial power. It was explained that the New Zealand troops were there, by wish of the local government, to co-operate with the local forces. Certainly they had no imperial purpose.

Where should New Zealand turn, if Uncle Sam were aloof and the Motherland had deserted her family? Various answers were dictated by circumstances or sought out by governments. The circumstances included the fact, now indubitable to the most British of 'Kiwis', that New Zealand was a group of Pacific islands, and that its neighbours, if somewhat distant ones, were Australia, Polynesia and Melanesia.

The National Government had sought, with some, though limited, success, to strengthen ties with Australia, which seemed more accurately described as 'neighbouring' now that distance had been diminished by jet aeroplanes. The result was the New Zealand–Australia Free Trade Agreement (N.A.F.T.A.) of 1965, which aimed at and achieved an expansion of trans-Tasman trade. Its scope was limited by the determination of both governments not to damage the interests of their own producers.

In the nineteen-sixties and seventies New Zealand also strengthened its connections with the Pacific island groups, now becoming independent one after another. New Zealand had taken part in the process of decolonization. It helped to promote the independence of Western Samoa (1962) and Nauru (1968) and self-government (a sort of 'dominion status') in 1965 in the Cook Islands, whose people remain New Zealand citizens. Niue also became self-governing, but in close association with New Zealand, in 1974. In 1971 New Zealand became a member of the South Pacific Forum, in which heads of Pacific governments and other ministers discuss their common problems.

From 1947 onwards New Zealand was a member of the South Pacific Commission, which was responsible for promoting research in Oceania. Increasingly, in the sixties and seventies, New Zealand aid has been directed to the Pacific. Although assistance was given to many other areas, such as India and Bangladesh and Africa, the South Pacific was the area in which aid on the scale New Zealand could afford was likely to be the most effective. By 1976 over half New Zealand's bilateral aid went there. (Total bilateral aid was $49,000,000, plus another $15,000,000 aid contributed through U.N. and other agencies.) In this period thousands of Pacific Islanders migrated to New Zealand. New Zealanders became aware of the Pacific far more than in the past, and aware that it was no longer a backwater, or remote from world affairs. All the great powers bordered on the Pacific.

Where should New Zealand turn, then? Norman Kirk inaugurated a short period of real creativity in foreign policy. He determined to pursue policies independent and seen to be such, not dictated, as so often in the past, by the U.K. or the U.S.A. Some degree of independence was, in any case, being forced upon the Government. Moreover, in the new, relatively fluid relations between the great powers there was some space for manoeuvre; between the big fishes there was more room for small fishes to move.

The third Labour Government reopened the embassy in Moscow, closed in 1950 during the Cold War. New Zealand exchanged ambassadors with China. Kirk (he was his own Minister of Foreign Affairs) began to cast about for some new grouping. There was talk of an Asian–Pacific forum, including China and Japan, perhaps something like the South Pacific Forum, but Thailand and other South-East Asian countries were not yet ready to come to terms with China. Another of Kirk's ideas, a sub-regional grouping of Australia, Indonesia, Papua–New Guinea and New Zealand, similarly came to nothing, although President Suharto agreed to 'explore' the possibility of some co-operative arrangement.

Norman Kirk's speeches consistently sounded a note of international idealism reminiscent of those of M. J. Savage or Walter Nash. He declared that New Zealand would 'find and hold a firm moral basis for its foreign policy'. There was a basic idealism in two striking government actions relating to foreign affairs. Kirk saw clearly that while fear of Communism was a declining element in international politics, racism was becoming a central issue. Labour had promised not to interfere in the affairs of sporting bodies, but, after receiving advice from the police about likely disorders if a South African rugby football team came to New Zealand, Kirk instructed the Rugby Union that a racially selected team could not come. There was an outcry from politically innocent rugby administrators and players, but the decision was wise. On an earlier occasion, in 1959, when the question had arisen whether a New Zealand rugby team, selected to exclude Maoris, should tour South Africa, Nash had dodged the moral issue. With Kirk there was no shilly-shallying.

In 1973 Australia and New Zealand applied to the International Court of Justice to try to stop French atmospheric nuclear tests in the Pacific. If the devices exploded were as harmless as the French claimed, why did they not test them nearer home? The Court called on the French to stop the tests while the case was being heard, but they persisted. In 1972 some small vessels had sailed from New Zealand into the test zone near Mururoa. Now the New Zealand Government sent the frigates *Otago* and *Canterbury* into the test zone. This official and startling protest received world-wide publicity.

Kirk died tragically in 1974. He had not lived to deal with the worst problems of the seventies, notably the inflationary furnace, although it was alight but ignored towards the end of his life and during his illness. He achieved little of his political hopes, yet he had made a great impact on New Zealanders. He was 'a big man', physically and in his broad sympathies for suffering humanity, in the Seddon mould. W. E. (Bill) Rowling, his Minister of Finance, who succeeded him as Prime Minister, was left to try to cope with unprecedented difficulties.

Inflation began to accelerate in the U.S.A. in the mid sixties, during the Vietnam War. It was noticeable in New Zealand by 1967–8. But in 1973 oil prices quadrupled in a few months. As the boom collapsed there was the worst drop in New Zealand's terms of trade (that is, the relationship between the prices of exports and imports) since the depression of the thirties: from June 1973 to March 1974 there was a forty-six per cent decline. A large surplus in the balance of payments in 1973 had become a deficit of $1,300,000,000 by 1975 and continued near $1,000,000,000 dollars in 1976 and 1977. The Labour Government tried to cope with this situation, not by old-fashioned deflationary policies but by overseas borrowing on a scale never known before. By 1975 the external public debt stood at $863,000,000.

Apart from the Coalition of 1931, when Liberals and Reformers joined forces against Labour, it is doubtful whether a single government had survived an economic crisis in New Zealand in the hundred years since Grey fell in 1879. In 1975 Labour was blown away in the most striking upset in the country's electoral history. The number of seats held by the parties was reversed: now National held fifty-five seats to Labour's thirty-two. The new Prime Minister, R. D. Muldoon, had denounced Labour's borrowing – and now borrowed. Vogel's ghost must have turned pale with fear and astonishment. By 1978 the external public debt had reached the remarkable figure of $2,447,000,000. There were several devaluations of the dollar. At the same time there was a huge internal budgetary deficit.

By the mid and late seventies New Zealand was experiencing its greatest economic difficulties since the depression of the thirties. For a time the currency revaluations of 1973 had helped to keep inflation below the soaring world rates. Nevertheless, in 1970–76 it averaged over ten per cent a year and was nearly eighteen per cent in mid 1976. In 1975–7 it was above world rates and continued to run at over twelve per cent in 1978. Unemployment began to climb, too, reaching nearly 25,000 in early 1979, with another 31,000 working on 'job creation' schemes. Although only a small proportion of the workforce in comparison with most countries, the sight of men on 'special work', planting trees and the like, was alarming to most citizens.

To New Zealanders perhaps the most startling fact was that there was an actual decline in their standard of living. Real income *per capita* fell by over eleven per cent in 1973–7. It was now below that in twenty countries, whereas for many years New Zealand had stood among the leaders. The significance of this change should not be exaggerated. The standard of living was still at about the level of 1971, before the most recent boom began. As in the depressions of the eighteen-eighties and nineteen-thirties, and the recession of 1967–8, New Zealanders indicated their lack of confidence by leaving in thousands – 45,000 in 1977–8. Since most of these were skilled young people, that was a massive 'brain drain'. In 1978, for the first time this century except during the Second World War, the New Zealand population actually fell. This was called the 'Irish solution' to unemployment; exporting the population. As wage rises fell behind price increases, another sign of malaise was an increase in industrial disputes. In 1976 there were four times as many stoppages as the average annual number for the nineteen-sixties; over forty per cent of the union members were involved in disputes. Though losses in productivity were not higher than in Australia or the U.S.A., for instance, they were still damaging. By the late sixties the Arbitration Court had declined in status as the unions lost faith in it and turned to direct bargaining with employers. In 1973 the machinery of industrial relations was reconstructed. An Industrial Commission, an Industrial Court and an Industrial Relations Council were set up to replace the old Arbitration Court, but in 1977 a single Arbitration Court was set up again. These rapid changes reflect a highly unstable industrial situation.

No one supposed that the great deficits in the balance of payments could be sustained for long. It was widely recognized in New Zealand that the country must 'trade its way' out of its troubles. But that was not easy. As in the nineteen-thirties, its greatest economic difficulties were those of marketing. As one of the most efficient producers and greatest exporters of meat and dairy foods, New Zealand suffered from the agricultural protectionism of most industrialized countries, which busily subsidized their own less efficient farmers. The governments of these countries almost all denounce industrial protectionism while practising agricultural protection.

Fearing the day when Great Britain would join the E.E.C., New Zealand had in large measure succeeded in diversifying her markets. Great Britain was still the biggest single export market, but took only twenty per cent of exports in 1970, in comparison with fifty in 1965. Major new markets had been established in Japan, Australia and North America, and important markets in the U.S.S.R., South America and South-East Asia. Nevertheless, in the mid seventies, those markets were inadequate and insecure.

	1938–9	1952–3	1976–7
United Kingdom	81·3	68·1	19·9
Australia	3·8	1·4	12·3
U.S.A. and Canada	10·3	10·7	14·1
Japan		2·0	12·5
E.E.C. (Excl. U.K.)		12·4	11·8
Middle East Oil Countries	4·6	5·4	3·0
Other			26·4
TOTALS	100·0	100·0	100·0

(from Ian Ward (ed.), *Thirteen Facets*, p. 107, Wellington, 1978)

The E.E.C., and therefore Great Britain, no longer took New Zealand cheese after 1977; the special arrangement for butter was extended only until 1980; and now there was talk of a 'sheep meat regime'. If the E.E.C. should turn a cold protectionist shoulder to New Zealand exports of lamb it would be a severe blow. In 1978 New Zealand lamb crossed a twenty per cent tariff and still sold in Great Britain at about eighty-five per cent of the price of British lamb and half the price of lamb in France. New Zealand sold twenty million carcasses, two fifths of the lamb eaten there, to Great Britain. In 1935 New Zealand feared the threatened British meat 'quotas' on imports; now it dreaded a 'sheep meat regime'.

Japan, the U.S.A., Western Europe and Australia all contrive to regulate and minimize New Zealand dairy and meat exports. So the Government's main problem in foreign relations have been those of economic foreign policy. The Prime Minister, R. D. Muldoon, chose sometimes to conduct foreign negotiations in his own abrasive and public style. He denounced Japan for pursuing a form of economic imperialism. When New Zealand extended its exclusive fishing zone to 200 miles in 1978, the Japanese were refused the right to fish unless they took more New Zealand beef. They declined to be bullied, although eventually they made some minor trading concessions.

Whether the recession will prove a phase or a trend remains to be seen. The pessimists believe that the country's high standard of living in recent years has rested on accidents – the booms following the Second World War and accompanying the Korean and Vietnam Wars. They say that even if export prices rise again, the terms of trade will remain unfavourable. Therefore New Zealand will have to be content to accept a long period of lower standards. The optimists hope that agricultural protectionism will not persist. They believe that in a world with exploding populations a major food-exporting country is bound to enjoy a high standard of living.

Mr Muldoon is certainly one of the more memorable of New Zealand Prime Ministers, and not merely because he has published his autobiography – twice. He can be overbearing, bullying. He seems to regard politics as a version of 'Gunfight at the O.K. Corral'. Some of his enemies have seen in him a potential dictator. His government overturned some of the principal legislation of the previous Labour Government, notably Labour's elaborate organization for broadcasting and television and its local government legislation. But it would be an error to see the National Government or its leader as reactionary, in the sense of seeking to turn the clock back politically. For instance, Labour had revised the whole system of benefits and pensions, introducing an 'actuarial scheme' whereby the citizen contributed throughout his life to a fund from which he would eventually draw his superannuation. The Muldoon Government reintroduced a system, like that of 1938, in which all benefits are paid from taxation. Muldoon's national superannuation scheme gives a retired, married couple eighty per cent of the average ordinary wage at the age of sixty. This must be the most expensive piece of legislation in New Zealand history. It might well be regarded as more radical a system than Labour's scheme.

A question often asked is whether the country can afford it. The health budget for 1978–9 was $984,000,000 while the vote for social welfare was $1,798,000,000. Altogether health and social welfare took nearly a third of government expenditure. The judgement of New Zealand voters has been made very clear. Social security is one of their most treasured possessions; it would be one of the last things they would give up. It may be, however, that the system is in some respects deteriorating. Hospital care absorbs about seventy per cent of government expenditure on health, which is far higher a proportion than in most countries, yet still there are complaints about delays in getting treatment. Large numbers of people have taken out insurance policies which pay for treatment in private hospitals. Already, there are signs of a return to the situation before 1938 of one health system for the rich and another for the poor.

Perhaps the most sustained drive of New Zealand society throughout its history has been towards what in Great Britain would be regarded as a middle-class standard of living and against the inequalities of the British class system; in short, towards a bourgeois equality. The high standard of living is threatened by balance of trade problems. But what about the equality? As long ago as 1962 political scientists claimed that New Zealand had been an 'equal society' but that equality was being eroded away. The evidence was then hard to perceive. More recently several left-wing critics of New Zealand society have repeated the claim that classes were developing.

It would be difficult to establish that there is great poverty in New Zealand, but of course some are poorer than others. The Kirk–Rowling Government gave exceptional attention to the needs of the least privileged – often recent Pacific Island immigrants or 'solo mums' – helping them, for instance, to get state houses, to the distress of many 'ordinary Kiwis' and former Labour voters, who felt neglected and had great political power, whereas the poor minorities did not. There are still people who, for various reasons, are poor, but poverty is not something likely to strike a visitor, as it does in parts of most of the world's great cities. Are there, however, signs that 'classes' are developing, whether Marxist and derived from the control of the means of production, or merely sections of the population with vastly differing incomes and life styles?

To this question an answer must be inconclusive. There are and have always been expensive and cheaper suburbs, the former inhabited mainly by professional and business people who vote National, the latter by manual workers who vote Labour. New Zealanders readily identify the prestige of different occupations in a hierarchy related to income, education, skill and relative dirtiness of the job, placing doctors, company directors, big businessmen, lawyers, wealthy farmers, near the top, and at the bottom unskilled labourers, road sweepers and charwomen. But there is no clear evidence to support the idea that class barriers are widening; indeed there is evidence that the share of wealth owned by the more wealthy people actually declined slightly in the years 1951–71. Another fact of importance is that the 'span' of incomes in New Zealand is low in comparison with, say, the U.S.A. The peak in incomes is low and very few people earn the highest and lowest incomes. Extreme differences between rich and poor are minimized, and social security and heavy taxes radically redistribute incomes. There is much less overt expression of class-consciousness than in the United Kingdom, and nothing like the British 'Establishment', an élite based on heredity, inherited wealth, and a separate upper-class education system and buttressed by

monarchy, aristocracy and established church. What New
Zealand does have is vestigial elements of the British class
structure, but without an aristocracy. Wakefield's ideal of a
cultured élite was until 1890 partially realized in the rule of
the 'gentry', but in that year the voters demonstrated a distaste for privilege which has persisted. Some remain richer than
others, but wealth carries no prerogative of leadership.

A sociologist has recently suggested that an 'eth class', a
truly indigenous local class, is developing. Certainly Maoris
and other Polynesians are usually less educated than the
Europeans and a much higher proportion of them are found
in unskilled occupations. There is no doubt that one of the
country's greatest problems, and the greatest danger to its
relative equality, lies in those facts.

In the nineteenth century many Maoris lived in or near the
European towns, but by the twentieth the overwhelming
majority lived in rural districts remote from the towns. In 1936
there were only 1,700 Maoris in Auckland, for instance. The
Maoris were not fully integrated into the European economy
but still lived partly on food from their own cultivations and
on fish, eels and birds. They formed a seasonal, rural labour
force for European farmers and public works projects. This
situation changed very rapidly. There was a massive *heke*
(migration) to the towns during and after the Second World
War. By 1945 twenty per cent of Maoris lived in towns; by
1976 seventy-six per cent did so.

At the same time thousands of Pacific Islanders migrated to
New Zealand, about 61,000 by 1976. Auckland became the
greatest city in Polynesia, with 38,000 Pacific Islanders. In
addition there were 86,000 Maoris and part-Maoris living there.
Over twelve per cent of the population were Maori, partly
Maori, or other Polynesians.

There are real social difficulties arising from the mixture of
races in the cities. For instance, Polynesians have tended to
congregate in less expensive suburbs where crimes of violence
have become too common, notably in or near hotels. Life in
large cities has presented Maoris and Pacific Islanders with
many problems of adaptation they have not encountered
before. It must not be supposed, however, that the tensions are

brown versus white. There are strong rivalries between Maoris and Pacific Islanders and among the Island groups too.

The Maoris have not yet achieved the full equality promised by the Treaty of Waitangi. In measurable respects, such as housing or income, they are 'disadvantaged'. Although Maoris are to be found in all professions and occupations, there are too few in higher-paid occupations; there is a very low proportion of them in the universities. Yet the situation could be described in a very different way. There are now 280,000 Maoris, probably more than when Captain Cook came. They have had a remarkable success in adapting to two centuries of challenge and change.

It must not be thought that the Maoris simply want to become brown *pakeha*. Many urban Maoris lose interest in tribal tradition and cease to speak Maori. But on the whole, Maori culture is very tenacious. The language is widely taught in schools and universities. Maori *marae* (meeting houses with a space in front) have been built in large numbers. There Maori customs are treasured. Very often the most educated Maoris, in European terms, are most conscious of their *Maoritanga*, their 'Maori-ness'. They have their own culture – 'modern Maori'.

The Maoris have lost – usually sold – most of their land, and have about as much land per person as the *pakeha*, about seventeen acres each. But the Maori still likes to have his *turanga waewae*, a place where he is entitled to stand, his stake in the country. In the nineteen-seventies several Maori movements arose to protest against the loss of Maori land. One was the Maori 'land march' of 1976. Another was the protest of a group of Maoris and others against the loss of land at Bastion Point in Auckland. There have also been 'brown power' movements demanding full equality.

'Amalgamation', the humanitarian ideal of the eighteen-forties, has not occurred physically or socially. But what may prove decisive is a very rapid increase in racial intermarriage. There are a very large number of people, 356,000 in 1976, who have some degree of Maori ancestry. The New Zealanders of the future who are not sun-tanned may have olive skins.

Some of the Pacific Islanders had difficulties different from those of the Maoris. In 1976 the Government believed that there were up to 10,000 Pacific Island 'over-stayers' living in the country. These were not people from Niue or the Cook Islands, who are New Zealand citizens, but those from Tonga, Samoa or elsewhere who had entered New Zealand on visitors' or short-term work permits and who had stayed on, many of them with families in New Zealand. In 1976 many 'over-stayers' were deported. The police handled the problem very roughly and the dawn raids and random street checks of anyone who looked Polynesian reminded people of the South African police state. This was the worst example of racial tension in recent years.

In its first years of office the Government of Mr Muldoon was at its most insensitive in areas of racial relations. Certainly the Prime Minister did not believe that racism had become a more contentious issue in international affairs than Communism. The Government had promised the voters not to interfere in sport, which meant that the one-eyed or myopic rugby administrators could send another All Black team to South Africa. The General Assembly of the United Nations had asked members to stop sporting contacts with South Africa, but this had little weight with the Government and none with the rugby administrators. 'The tour' was 'on'; the Prime Minister treated Abraham Ordia, the secretary of the Supreme Council of Sport in Africa, with contumely. The outcome was that the African and other athletes walked out of the next Olympic Games in Montreal and New Zealand's name was held in very wide contempt. Like Kirk, Muldoon had to change his mind. In the end the Prime Minister was rescued by the Commonwealth connection. At a meeting of Commonwealth Prime Ministers in Great Britain in 1977 a formula was worked out acceptable to the New Zealand Government. Each Commonwealth government accepted it as its urgent duty 'to vigorously combat the evil of apartheid . . . by taking every practical step to discourage contact or competition by their nationals with sporting organizations . . . from South Africa . . .' In New Zealand rugby football, a game played in a few small countries and by small minorities in a few large ones, was a significant political issue for twenty years after 1958. It must be stressed, however, that rugby was not a racial issue within New Zealand as it was in the United Nations. Large numbers of Maoris and Pacific Islanders were ardent fans who were eager to beat the Springboks and not very aware of apartheid in sport on the international field.

The other group who became more aware in the sixties and seventies that they were not equal was the women. In New Zealand the image of the female as Little Mother had always been powerfully imprinted on the minds of both sexes at an early age. The women became aware that, since they had won the vote in 1893, almost first in the world, nothing much had happened. A handful of women were elected to Parliament; a couple became cabinet ministers; the National Council of Women inspired some of the relatively few measures of social legislation between 1911 and 1935; that was about all. Consequently a new women's movement was needed and arose in the nineteen-sixties and seventies, partly inspired by the rise of women's movements overseas. Women began to enter the work force in large numbers: the proportion of women aged fifteen to sixty-four who worked rose from twenty-eight per cent in 1951 to forty-two per cent in 1976. This was a social change of immense significance, influencing all sorts of other customs, such as child-raising. Women began to enter the legal and other professions in force, though there were still few in Parliament. Equal pay was at last secured. Another important result was a greater feeling of solidarity among women, thousands attending the women's conventions.

A movement associated with women's rights, though not exclusively female, was abortion. On the question of easy access to abortion the women were perhaps as divided as the men, but often took the lead on both sides. This enormously explosive issue vexed the governments of the seventies and stirred up residual sectarian feeling, for Roman Catholics were the strength of the anti-abortionists. Abortion, too, is an issue of great moment in society. The birthrate, which was already falling in the sixties and seventies, might conceivably (it was argued) be further reduced.

The nineteen-seventies proved a turbulent decade. There were few certainties to cling to. On what was New Zealand's 'dependent economy' to depend? Citizens noted with a new irony that the country's national song was 'God defend New Zealand'. Few other allies were in sight. Politics were unusually volatile, with extraordinary swings in public opinion. In the 1975 election Labour's share of the votes cast had dropped by eight point eight per cent. In 1978 the Muldoon Government received almost as severe a hammering. Its share of the votes dropped by nearly eight per cent, but it did succeed in keeping power because Labour's vote rose by only point eight per cent. Sixteen per cent of the voters swung to Social Credit whose leader, Bruce Beetham, was elected to Parliament. (His party had in 1969 lost the seat held by Vernon Cracknell.) National now held fifty seats and Labour forty-one, so National had succeeded, at least for the rest of the nineteen-seventies, in surviving an economic crisis, even though Labour actually won more votes.

In the seventies many of the things for which the pioneers had fought, including equality, were threatened. Yet there was something which could perhaps be put on the other side of the balance. New Zealanders seemed more sure of themselves, of their identity, of their national identity, than ever before.

THE SEARCH FOR NATIONAL IDENTITY

> Nick and I were sitting on the hillside and Nick was saying
> he was a New Zealander, but he knew he wasn't a New
> Zealander. And he knew he wasn't a Dalmatian any more.
>
> FRANK SARGESON, 'The Making of a New Zealander'

THE chief result of recent events has been to bring home to
New Zealanders a fact which they have not always seemed to
regard as important: New Zealand is in the Pacific. And in
emphasizing geography and its consequences, world politics
since 1941 serve as a reminder of another circumstance; that
for a century and a half, since the Americans and Australians
came for timber, flax, or sealskins, the islands have been part
of the New World. To understand their history we must turn
continually to experience in other lands settled by Europeans
since Columbus: to the Indian wars in the United States; to
the Australian squatters; to the Californian and Australian
gold-rushes; to American, Canadian or Australian politics – for
parallels to the Liberal Party and its radical labour and land
legislation, or the Reform Party and the credit reform movements.

In its turn, the development of New Zealand followed that
of the United States and Australia. Inequality was the dynamic
of the Old World, equality of the New. The New Zealanders'
egalitarianism, their easy-going good fellowship, their devotion
to mechanical appliances, are also characteristics of Australians
and Americans. The resemblance was forecast more than a
century ago by Thomas Cholmondeley: 'New Zealand must
daily Americanize.' It is a resemblance already remarked on in
1903 by an American historian, Frank Parsons, who wrote of
the New Zealanders:

They are the Yankees of the South Pacific. In fact, New
Zealand is a little America, a sort of condensed United States.
If all the nations of the world were classed according to the
number and importance of their points of resemblance, the
United States, New Zealand and Australia would stand in a

324 A HISTORY OF NEW ZEALAND

group together, with England, Switzerland and France close by, and Belgium, Denmark, Germany, and Scandinavia not far off.

Great Britain, Germany, the Netherlands and Scandinavia might, more aptly, be grouped 'close by'; but it still seems today, that, in their way of life, the New Zealanders belong to a branch of New World civilization the main centres of which are Sydney, San Francisco and Auckland – the Pacific Triangle.

The east coast of Australia, the western shores of the United States and Canada, lie on the same ocean, were washed by the same historical seas, as New Zealand. They were settled in the same age and exchanged their menfolk impartially according to the chance of gold discoveries. Three of the most common exotic trees in New Zealand are the Monterey cypress (*Cupressus macrocarpa*), the Monterey pine (*Pinus radiata*), both of these from a small peninsula in California, and the Australian eucalypt or wattle. Along the Californian coast innumerable magnificent Australian gums and hedges of 'mirror-leaf' (the New Zealand *taupata*) remind us of the same connexion. In all three places may be seen the ornate wooden architecture of late last century. The 'Californian bungalow' was the popular New Zealand house of the twenties. It is impossible for the scholar or the traveller not to see the fraternal resemblances. New Zealand grew up like its colonial brothers.

Such is one of the conclusions which arise from this account of New Zealand's history; it is not one which would be drawn from earlier or popular accounts of New Zealand's past, or, indeed, from the earliest New Zealand Company publicity forecasts of its future. Always the emphasis was on Britishness.

'The stock from which the New Zealanders are sprung,' two historians announced flatly in 1902, 'is not only British, but the best British.' The legend lives on: as late as 1930 J. B. Condliffe wrote in *New Zealand in the Making* (and repeated the statement in another book in 1959): 'New Zealand's social health depends primarily upon the quality of the stock from which the present generation has been recruited. Physically, mentally, and morally, the original stock was rigidly selected.'

It is commonly assumed that New Zealand was annexed solely because of the insistence of Wakefield, who wished to found a second England, and forced the British Government to forestall the French. His aims are confused with the result. The experiment in 'scientific colonization' is supposed to have succeeded: New Zealand was settled chiefly by cultivated representatives of English county families, together with their respectable followers – though these are rarely mentioned – who established a 'Britain of the South'.

Scholars and journalists alike have helped to perpetuate this portrait of New Zealand. As recently as 1977 a leading New Zealand newspaper asserted in an editorial: 'Our population is well over ninety per cent of British origin . . .' This statement is almost meaningless and quite misleading. If it means anything it is that most New Zealanders – including Indians, Fijians, Chinese, Samoans, as well as every single person born in New Zealand, including Maoris – were born in the British Commonwealth. The European population is undoubtedly predominantly of British descent, but what proportion may have one or more German, French, Scandinavian, Yugoslav or other non-British ancestors within the past century is quite unknown. From this (and from many other points of view), the proud boast of many New Zealanders, that they are 'More British than the British', would be more meaningful if it read: 'More British than the Americans and Australians.'

'More British than the British' is a statement of no verifiable meaning, but it has had several psychological roles. For many New Zealanders it has meant 'better than the British', the majority of whom have long been regarded as under-paid, under-fed, under-privileged folk who lack the initiative to migrate to New Zealand. In this sense it has not been incompatible with dislike of some sections of the British people. In the depressed twenties and thirties there was, in the trade unions, some antagonism towards British immigrants, who increased the competition for jobs. There has, from the earliest days, been a certain hostility towards educated southern Englishmen and their speech. One may sometimes detect among New Zealanders what V. S. Pritchett observed among Americans, 'the anti-English rancour, the craving for English approval, the resentment of it' – resentment because it is interpreted as patronage. In general, however, such feeling is muted and good-humoured. Understatement and unemotional conduct, after all, are reputedly British characteristics.

The claim to be ultra-British has served another subjective function. Like most people, the New Zealanders like to think that they are a superior breed of men. Just as the claim to descend from 'selected stock' implies a superiority to the British Australians, so the emphasis on British ancestry implies superiority to non-British people, and especially to the Americans or other ex-colonials who are of mixed – and supposedly inferior – descent. Only eighty years ago, Americans used similarly to stress that they were a Teutonic and Anglo-Saxon people.

Above all, to be British has meant to claim a share of the traditional British qualities of sportsmanship, fair play, modesty, discipline, courage. And it has enabled New Zealanders to identify themselves with British greatness. If the emphasis on the 'British' characteristics of the early settlements has been out of focus, it remains true that, for European New Zealanders, tradition begins not with Governor Hobson but with King Alfred. By thinking of themselves as a British people, many New Zealanders have provided themselves with an answer to the question which has perplexed the Americans: What am I? It is a ready-made answer, but for those for whom it is an article of faith, it gives great comfort.

When, in 1854, Sir George Grey wrote his *Mythology and Traditions of the New Zealanders*, the 'New Zealanders' were the Maoris. Now Maui has fallen, with his divine ancestors. What Grey remarked of Maori traditions – that 'they contain much that is fabulous and highly extravagant, but it is highly probable that many of the fabulous tales are strung on to much that is true as regards their history' – might be said of modern legends about the highly civilized founding fathers and their respectable virtues. Such tales, like the Maori legends about the 'Fleet', obviously embody certain facts from the past; but they omit most of the facts. They give an impression of New Zealand, past or present, much less varied and colourful than the reality.

The attempt to explain New Zealand in terms of Britishness led to some odd editing of the facts. For instance, the attitude of Massey towards imperial affairs was often attributed to his predecessors. A survey of New Zealand life assured the reader, with regard to the country's external policy: 'We have never pushed precociously forward. We have not bombastically beaten our breasts and congratulated ourselves on achievements as an individual state . . .' King Dick must have felt most uncomfortable – forgotten, and yet, by implication, rebuked.

Such statements as this point to one important aspect of the New Zealand–British tradition: it was a 'genteel' tradition. It derived from the Great Britain, not of the aristocracy or the trade unionist, but of the middle or the aspiring lower middle class; the Great Britain, not of St James's or the East End, but of South Kensington or the garden suburbs. It saw New Zealand, not in the image of the Britain of George IV or Edward VII, but of Queen Victoria; a Britain thought of as respectable, moral – and the most powerful state in the world. This idealized conception of Britain gave way only slowly to the facts of its decline as a great power.

Although by 1890 most Europeans in New Zealand were native-born, immigrants formed a majority of adults over, say, fifty, until the nineteen-twenties. They were colonials; they *were* British. They did not quite belong. There was another and indigenous New Zealand myth which was concerned with the same problem of definition and which stressed not belonging. Some of the poets of the nineteen-thirties and forties, and the critic, M. H. Holcroft, were preoccupied with themes of loneliness, estrangement, exile. Their interpretation of New Zealand life emphasized the brevity and insignificance of the European past. Allen Curnow noticed in a critical essay the frequent appearance in New Zealand poetry of the idea that 'our presence in these islands is accidental, irrelevant; that we are interlopers on an indifferent or hostile scene.' The towns, one would gather, are merely the encampments of nomads who have broken into the natural order like robbers into a temple, blind to its beauties, proportions, or wisdom. Humanity in New Zealand feels insecure, oppressed, because it is rootless; it has failed to make the land its own. Such themes recur continually in the verse of Curnow, Brasch, Ursula Bethell and other poets.

The plains are nameless and the cities cry for meaning . . .

Homestead? Nay, halting-place, accommodation . . .

Waiting for our songs, the woods are still,
The stones are bare for us to write upon.

Not I, some child, born in a marvellous year,
Will learn the trick of standing upright here.

One is reminded of Robert Frost's poem, 'The Gift Outright'.

The land was ours before we were the land's.
She was our land more than a hundred years
Before we were her people. She was ours
In Massachusetts, in Virginia.
But we were England's, still colonials . . .

It would be misleading to imply that the New Zealand poets
who expressed this theme were still colonials. As we have already seen, these writers had at last accepted that they were
New Zealanders. But what was the New Zealander? They were
impressed with the fact that their people were culturally still
Europeans; impressed with the inadequacy of the past; with
the rootlessness of present behaviour. They thought their land,
like the America of Robert Frost's poem, 'unstoried, artless,
unenhanced'. The fact that the majority of their countrymen
were unaware of most of the symptoms they observed does not
invalidate their diagnosis. The intellectuals, as in America,
were more aware of the need for assurances as to their identity.
They wished for precision, whereas the 'digger' of the First
World War had been content to feel that he was an 'Anzac', the
'dig' of the Second World War that he was a 'Kiwi', without
asking further questions, or others again had been satisfied
with the vague idea that the New Zealanders were a new branch
of the British people.

It is worth noting that almost all the writers whose work expresses this attitude were South Islanders. It is a regional
myth, which has had little appeal in the North Island, with its
monuments to ancient Maori occupation and its denser population. It should also be remarked that this South Island myth
has been rejected in recent years by younger men and women

who have accepted their role as writers without worrying unduly about being New Zealand writers.

Perhaps the first identifiable New Zealanders were the soldiers who went to the First World War. Going overseas in a body, and encountering large numbers of British, Canadian, Australian and other English-speaking people, they became aware that they were different; not very different from Australians, but different. Certainly they sounded like New Zealanders. Possibly – the hypothesis is difficult to test – this was also true of some of the troops who fought in the Boer War. Some of the ex-servicemen returned from France, like John A. Lee, became self-conscious New Zealand nationalists. By the Second World War most of the servicemen simply assumed that they belonged to a nation. It was still possible, however, even then, to be and feel both a New Zealander and British. And for long after that war a New Zealand passport said that its holder was 'a New Zealand citizen and British subject'.

From this point of view a decisive influence was not the decline of the Commonwealth, for the ties with Britain continued, but the entry of Great Britain into the E.E.C. Mother had deserted. Instead of an ennobling American revolution, New Zealand experienced a somewhat humiliating rejection by the Motherland. Of many New Zealanders it may be said that they were not born to it and did not achieve it, but had nationalism thrust upon them.

By about 1940, if asked to identify themselves, most people born in New Zealand would, without hesitation, have said that they were New Zealanders. But, again, what is a New Zealander? No international stereotype exists, as there does of the thrifty Scot, the wild Irishman, the drunken and chundering Australian. Perhaps people in Great Britain would think of New Zealanders as an outdoor people, vigorous at rugby, but less abrasive than the Australians – in short, think of them as genteel Aussies.

Has any local stereotype emerged? In literature the most frequent character has been a bachelor, a man alone. *Man Alone* is the title of a novel by John Mulgan, but he appears in numerous other works of fiction. He is the outsider, a misfit, at odds with society. He is a close relative of the 'masterless man' in American literature, who left Europe in order to become masterless.

There is another lonely man in New Zealand literature, who first appeared, perhaps, in the short stories of Frank S. Anthony about 'Me and Gus'. He is a dairy farmer who lives with his mate and practises – but does not, like some Australian characters, preach – 'mateship'. He is shy with women, awkward in mixed company. This man alone reappears in the early stories of Frank Sargeson. Considered as a comic character, he is also related to the television personality, Fred Dagg, invented by the comedian, John Clarke.

What inferences may be drawn from the frequency with which such men appear in literature is questionable. Certainly they live in a New Zealand out-of-date, the country dominated by small farmers from, say, the eighteen-nineties to the nineteen-thirties. The Australians, too, highly urbanized, had a rural hero, the stock-rider of fiction. No doubt the 'man alone' did express some common experiences of the New Zealand pioneer, and symbolize some of his hopes and frustrations. The real life of Maoris, women and urban New Zealanders has not yet crystallized into any recognizable stereotype in literature. They have not fully emerged.

R. G. Collingwood wrote in *The Idea of History*, 'Man, who desires to know everything, desires to know himself.' In modern times it has been a common, almost an invariable feature of the rise of new nations, or national movements, that their leaders or writers, like self-conscious New Zealanders, should seek to define their nationhood in terms of the past. But it must not be supposed that any considerable number of New Zealanders devote any considerable energy to ransacking history or, indeed, literature for clues to explain their present situation. In general, they have had little sense of their past in the new land; nor is the assumption that there is value in a long past or in ancient tradition at all widely accepted. As the *New Zealand Herald* remarked in 1925, on the election of Gordon Coates to office as Prime Minister: 'All is yet molten, mercurial. There are more departures to make than precedents to follow. To have a history may be an old land's glory and safeguard: to make history is a new land's perilous employment.'

GLOSSARY OF MAORI, COLONIAL, AND NEW ZEALAND TERMS

MAORI

ariki	high chief
atua	god, demon
hapu	sub-tribe
hei-tiki	greenstone pendant hung from neck
kaikomako	small tree (*Pennantia corymbosa*)
karakia	charm, spell, incantation
kauri	large pine tree (*Agathis australis*)
kiwi	small flightless bird (*Apteryx* of several species)
kotahitanga	unity: name of Maori national movements
kowhai	tree (*Edwardsia microphylla*)
kumara	sweet potato (*Ipomoea batatas*)
kuri	dog
makutu	bewitch; witchcraft
mana	prestige; influence; authority
mangai	mouth
marae	space in front of meeting-house; plaza
mere	short, flat stone club; a variety of *patu*, often made of greenstone
moa	extinct flightless bird of various genera; e.g. *Dinornis, Euryapteryx*
ngarara	reptile, monster
niu	small sticks used in divining; a pole
pa	stockade; fortified village
pakeha	foreigner; (pop.) white man
patu	short club of stone, whalebone, etc.
pohutukawa	tree (*Metrosideros tomentosa*)
pu	gun
rangatira	chief
runanga	assembly
takahe	small flightless bird (*Notornis hochstetteri*)
take	root; cause
tapu	sacred; holy; taboo
taro	food plant (*Colocasia antiquorum*)
taupata	tree (*Coprosma retusa*)
tohunga	wizard; priest; skilled person
tui	bird (*Prosthemadera novaeseelandiae*)
tutua	low-born (person)

utu	satisfaction for injuries received; payment; revenge
whanau	offspring; extended family group
whare wananga	house of learning

A FEW COLONIAL OR NEW ZEALAND TERMS

Anzac	Australian and New Zealand Army Corps (First World War, 1914–18)
bach	seaside cottage (from 'bachelor')
back-blocks	remote rural districts
billy	tin can used as jug or kettle
boo-ay	(spelling doubtful); see 'back-blocks' (Corruption of Puhoi, the name of a settlement?); pron. bu: aɪ; used in the expression 'up the boo-ay'
bush	the forest
cow cockie	dairy farmer
crib	seaside cottage
dally	Dalmatian, made by Yugoslav immigrants; e.g. 'Dally plonk' – Dalmatian wine
damper	unleavened loaf or cake cooked in ashes
digger	gold-digger; soldier (First World War and, in the form 'dig', Second World War)
Lib-Lab	member of Liberal–Labour Federation, 1899 (a term also used in England)
paddock	field; often very large
Pakeha-Maori	European living with Maoris
Red Fed	member of the ('Red') Federation of Labour, 1909
scrub	stunted trees; country covered with this
shagroon	term used in Canterbury for Australian stock-drovers, 1851 (derived from Irish Shaughraun, Saxon (hence foreigner)?)
sly-grogging	selling alcoholic liquor illegally
wowser	opponent of gambling, drinking alcohol, etc.; a Puritan

TABLE I

EUROPEAN LAND TENURE, 1891–1956

In millions of acres to nearest half-million	1891	1911	1928	1956
Occupied land	32	40	43.5	43
Freehold	12.5	16.5	20.5	21.5
Crown leases	14	19	19	16.5
Private and public leases	3	4	2.5	2
Maori leases	2	2	1.5	1
Freehold as % of occupied land	39%	41%	37%	50%
Crown leases as % of occupied land	44%	48%	44%	38%

This table is based on figures in the *New Zealand Year Book*
1911, 1928 and 1956, and *New Zealand Statistics*, 1891. The
actual area of occupied land is greater than the figures given for
1928 and 1956 because holdings of under one acre and lands
within borough boundaries were excluded from the official
estimate. With regard to Crown leases, it should be remarked
that the bulk are pastoral leases – poor land held in large holdings.
In 1891 pastoral leases accounted for 12.5 million acres of Crown
leases; 11 million in 1911; 9.5 million in 1928; an, as nearly as
can be discovered, some 8 million in 1956. Crown waste lands,
reserves, etc., are not included in this table. (See Table II for a
fuller picture).

TABLE II

TENURE AND CONDITION OF LAND, 1951

Description	Area in acres	per cent of total
Freehold	21,869,100	32.9
Public Reserves	16,661,600	25.1
Crown leases (excluding reserves leased by Crown)	15,890,700	23.9
Crown land available for disposal	2,327,300[1]	3.5
Maori land	4,477,500[2]	6.8
Land unfit for settlement (rivers, roads, etc)	5,164,500	7.8
Total	66,390,700	100.0

1. Mostly unfit for settlement.
2. Includes some land sold to Europeans.

SUGGESTIONS FOR FURTHER READING

THERE is no adequate substantial work on New Zealand history. The nearest approach to a full-scale treatment is J. B. Condliffe's *New Zealand in the Making* (1930) which surveys economic development and, to some extent, social and political history. The second edition (1959) is not an improvement on the first. *Speeches and Documents on New Zealand History* (1971) edited by W. D. McIntyre and W. J. Gardner is a useful work of reference. *Looking Back: A Photographic History of New Zealand* (1978) by Keith Sinclair and Wendy Harrex illustrates some major themes in New Zealand history in visual and photographic essays.

There are several excellent books on the pre-European Maori. Roger Duff's *The Moa-Hunter Period of Maori Culture* (second edition 1956) is fascinating but out of date. R. C. Green's *Adaptation and Change in Maori Culture* (1977) is the most recent summary account of New Zealand pre-history. Andrew Sharp's *Ancient Voyagers in Polynesia* (1963) is the most provocative and stimulating work on its subject. Peter H. Buck's *The Coming of the Maori* (1949) and Raymond Firth's *Primitive Economics of the New Zealand Maori* (1929) are the best works on 'classical' Maori culture.

The authoritative work on the European explorers is J. C. Beaglehole's *Discovery of New Zealand* (second edition 1961) but the serious student can turn to nothing more fascinating than his superb edition of *The Journals of Captain James Cook* (1955–67). Beaglehole died before he quite completed his large biography, *The Life of Captain James Cook* (1974), which is very thorough but in which the man gets lost in the details.

There are few good books on the missionaries. The best is Judith Binney's *The Legacy of Guilt: A Life of Thomas Kendall* (1968). J. M. R. Owen's *Prophets in the Wilderness: The Wesleyan Mission in New Zealand, 1819–1827* (1974) is another useful work on the subject.

The effects of European contacts on the Maoris are best discussed in H. M. Wright's *New Zealand, 1769–1840* (1959). For the study of early European settlement J. S. Marais's *The Colonization of New Zealand* (1927) and John Miller's *Early Victorian New Zealand* (1958) should be consulted. Michael Turnbull's *The New Zealand Bubble* (1959) provides a short, critical account of the 'Wakefield system'. *Fatal Necessity: British Intervention in New Zealand, 1830–1847* by Peter Adams (1977) examines in detail the events leading up to annexation. Ian Wards' *The Shadow of the Land: A Study of British Policy and Racial Conflict in New Zealand, 1832–1852* (1968) gives the best account of the warfare in the 1840s. Alan Ward's *A Show of Justice: Racial 'Amalgamation' in Nineteenth Century New Zealand* (1973) discusses government policy towards the Maoris, which was also examined in K. Sinclair's *The Origins of the Maori Wars* (1957). B. J. Dalton's *War and Politics in New Zealand, 1855–1870* (1967) gives more detail about political and military aspects and about the Waikato campaign. J. E. Gorst's *The Maori King* (1864; second edition 1959) is still a very interesting and valuable study.

On more recent Maori history there are some fascinating books, including Paul Clark's *'Hauhau': The Pai Marire Search for Maori Identity* (1975), J. M. Henderson's *Ratana: The Man, the Church, the Political Movement* (1972 edition) and John A. Williams's *Politics of the New Zealand Maori: Protest and Cooperation, 1891–1909* (1969). Michael King's *Te Puea: A Biography* (1977) is a very interesting study, largely based on oral evidence.

There are a number of books on nineteenth-century government and politics. A. H. McLintock's *Crown Colony Government in New Zealand* (1958) and J. Rutherford's political biography, *Sir George Grey* (1961), are detailed accounts. W. P. Morrell's *The Provincial System in New Zealand* (1932) has not been superseded. R. M. Burdon's *Life and Times of Sir Julius Vogel* (1948) and his *King Dick* (1955), Keith Sinclair's *William Pember Reeves* (1965) and Judith Bassett's *Sir Harry Atkinson, 1831–1892* (1975) provide biographical and political studies. Patricia Grimshaw's *Woman's Suffrage in New Zealand* (1972) is an important work on women's (and men's) politics. R. M. Chapman's *The Political Scene, 1919–1931* (1969) is unrivalled on the twenties. More modern political history is discussed in R. M Chapman, W. K. Jackson and A. V. Mitchell's *New Zealand Politics in Action: The 1960 General Election* (1962); Bruce Brown's *The Rise of New Zealand Labour* (1962); and R. S. Milne's *Political Parties in New Zealand* (1966). P. J. O'Farrell's *Harry Holland* (1964), Michael Bassett's *Confrontation '51: The 1951 Waterfront Dispute* (1971), H. Roth's *Trade Unions in New Zealand: Past and Present* (1973), Erik Olssen's *John A. Lee* (1977) and Keith Sinclair's *Walter Nash* (1976) should also be consulted on Labour history. Lipson's survey *The Politics of Equality* (1948) is somewhat out of date. The most provocative and controversial account of recent politics is W. B. Sutch's *The*

Quest for Security in New Zealand, 1840–1966 (1966). Austin Mitchell's *Politics and People in New Zealand* (1969) is a fairly popular collection of essays. Stephen Levine edited *Politics in New Zealand: A Reader* (1978).

Various constitutional and administrative issues are outlined in R. J. Polaschek's *Government Administration in New Zealand* (1958); N. S. Wood's *Industrial Conciliation and Arbitration in New Zealand* (1963); and in K. J. Scott's *The New Zealand Constitution* (1962).

The most important treatment of economic history will be found in C. G. F. Simkin's *The Instability of a Dependent Economy* (1951) which stops, unfortunately, in 1914. J. B. Condliffe's *The Welfare State in New Zealand* (1959) and C. Westrate's *Portrait of a Modern Mixed Economy* (1959) examine more recent trends. There are two useful books on the gold rushes, P. R. May's *The West Coast Gold Rushes* (1962) and J. H. M. Salmon's *A History of Goldmining in New Zealand* (1963). A 'business history', *Makers of Fortune: A Colonial Business Community and its Fall* (1973), a study of Auckland in the 1880s by R. C. J. Stone, is well worth reading, as is G. R. Hawkes' *Between Governments and Banks: A History of the Reserve Bank of New Zealand* (1973).

On foreign and imperial relations the chief works are J. C. Beaglehole (editor), *New Zealand and the Statute of Westminster* (1944); two books by F. L. W. Wood, *New Zealand in the World* (1940) and *The New Zealand People at War* (1958), which deals not with 'the people' but high policy; and *New Zealand's External Relations* (1962), edited by T. C. Larkin. Angus Ross analyses New Zealand's form of 'sub-imperialism' in *New Zealand Aspirations in the Pacific in the Nineteenth Century* (1964). New Zealand's record in Samoa is authoritatively examined in J. W. Davidson's *Samoa mo Samoa: The Emergence of the Independent State of Western Samoa* (1967). R. M. Dalziel's *The Origins of New Zealand Diplomacy: The Agent-General in London, 1870–1905* (1975) examines imperial relationships. *New Zealand in World Affairs*, vol. 1 (New Zealand Institute of International Affairs), includes some valuable articles. M. P. Lissington's two books, *New Zealand and the United States, 1840–1944* and *New Zealand and Japan, 1900–1941* (both 1972), are indispensable studies, as is *The Australian–New Zealand Agreement 1944*, edited by Robin Kay (1972). The Ministry of Foreign Affairs has published *New Zealand Foreign Policy: Statements and Documents, 1943–1957* (1972).

There are several excellent studies of modern Maori communities. Joan Metge's *A New Maori Migration: Rural and Urban Relations in North New Zealand* (1964) and her survey *The Maoris of New Zealand* (1967) are important studies. John Harré's *Maori and Pakeha* (1966), James E. Ritchie's *The Making of a Maori* (1963) and P. W. Hohepa's *A Maori Community in Northland* (1964) are all essential reading. M. P. K. Sorrenson's booklet, *Maori and European Since 1870* (1967), gives an excellent short survey.

The best scholarly books on the arts in New Zealand are E. H. McCormick's *Letters and Art in New Zealand* (1940), *New Zealand Literature* (1959) and *The Expatriate: A Study of Frances Hodgkins* (1954). Antony Alpers' *Katherine Mansfield* (1953) and Jeffrey Meyers' *Katherine Mansfield: A Biography* (1978) are both valuable, the first perceptive, the second informative. Charles Doyle's *James K. Baxter* and Vincent O'Sullivan's booklet with the same title, both published in 1976, provide studies of an outstanding New Zealand poet. Dennis McEldowney's *Frank Sargeson in his Time* (1976) discusses a leading short story writer and autobiographer. Wystan Curnow edited *Essays on New Zealand Literature* (1973) and Cherry Hankin edited *Critical Essays on the New Zealand Novel* (1976).

There are several anthologies of New Zealand verse, including Allen Curnow's *The Penguin Book of New Zealand Verse* (1960; second edition 1966), R. M. Chapman and Jonathan Bennett's *An Anthology of New Zealand Verse* (1956), Charles Doyle's *Recent Poetry in New Zealand* (1965), Vincent O'Sullivan's *An Anthology of Twentieth Century New Zealand Poetry* (second edition 1967) and Arthur Baysting's *The Young New Zealand Poets* (1973). D. M. Davin's *New Zealand Short Stories* (1953) and C. K. Stead's 'Second Series' of this Oxford University Press anthology (1966) collect examples of an art at which New Zealanders have excelled.

For recent detailed articles, readers should consult *The New Zealand Journal of History*, *Political Science* (Wellington) and *The Journal of the Polynesian Society*. The leading literary journal is now *Islands*.

The three-volume *Encyclopaedia of New Zealand*, edited by A. H. McLintock (1966), may be consulted on most aspects of New Zealand history and life.

UNPUBLISHED THESES

Much of the best work on New Zealand history is still to be found in unpublished university theses. In addition to those listed in the first edition of this book. I am indebted to the following: R. J. Bremer, 'The New Zealand Farmers' Union as an Interest Group . . .' (Victoria University of Wellington); R. Clifton, 'Douglas Social Credit and the Labour Party 1930–35' (Victoria); J. R. S. Daniels, 'The General Election of 1943' (Victoria); B. H. Farland, 'The Political Career of J. G. Coates' (Victoria); B. S. Gustafson, 'The Advent of the New Zealand Labour Party, 1900–19' (Auckland); R. J. Martin, 'Aspects of Maori Affairs in the Liberal Period' (Victoria); R. K. Newman, 'Liberal Policy and the Left-wing, 1908–11' (Auckland); H. S. Moores, 'Sectarian Conflict in New Zealand, 1911–20' (Auckland); J. R. Phillips, 'A Social History of Auckland 1840–53' (Auckland); A. D. Robinson, 'The Rise of the National Party' (Victoria); K. Shawcross, 'Maoris of the Bay of Islands, 1769–1840' (Auckland); J. A. Williams, 'Maori Society and Politics, 1891–1909' (Wisconsin).

INDEX